Eleanor Herman is the author of the *New York Times* bestseller *Sex with Kings*, *Sex with the Queen*, *Mistress of the Vatican*, and *The Royal Art of Poison*. *King Peggy* has been optioned as a movie starring Queen Latifah. Her non-fiction books – which read like novels – explore the intersection of women, royalty, and power.

MURDER IN THE GARDEN OF GOD

A TRUE STORY OF RENAISSANCE AMBITION, BETRAYAL AND REVENGE

Eleanor Herman

This book is dedicated to all those who tend God's garden.

CONTENTS

INTRODUCTION

I will open my mouth in parables, I will utter hidden things, things from of old.

– Psalm 78:2

Revenge, it is said, is a dish best served cold. Felice Peretti, who became Pope Sixtus V in 1585, served perhaps the coldest dish of revenge ever, prepared with deceit, salted with calculation, and spiced with the overpowering belief in his own glorious destiny. Raised to the cardinalate in 1570 (he took the name of Cardinal Montalto), he was among the least influential members of the Sacred College. Perhaps that is why the powerful Duke Paolo Giordano Orsini didn't fear taking away that which the cardinal cherished most in the world. Montalto bided his time in prayerful forgiveness – until he was elected pope. From that day forward, all his formidable power would be directed toward punishing both his transgressor and those noblemen like him who had ever harmed the poor, the powerless, and the innocent. Italy shuddered as hundreds of heads with their mouths agape adorned the streets of Rome, grisly testament to the ruthlessness of the pope's retaliation.

Many contemporary authors report that Cardinal Montalto feigned his illness to win the papal election; cardinals sometimes preferred to elect a sickly, kind old pope, one who would require their advice, rather than a vigorous, independent one. Some twentieth-century historians have questioned the accuracy of these reports. Such a commanding, straightforward individual as Sixtus, they claim, would never have bamboozled his fellow cardinals regarding his health, coughing and leaning on a stick for several years before the papal election. Yet modern historians cannot deny that he lied when he repeatedly and publicly forgave the murderers who caused him pain, and then pounced on them as soon as he ascended to the papacy. Deceit, it seems, was a tool he used to accomplish his goals, as it was with most Renaissance princes.

At the center of the pope's vendetta stood Vittoria Accoramboni, widely acknowledged as the most beautiful girl in Rome. She possessed loveliness so astonishing and a manner so ingratiating that they allowed her weaknesses – vanity, selfishness, and shallowness, to name but a few – to escape scrutiny. She was never content with one day's blessings, but always impatient for what tomorrow would bring. Ultimately, she may have realized the error of her ways, but by then, of course, it was too late.

The story of Vittoria Accoramboni and her obese, powerful, lust-addled admirer, Duke Paolo Giordano Orsini, is strikingly reminiscent of that of Henry VIII and Anne Boleyn, whose passionate and bloody saga had occurred only fifty years earlier. Both women were raven-haired sex kittens bent on trading their bodies for wealth and position, refusing to assuage their suitors' desires until after the wedding. Both Henry VIII and the duke were apoplectic with frustration when they didn't get their own way. Both boldly fought the Church and the pope to have their dubious marriages validated.

Perhaps it is no coincidence that the riveting story of Pope Sixtus took place when William Shakespeare was a young man, scanning foreign tales to source ideas for his plays. This story has elements of *Macbeth*, *Hamlet*, *Romeo and Juliet*, and *Othello* – ambition, jealousy, and hatred that lead to murder, dead lovers, revenge, and a grand finale with cadavers piled high on the stage. The epilogue, which offers a gratifying morality lesson, is loudly declaimed by the last man standing.

We think of Renaissance thought as a civilizing influence on brutish medieval ways, and for good reason. Fueled by the invention of the printing press, literacy was on the rise; dark, forbidding castles became gracious, light-filled palaces. The first books of etiquette appeared where readers were informed that it was impolite to fart at the dinner table or blow their noses on the bread. Many of the artistic achievements of the period – in sculpture, painting and architecture

– represent what some historians consider to be the pinnacle of Western civilization.

Sadly, such refinements did not take root in men's hearts, but merely created a veneer of cultivation that masked ever-present medieval savagery. In examining this story, we will find a shocking dichotomy: a world where faith and sin, charity and murder, magnificence and filth flourished side by side, often within the psyche of the same individual. Noblemen might lay aside their weapons to study ancient Latin love poetry but would pick them up again at the slightest provocation. Inside the most refined nobleman, clad in gorgeous bejeweled velvet, a pendulum oscillated wildly between the extremes of cultured generosity and primitive violence. What's more, developments in the design of firearms throughout the fourteenth century – making them smaller and more portable – added an extra dimension to this violence from around 1500.

In the Renaissance, the wealthiest members of society were highly sensitive to perceived disrespect and would even commit murder with little cause. One reason for this noble propensity to violence is clear – the law rarely punished a nobleman, whose blue blood was a source of awe and wonder. Such a distinguished individual was let off with an admonishment, or temporarily banished from the city, or sentenced to open a soup kitchen. If a poor man committed a murder, he stood a greater chance of being executed.

Another reason for noble atrocities was the Renaissance ideal of honor, which was often connected to murder. Honor demanded that a man rely on valorous deeds to keep himself and his family safe. Only cowards and women took their cases to court, where they had little hope of justice anyway. Many judges were corrupt, favoring the side that could pay them the most substantial bribe.

In the name of honor, straying noble wives were strangled with red silk ribbons by husbands freshly returned from the whorehouse; defenseless enemies were mercilessly cut down in nighttime ambushes or poisoned during daytime dining. Some three centuries after our story, murder ceased to be an acceptable way to restore honour to oneself or one's family in Western nations, but here they were inextricably bound together.

Astonishing contradictions existed at all levels of society. Having burgled a home, the thief might stop off at the nearest church to donate some of his booty as alms. Prostitutes would keep a picture of the Virgin Mary next to their beds, and when the church bells rang, perplexed customers would be pushed aside as the women knelt down to pray. Assassins would often wait for their wounded victims to give their last confessions before administering the *coup de grâce* and would make the sign of the cross over the blood-soaked body.

In such a world, Cardinal Montalto would have felt justified in using deceit as his weapon of choice, hiding his anger and thirst for revenge until the time was right to reveal them. Indeed, the most compelling character in this curious assembly of murderous noblemen and sensuous women is the pontiff himself. Raised as an impoverished peasant with a penchant for plants, he saw himself as God's gardener.

At his accession to the papal throne, Rome was a long-neglected garden, untended, thirsty, overrun with creepers and thorns. As pope, he brought water to a parched Rome by repairing the ancient aqueducts; he weeded out the noxious elements of society and he fertilized his garden – God knew there was a great deal of fertilizer in Rome; he hoed wide paths straight across the city, ridding Rome of its maze of narrow medieval alleys and creating today's modern street system; he planted great trees of stone, raising ancient fallen obelisks and, in the case of the still-standing one on the side of the Vatican, moved it to the center of St. Peter's Square. These obelisks continue to serve as landmarks today.

For over a thousand years, from the founding of the Papal States in the eighth century until their loss following the unification of Italy in 1870, popes found themselves in a nearly impossible situation requiring completely contradictory talents. A saintly pope devoted to the spiritual interests of the Church was usually not a general or executioner, nor even much of an administrator or statesman. Likewise, popes who rode into battle in full armor and gladly executed enemies were unlikely to have been effective spiritual leaders.

Sixtus V was one of those rare pontiffs who had everything the job required: he was a statesman, administrator, judge, theologian and orator, whilst also a devout Catholic and a model of moral probity. He saw himself as a terrifying avatar descended from the heavens to enforce justice so long denied, an avenging fury sent by God to punish the wicked. At the root of his severity was a deeply personal wound that would never heal, caused by Vittoria Accoramboni, the most beautiful girl in Rome.

SOURCES

Countless manuscripts – or *relationi* – about Sixtus V exist in Italian archives. The authors write of his early years, the conclave in which he was elected, and the blow which changed his life forever. A *relatione* located at the Shakespeare Folger Library in Washington, D.C. is attributed to Cardinal Orazio Maffei, who died in 1610. A *relatione* consisting of six hundred pages in my personal collection was written by an anonymous author, and I refer to him as "the chronicler" in the following pages.

In addition to the *relationi,* there are two interesting English translations of books on the life of this extraordinary pontiff. In 1669, Gregorio Leti created his Italian *History of Sixtus V.* Though Leti was vociferously anti-Catholic, and generations of Church historians have been horrified by his somewhat undignified anecdotes, I found his biography surprisingly positive. Clearly, Leti admired the pope's tough stance on crime. In 1870, Baron Joseph Huebner, former Austrian ambassador to Italy, wrote his French *Life and Times of Sixtus the Fifth.*

Domenico Gnoli's *Vittoria Accoramboni, Storia del Secolo XVI* (1872) is priceless in its documentation of original archival sources. Cardinal Giulio Antonio Santorio, who was created cardinal along with Felice Peretti in 1570, wrote his autobiography in about 1600, where he mentioned Vittoria several times.

The Correr Museum Library in Venice has the last touching letter to his wife of Lodovico Orsini, Duke Paolo Giordano Orsini's violent cousin, as well as the "Defense" of the duke's secretary, Francesco Filelfo, of his actions in the great final conflict.

Diplomatic dispatches provide another rich source for our story. Foreign ambassadors living in Rome wrote in-depth weekly reports to their home governments, mixing in scurrilous street gossip with summaries of the pope's latest theological decrees. The Venetian diplomats showed exceptional ability in worming their way into a pontiff's confidence and reported every detail immediately to the Venetian Senate. Such diplomatic records still exist in national archives across Europe.

Early newssheets known as *avvisi* – or notices – have served as another source. These were handwritten documents of two to eight pages, consisting of small paragraphs in chronological order with no headlines. An *avvisi* writer sold subscriptions to foreign courts, banking houses, and wealthy individuals. In 1580s Rome, countless *avvisi* reported the riveting story of Vittoria Accoramboni amongst other news. Roman *avvisi* often had to be smuggled out of town, as local authorities took a dim view of spreading gossip abroad about Church corruption or bad government. Venice, however, operated presses more freely than Rome, and printed newssheets could be bought on the street for a Venetian penny – a *gazette*. They soon became known as gazettes themselves.

Two travel diaries have provided us with tantalizing glimpses of late Renaissance Rome, Venice, and Padua as seen by outsiders. A visitor's description of a city can be more useful to historians than that of a native, describing in detail sights and customs that residents might take for granted or fail to mention. From 1580-1581, Michel de Montaigne, a French nobleman, traveled throughout Italy seeking a cure for his appalling kidney stones at the salutary baths. He recorded in great detail the filth of the inns, the monuments of the cities, and even the beauty – or lack thereof – of the prostitutes.

In 1608, an Englishman named Thomas Coryat walked to Venice and back with the express purpose of writing the first tourism book. At the time, the idea of travel for sightseeing alone was laughable, given the paramount discomforts. Coryat is credited with introducing the fork to England and the Italian word *umbrella* into the English language. Coryat's book, *Coryat's Crudities: Hastily gobled up in Five Moneth's Travels*, was so successful that it launched the Grand Tour of the seventeenth–nineteenth centuries, a kind of traveling finishing school, whereby young British gentlemen perfected their education by visiting the continent, and, especially, Italy.

PART I

THE PURSUIT OF SPLENDOR

Chapter 1

THE MOST BEAUTIFUL
GIRL IN ROME

*Charm is deceptive, and beauty is fleeting; but a woman who fears the
Lord is to be praised.*

– Proverbs 31:30

It was a truth universally acknowledged in sixteenth-century Italy
that a girl whose dowry consisted mainly of her beauty was of far
greater interest to her suitors than to the suitors' families. Such women
may have been admired, but family members generally preferred an
infusion of cold, hard cash into the family. An ungainly girl with bad
skin and rotten teeth would have been welcomed as long as she trailed
rich booty in her wake.

In 1573, such was the problem faced by the raven-haired
Vittoria Accoramboni who, at sixteen, was widely acknowledged as
the most beautiful girl in Rome. Her face was a perfect ivory oval;
her nose and mouth were exquisitely sculpted, and her eyes were dark
and expressive. Many who saw her exclaimed that her beauty was a
miraculous gift from God.

Vittoria was praised not just for her looks, but for her seeming
sincerity and compassion, which bewitched her listeners. Cardinal
Orazio Maffei, who knew her, reported, "She had an extraordinary,
almost a miraculous attraction in conversation and comportment,
accompanied with no affectation or art. If it were possible for someone
not to be impressed with seeing her, he could not help but become
entangled as soon as he listened to her."[†]

---

† Strozzi, *Vita del Sommo*, folio 4b.

Vittoria's grace and beauty were burnished by a pedigree which could be traced back several centuries. In the 1200s, the Accorambonis had owned a castle in the town of Tolentino, two hundred miles northeast of Rome, but this had been confiscated by the pope when they rebelled against him. The family ended up in Gubbio, some one hundred miles north of the capital, where they owned an old palazzo. Many Accoramboni men found success in Rome, where they worked for the Church in diplomatic or governmental positions. Vittoria's grandfather, Girolamo, for example, was the personal physician of Pope Adrian VI (reigned 1522-1523). Her father, Claudio, was a military man who, having fought in France in his youth, turned to law, and worked for the Roman government. In the 1530s, Pope Paul III demonstrated his fondness for Claudio by arranging his marriage to a girl of good family, Tarquinia Albertoni.

Although Vittoria was blessed by the robust constitution which Tarquinia imparted to all her offspring, her mother's extraordinary fecundity was a distinct misfortune. Baptized in Gubbio on February 15, 1557, she was the tenth of eleven children – eight boys and three girls. The meager means of the Accorambonis weren't remotely sufficient to provide the girls with dowries and the boys with enough property to live honorably. Normally, the high childhood mortality rate of the time solved such a dilemma, but at least nine of the Accoramboni offspring grew stubbornly toward adulthood, radiating rude good health.

When a family suffered such financial constraints, some of the sons went into the Church. Here, with diligence and the patronage of a great bishop or cardinal, they could earn a comfortable living and rise in the Church hierarchy. And, indeed, two of Vittoria's brothers – Ottavio and Mario – chose that path. Others might enter the military where, if they survived, they would be enriched by the spoils of war. Such was the career of her brother, Camillo. Unfortunately, providing dowries for the girls to marry well was beyond the limited family resources. In such cases, most families would send their daughters to convents where their heavenly bridegroom, Jesus, required only a tenth of the dowry of a mortal husband. And so Vittoria's sisters,

Massimilla and Settimia, were bundled away to that great warehouse of unwanted women.

But it would have been a grievous waste to hide Vittoria's beauty in a place where it would do nothing to raise the family fortunes. The right marital alliances would not only help Vittoria attain an opulent lifestyle but would also boost the careers of her many brothers. Perhaps some elite family, with wealth, property, and ecclesiastical and governmental connections, would accept her with a small dowry. The Accorambonis could scrape together some 5,000 scudi, a respectable sum for a middle-class groom, but not nearly the going rate of 20,000 scudi required to secure the son of a noble and powerful family.

By the time Vittoria entered the marriage market, her family had moved to Rome, the capital of both the Catholic world and the nation known as the Papal States, which stretched roughly across the center of the Italian peninsula. There they settled into the Palazzo Albertoni which, despite its name, was really quite a modest house. Evidently, Vittoria's maternal relations, the Albertonis, had donated it, perhaps as part of Tarquinia's dowry, or perhaps out of pity for her limited circumstances. Three stories tall, with six narrow windows set closely together, today it is a patchwork of shades of red burnished by rain, wind, and time. To the left is a carriage entrance which leads to a small courtyard. Modest though it may have been, the location of their palazzo was excellent, conveniently close to the Piazza Navona, a large and bustling square in the heart of the city.

Vittoria's family must have been well aware that Rome – with its dozens of noble families boasting strapping single sons – offered greater marriage opportunities than Gubbio. As paterfamilias, Vittoria's father, Claudio, should have been instrumental in arranging her marriage and helping her with her many subsequent legal matters. But Claudio is conspicuously absent from contemporary records. It is her mother, Tarquinia, whose Machiavellian scheming would reputedly further her daughter's rise.

Surely, she must have reasoned, Vittoria's luminous beauty – a miraculous gift from God himself – was worth more than the grandest dowry? It was not, alas. Tarquinia was dissatisfied with the proposals that came in. Not one of them offered the grandeur that her daughter's beauty deserved. But one proposal offered *potential* grandeur, and this one she examined closely.

At twenty, Francesco Peretti was an easygoing youth of unimpressive background, whose family hailed from the Marches, a province of the Papal States on the east coast of Italy. His grandfather had been a subsistence farmer, eking out a living by growing vegetables and tending pigs on a rented strip of land. His grandmother had been a housekeeper for a wealthy matron. "The family of Peretti was so poor," according to one early biographer, "that they had not bread to eat, being fain to beg here and there."[†]

Francesco's mother, Camilla, had been a laundress married to a farmer, Gianbattista Mignucci, from her hometown of Montalto. Widowed, she had two surviving children, Francesco, and his sister Maria who was close to him in age. But the wild card in the family was Francesco's uncle, the distinguished theologian and orator, Cardinal Felice Peretti, known as Cardinal Montalto after his place of birth. Though the cardinal had suffered great poverty as a child and had helped his father raise pigs, his entrance into a monastery had provided him with an excellent education and a brilliant career.

Upon becoming a cardinal in 1570, Montalto plucked his sister and her children from the utter poverty of the country and installed them in greater comfort in Rome. "Camilla was so beloved by him," according to Cardinal Maffei, "that upon receiving his cardinalate and lacking other nephews by way of a brother, he adopted her children into his house, giving them his last name, his coat of arms, and making his heirs the two children… who were now no longer known as Mignucci, but would always be known as Peretti."[‡]

Cardinal Montalto loved Francesco as if he were his own son. Cardinals, of course, were not supposed to have sons – though many did – and it was their nephews whom they raised and educated, who became their heirs. Cardinal Montalto, having only one surviving nephew, placed all his hopes for the family in him. Francesco was

† Leti, *Nipotismo*, p. 70.
‡ Strozzi, *Vita del Sommo*, folio 5a.

seventeen when his uncle brought him to Rome and enrolled him in a humanities course supervised by a Jesuit friend. To prevent his nephew from developing inflated ideas of his new position, he made him wear middle-class clothing without any fashionable ornaments such as gold and silver embroidery, furred sleeves, or bejeweled buttons. One day, Cardinal Michele Bonelli remarked to Montalto, "He should appear a bit more noble." But Montalto replied, "What does your Excellency want? I was born poor and live poor. How can I permit that in my presence my nephew becomes rich and noble?"[†]

Cardinal Montalto kept his nephew's nose to the grindstone, far from sumptuous parties, where he would have learned both refined manners and bad habits. He used to say to Francesco, "Remember, my nephew, that you are the only support of our family. The only way you can rise in the world is to have good judgment towards your conduct and apply yourself to your studies. I have done my part, and you must do yours."[‡]

Although most cardinals lived princely lives in sumptuous palaces, surrounded by exquisite furnishings and supported by servants, Cardinal Montalto was one of the "poor cardinals", those whose income was below what was deemed necessary for a decent lifestyle. Poor cardinals received an extra subsidy from the pope so that a prince of the Church needed not be ashamed of his living conditions.

For Tarquinia, the cardinal's financial limitations were certainly a drawback as he was in no position to set up the young couple in a luxurious home. But the Accoramboni family was intrigued by the fact that Montalto was being touted by many in Rome as the next pope. Even as a child, Felice was believed by his family to be a future Vicar of Christ. The fascinating family story of his conception was recorded in a contemporary manuscript corrected by Sixtus V himself. One night when Piero Peretti's wife, Marianna, was residing with her employers, the voice of God woke up her husband, commanding him to pay her a conjugal visit.

[†] Cicogna, 1204, *Vita di Sisto V*, Part 2, folio 67b.
[‡] Ibid., folio 68a.

"Rise, Peretti," it said, "and go seek thy wife, for a son is about to be born to thee, to whom thou shalt give the name Felice since he is one day to be the greatest among mortals."[†] To sixteenth-century Italians, the greatest mortal was clearly the pope.

Their son was conceived that night and born on December 13, 1521, the fourth of seven children. Following the command of the angelic voice, they named him Felice – which means *happy* in Italian – for the joyous future that awaited him.

Four children survived childhood: Felice, Camilla, a sister named Flora – who died sometime after giving birth to a daughter around 1550 – and a brother named Prospero, who died in middle age in the 1560s. Felice and Camilla were extremely close. To raise money for the struggling family to buy food, sometimes the ragged little girl stood on the main road, holding her baby brother, offering to let passersby kiss the feet of a future pope in return for alms.

The boy's seemingly miraculous survival of childhood accidents confirmed the family's beliefs in his great destiny. One night while he was sleeping, his bed caught fire from a nearby lamp, but he escaped unharmed. As a toddler, he was found floating face down in a pond and was fished out suffering no ill effects. And the plague, which killed a brother who slept in his bed, left him unscathed.

As he faced the numerous challenges of his long Church career, Felice often spoke of what he would do when he finally became pope. Though noble cardinals and jealous monks might laugh at the aspirations of a low-born nobody from the Marches, Felice was completely convinced of his destiny. The people of Rome, eagerly believing heavenly signs and divine prognostications, looked on him with an uneasy awe. Hadn't his ascension to the papal throne been prophesied even before his conception? Surely, he would indeed become pope one day.

Tarquinia knew that if Uncle Felice fulfilled the prophecy to become pope, the family would become rich and powerful overnight. For centuries, nepotism – which comes from the Italian word *nipote* for *nephew* – had been an accepted practive within the

† Ranke, Vol. 3, p. 225.

Vatican. Most new popes would appoint an unmarried nephew to the position of "cardinal nephew" – a kind of secretary of state – the second-in-command in both Church and nation. If Vittoria married Francesco, the pope's only nephew would be ineligible to become a cardinal. The pope would, in all likelihood, select one of Vittoria's brothers who had already entered the Church. And once a cardinal, there was always the possibility of becoming pope. The cardinal nephew of Calixtus III (reigned 1455-1458) became Pope Alexander VI in 1492; and the cardinal nephew of Pope Sixtus IV (reigned 1472-1484) became Pope Julius II in 1502. And there were many others.

Lay nephews would also be richly rewarded. If Cardinal Montalto became pope, he would no doubt make Francesco a prince and Vittoria a princess. Sometimes popes purchased principalities for their nephews; occasionally they inherited them when a ruling dynasty died out, and sometimes they simply sent troops to wrest them in bloody battles from their rightful owners. This way, after the pope died, the nephew would still be a prince, living in a palace and ruling over a territory.

Usually, a new pope immediately made his lay nephew captain general of the Church and governor of the papal fortress, Castel Sant'Angelo – positions of great honor with even greater salaries. The pope arranged marriages for his family members, not only with the ducal houses of Italy but also the royal houses of Europe. Catherine de Medici, the niece of Clement VII (reigned 1523–1534), married the son of the King of France, eventually becoming queen. If Francesco's uncle, when he became pope, ruled for many years, Vittoria's teenaged children, too, could become cardinals or marry into royal families.

Considering the lacklustre nature of the other offers for Vittoria's hand, her parents decided to take a gamble on Francesco Peretti. His uncle, however, was not entirely pleased that the offer had been accepted. Given the scanty Peretti fortune, the cardinal wanted his nephew to marry a rich, virtuous girl from the Marches, not the spoilt, impoverished Vittoria, darling of Rome or not. Many wealthy families in his native area had watched the cardinal's career with pride and would have been honored by such a connection. But Francesco had his heart set on the enchanting Vittoria. He absolutely had to have her; no other bride would do.

Cardinal Montalto himself was not unmoved by the prospective bride's beauty and charm. And it was an honor for the pig farmers of Montalto to marry into an ancient and noble line. But the limitation of funds on both sides of the family was a severe handicap, given the bride's worldly ambitions. A girl like Vittoria would not be happy with anything but the most elegant clothing and furniture. Wise in the ways of human nature, the cardinal nevertheless agreed to the match, although perhaps with a sigh or a shudder of foreboding.

And so it came to pass that Francesco Peretti, son of a farmer and a laundress, married above his station for love, and Vittoria Accoramboni, a beautiful but poor noblewoman, married beneath herself for a chance at winning in the papal lottery. The dowry documents were signed on June 20, 1573, stating that the bride would bring with her the sum of 5,000 scudi, payable in installments. At dawn on June 28, 1573, the wedding cortege walked from the Accoramboni palazzo to the Church of Santa Maria della Corte.

Sometimes it is fortunate that young couples at the altar have no premonitions of their future together. They cannot see the day when indifference replaces love, when monotony replaces excitement, when sexual ardor is forgotten or only remembered with bitterness. The possibility of adultery is incomprehensible, the idea of murder ridiculous. We can imagine that, lacking this bitter foresight, Francesco and Vittoria were truly happy on that day, and perhaps for many days thereafter.

Following the ceremony, the wedding party walked to the palazzo of Vittoria's family for the traditional nuptial feast given by her father, Claudio, for all his acquaintances and their families. After the reception, the guests, to the accompaniment of fiddlers and dancing buffoons, escorted Vittoria and Francesco in a festive procession to the Peretti house on the nearby Via dei Leutari. It was common for brides to be led on a white horse, their long hair worn simply – hanging loose to indicate their virginity – but their clothing designed to impress. Given the stretched family finances, Vittoria's gown was, most likely, rented, though the family would never have admitted it. It could subsequently be rented again periodically for festive occasions to give the impression that she really did own it.

Vittoria's wedding cortege carried her trousseau, those items considered essential for married life in her new household. It consisted primarily of clothing – petticoats, corsets, ruffs, cuffs, stockings, nightgowns, dozens of embroidered linen shifts, and dresses – as well as household textiles such as bed curtains, sheets, towels, tablecloths, and napkins. To show off his wealth and generosity, perhaps her father contributed more expensive items for the young couple, such as cupboards, silverware, or glazed blue and yellow majolica plates. Heavy objects were rolled on carts to her new home. But the traditional items that brought good luck – that even the humblest bride brought to her new home – were a wedding chest containing her linens, a washbasin, a tankard, and a deep bowl from which she would drink fortifying broth after childbirth.

The day after the wedding, Vittoria was served a special breakfast of eggs for fertility and candy to encourage sweet love between the new couple. Such a meal was also meant to balance her bodily humors after the conjugal shock they had received the night before. As a reward for her virginity, on this day, too, Francesco was expected to give his bride additional wedding finery – gowns, headdresses, and jewels – which she was to wear publicly to honor the Peretti family. Like the gown, these as well were, in all likelihood, rented. After a few weeks, or days, Vittoria's in-laws would have relieved her of her fine raiment and plucked the jewels from her slender hands.

If Vittoria regretted the financial restraint necessary in the wedding festivities, at least she knew that things would change as soon as old Pope Gregory XIII died and Uncle Felice became the new pontiff. Then she would then be catapulted to fame and fortune, with enough money buy all the rubies and silks she desired. For now, exploring the world of sex with a husband who adored her, and beloved by his entire family, she was, perhaps, satisfied.

Chapter 2

AFTER THE HONEYMOON

I find more bitter than death the woman who is a snare, whose heart is a trap and whose hands are chains. The man who pleases God will escape her, but the sinner she will ensnare.

– Ecclesiastes 7:26

Tarquinia's hopes that Cardinal Montalto would boost the careers of her sons were quickly realized. Ottavio became the bishop of Fossombrone, a town in central Italy. Scipione obtained a position working for Cardinal Alessandro Sforza, one of the most influential cardinals, and quickly rose to manage his most important business. Mario became a Monsignor and an abbot.

But if Vittoria's marriage brought good fortune to her brothers, it failed to boost her own. While she found herself living in a respectable house at the corner of Via dei Leutari in a bustling area of booksellers, copyists, and map-makers, she was less happy that the house was crammed with her in-laws and their servants. In addition to Francesco's mother, his sister Maria, her husband and their increasing brood of children also lived there. At the time of Vittoria's marriage, Maria had a boy, Alessandro, born in 1571, and would that year give birth to a girl, Flavia. She would go on to have another girl, Felice, in 1575, and a son Michele, in 1577.

The house, which still stands, was accessed through an arched tunnel which opened up into a small courtyard. The space was not large enough for horses and carriages to turn around in, and its main purpose was to give light to the surrounding rooms. We can assume that in the sixteenth century the courtyard was home to various animals. At the far end was a covered circular staircase which rose for four stories; on each landing were two doors with thick rectangular stone lintels. Here, in these plain rooms, lived the cardinal's family. The cardinal did not live in the same house. He owned several contiguous buildings on the short Via dei Leutari and, because of his position, required a home with less din and greater dignity. His abode would have had a waiting room, an audience chamber and possibly even a throne. His residence was nevertheless small compared to those of the richest cardinals, such as Alessandro Farnese and Ferdinando de Medici.

We have an interesting description of Camilla's household a few years later, in 1585, when the Venetian ambassador visited her. It smacked of poverty, he wrote, and was almost bereft of furniture. He was particularly appalled at the garments of Maria's fourteen-year-old son Alessandro, "who went around in front of everybody with worn-out ragged clothes."[†]

Camilla, for her part, must have felt her life in Via dei Leutari was positively luxurious compared to her country home. Before her brother's summons, Camilla had been a laundress in Montalto, earning pennies for the most grueling work imaginable. She heated enormous cauldrons over raging fires, pushed disgusting soiled linens around with a paddle for hours, bleached them in a vat of human urine, hung them in the sun to dry, and ironed them slowly with a heavy iron heated repeatedly in the fireplace. Laundresses were known for their raw, chapped hands and red, puffy faces. Now, however, Camilla didn't have to do the laundry of others all day long; she would do it only for her own household and that of the cardinal.

Given the circumstances, it is no wonder that Camilla was famous for her frugality. In a society that valued ostentatious display – mostly on borrowed money – Camilla well understood the value of a scudo. She ran her household to avoid waste at all costs and tucked away the extra coins for a rainy day. On paper, at least, she was a wealthy woman because as her brother acquired property in Rome he put it all in Camilla's name so as to continue receiving his annual 1,200 scudi subsidy as a "poor" cardinal.

[†] Gnoli, p. 251.

Camilla was a scrappy, gritty woman, all bone and sinew. No job was beneath her, no work too hard for her. She ran her own household and that of her brother like a drill sergeant. But she welcomed the elegant Vittoria into her family with open arms. Camilla's beloved son had improved the family status not only by marrying a noblewoman, but the most beautiful girl in Rome, at that. And Camilla was delighted that her son was head over heels in love with his wife, a rarity among married couples of the time. Yet it is unlikely that Camilla's new daughter-in-law pitched in much with the housework. It is difficult to imagine Vittoria joining Camilla in scrubbing floors, bleaching ruffs in urine, or trudging to the market each morning with a basket over her arm to buy cabbages. And it is possible that Camilla, awed by her noble daughter-in-law, didn't expect it of her.

One of the only honorable, noble, and ladylike contributions Vittoria could offer the family was sewing and embroidery. Needlework was considered highly ethical for members of the gentler sex, protecting them from the perils of an idle mind, which was particularly dangerous for a woman. According to contemporary beliefs, if a woman's mind had nothing in it, the vacuum between her ears would suction up the "naughty vapors" from her private parts directly into her brain, causing "the unruly motions of tickling lust."[†] If she did not start having orgies with strange men, she would break out in pimples and lose her wits.

Luckily, there was plenty of needlework to keep the vapors firmly where they belonged. In sixteenth-century Rome, even an artisan would have a score of white linen shirts. In addition, women of all classes had dozens of large handkerchiefs, a fashion accessory used as a headdress, a shawl tucked into the bodice or hanging from a belt. Many women chose patterns from embroidery books, which had recently become popular, and were sold on the Via Pasquino, around the corner from Vittoria's home. Homemade fan kits were popular, and perhaps Vittoria, who could not afford an exquisite mother-of-pearl jeweled fan, cut out her own and glued feathers and ribbons onto it. And so we can imagine Camilla cheerfully emptying

† Somerset, p. 90.

chamber pots and plucking chickens while her daughter-in-law sedately embroidered a pillowcase or fidgeted with a fan.

While Vittoria embroidered, it is not certain what kept Francesco busy. When he married Vittoria, he had probably just completed his university education, as most young men received their degrees at the age of nineteen or twenty. Given his uncle's work ethic, it is certain that the cardinal would have found him gainful employment. Cardinal Montalto didn't want Francesco to live in indolence off his uncle's position but wanted "to see sweat with honor to be able to live hand-to-mouth", according to the chronicler.[†]

Francesco very possibly worked for the cardinal himself, writing his letters and keeping track of his appointments. Or maybe Montalto had obtained for him a job in the Vatican administration. Few details emerge about Francesco, though contemporary records leave us with the impression that he was a good-natured youth, if a bit thick-headed. He was certainly ill-equipped to deal with the increasing demands of his beautiful bride.

For as the years wore on – unbearably the same, unbearably impoverished – the sweet girl morphed into an angry, demanding woman. Her beauty was worth more than a wretched room in a cramped house. She was worthy of a grand palace boasting dozens of servants in gorgeous livery. Her courtyard should be stuffed with gilded carriages and matched teams of proud horses instead of chickens, pigs, and their dung. Her wardrobe should consist of a rainbow of bejeweled gowns of velvet and silk, trimmed with fur.

At the dining table, as she daubed her shapely mouth with a napkin which she had gracefully embroidered herself, Vittoria saw that she was surrounded by country bumpkins. The cardinal uncle, despite his two decades of hobnobbing with the most eminent men in Rome, retained his rural ways. Years later, when foreign ambassadors carefully observed his manners, they wrote of his digging into his food and gulping his wine with dishonorable gusto. He had the alarming habit of dribbling food on his chin and then wiping it off with the

† Anon., p. 118.

back of his hand. And he had made sure his nephew retained the humble habits of the countryside lest he succumb to the sin of pride.

Rome was full of up-and-coming country clodhoppers hoping to win the patronage of a cardinal or powerful nobleman. Europe's first etiquette book, *Il Galatheo*, written in 1559 by Giovanni della Casa, attempted to teach them good manners so they would not disgrace themselves when spending time with the better bred. Reading the instructions, perhaps we can understand some of Vittoria's frustrations.

"And when thou hast blowne thy nose," della Casa advises, "use not to open thy handkerchief, to glare uppon thy snot, as if thou hadst pearles and Rubies fallen from thy braynes."[†]

Though della Casa stated that it was impolite to urinate in front of others, many men stepped away from the dinner table to pee nonchalantly into the fireplace or in a bowl in the corner. The author considered it in bad taste in company to fart, belch, pick one's teeth, nose, or ears, or thrust a hand down one's breeches to scratch at fleas devouring the private parts.

The poorly bred were known to cough and sneeze loudly, without so much as covering their mouths with their hands. "So there be some kinde of men, that in coffing or neesing [sneezing], make suche noise, that they make a man deafe to here them, and spray upon all those nearby. Besides these there be some, that in yauning, braye and crye out like Asses."[‡]

Della Casa was disgusted by those who dine "like swine with their snouts in the washe, all begroined, and never lift up their heads nor looke up, muche lesse kepe their hands from the meate, and with both their cheeks blowne, as if they should sound a trumpet or blowe the fier, not eate but ravon: who, besmearing their hands almost up to their elbowes, so bedawbe the napkins, that the cloaths in the places of easement [toilet paper] be other while cleaner... Neither is it good maner, to rubbe your gresie fingers uppon the bread you must eat."[§]

[†] della Casa, folio 7b.
[‡] Ibid., folio 6b–7a.
[§] Ibid., folio 9b–10a.

Understanding the vast gulf of breeding that yawned between themselves and this prodigy of beauty who had condescended to join their family, the Perettis bent over backwards to keep her happy. "Vittoria entered into the Peretti house with such superiority that was fatally conceded to her," wrote Cardinal Maffei, "that wherever she turned, she was not only specially received, but universally loved. And not only by Francesco, who adored her almost to the point of craziness, but also by his mother, Camilla. Cardinal Montalto was seen to have such a tenderness of affection that he didn't study anything else but her satisfaction … treating also her brothers as if they were his own nephews."[†]

Vittoria "had youthful feminine inclinations, so that the cardinal, as well as Camilla, both known as frugal people, satisfied her with happy liberality, almost without being asked, and almost competed to spoil her and enrich her with much, and rich pearls, and jewels, and splendid things much superior to their state."[‡] Unfortunately, although the family stretched its budget to accommodate her expensive tastes, it was never enough.

Despite Vittoria's improved wardrobe, she found to her grinding chagrin that when she attended banquets and balls, noblewomen far less attractive than she outshone her in gorgeous gowns and blazing jewels. It was a great injustice, this dimming of her God-given beauty, and Vittoria was determined to see justice done. And so, while Camilla was carefully saving used candle stubs to melt together into new candles and scraping ashes from the hearth to be used for making soap, Vittoria went shopping. She bought gowns and jewels, and dainty pieces of furniture inlaid with mother-of-pearl for her bedroom, and heady perfumes, and ostrich-feather fans, and gauzy headdresses embroidered with pearls.

She quickly ran up enormous debts. Most of the Italian Renaissance economy was based on debt. Hard cash was a rarity, so even a loaf of bread was often paid for with a promise. Most of the carriages of Rome's great nobles had been bought on credit, as well

[†] Strozzi, *Vita del Sommo*, folio 5a–b.
[‡] Strozzi, *Vita del Sommo*, folio 5b.

as their velvet clothes bedecked with pearls and rubies. Butchers and bakers who provided sumptuous banquets at the palaces of the rich might remain unpaid for years. Debt was nothing to be ashamed of; indeed, many debtors prided themselves on their long lists of creditors – proof on paper that their honorable names alone guaranteed easy credit.

Small infusions of cash were enough to keep the creditors from bringing in the bailiff. These sums were easily obtained by pawning household goods. According to family account books in Italian archives, some valuable items were pawned twenty times or more over the life of their owners to meet pressing debts. As it was, most Italians who made wills furnished their heirs with a long list of creditors, some of them going back decades, who needed to be paid promptly so that the deceased would find no obstacles barring his path to heaven.

Bartering was also common, and a cash-deprived nobleman who brought in barrels of wine and olive oil from his country estate at harvest time might pay his butcher or baker with those. But not just items of value were bartered. We have difficulty today imagining going into a bar and paying for a glass of wine with a pair of dirty socks or a stained napkin, but such was Rome in the sixteenth century.

Sometimes creditors accepted favors in lieu of payments. If Vittoria could convince her cardinal uncle to obtain a Vatican position for her dressmaker's son, it was likely the dressmaker's invoice would magically disappear. Or her brother serving in the Duke of Savoy's army might welcome as his aide the promising younger brother of her jeweler. But in the end Vittoria's retail desires were greater than any favors she could provide.

Chapter 3

GREED

He that is greedy of gain troubleth his own house, but he who hateth gifts shall live.

– Proverbs 15:27

When Vittoria's tangled web of debts became too much, and she needed cash to keep her creditors at bay, she began to think of her dowry. According to custom, a bride's dowry was legally hers and would be returned to her if her husband died, or if he beat her so brutally that she left him. In the meantime, the groom's family had the right to invest the dowry as they saw fit. The only stipulation was that the bride should be given a monthly allowance from the investment.

When Vittoria's father paid out the last quarterly installment of her dowry on May 24, 1576, Cardinal Montalto used the 1,250 scudi to buy land near his favorite church, Saint Mary Major, land which he put in Camilla's name. This was the breeziest, highest point in Rome, some 250 feet above sea level, adorned with the towering stone ruins of the Servian Walls, a barricade built around the city in the fourth century BC. Becoming a prince of the Catholic Church had not changed Montalto's love of hard physical labor, and within a year he had personally turned the overgrown hill into a fragrant, blooming slice of Paradise.

Perhaps it was a mistake for him to proudly show Vittoria the fruits of his efforts. The moment she saw the beautiful spot, she wanted it for herself. Hadn't her dowry gone to pay for it? Why shouldn't she have it, and use the sale of olive oil and wine for her maintenance? Remarkably, she managed to persuade Montalto of the righteousness of her cause and, although he adored his garden, he signed it over to Francesco and Vittoria on October 2, 1577.

Vittoria's expenses were increasingly competing with the cardinal's good works. Montalto's income was only 8,000 scudi a year – tiny for a cardinal. Out of this, he maintained his own household and that of Camilla. He provided houses for poor families in his impoverished hometown of Montalto, where, in 1578, he built a grammar school and hired a teacher. In 1579, he arranged to pay the salary of a doctor to provide free medical care to the community.

In June 1579, the cardinal provided Valeria, daughter of his dead sister Flora, a dowry of 3,000 scudi, the same amount he had paid for the dowry of Camilla's daughter Maria back in 1570, when she had married a Roman gentleman of moderate means. He squirreled away another 3,000 scudi for the future marriage of Maria's daughter, Flavia. He even gave Camilla's maidservant, Franceschina, a dowry of 200 scudi. This was not all. One of the duties of a cardinal, even a poor one, was to embellish churches; Montalto erected a beautiful marble chapel in Saint Mary Major.

But Vittoria kept angling for more luxuries. She found it shameful that she didn't have a coach and peppered the cardinal with requests to buy her one. Roman streets were clogged with several inches of filth – manure from horses, donkeys, and oxen, as well as rotten food and the contents of chamber pots cavalierly tossed out of windows. When forced to walk in the street, Roman noblewomen were careful to avoid soiling the hems of their gowns. They wore high platform clogs over their velvet slippers. These clogs would squelch down a couple inches into the stinking muck and still leave the gowns unscathed and the dainty slippers inside as good as new. But it was better not to walk at all, and any woman worth her salt had to have her own coach.

Coaches had only recently come into fashion. Before that, Romans were carried in sedan chairs in town. For longer journeys, they rode horses or mules, the women often traveling in litters – long boxlike structures swinging between wheels, in which passengers lay down on pillows. But in the early sixteenth century, Hungarians invented a rudimentary spring suspension system for carriages. As long as the roads were good and the trip was short, the new carriages provided a faster and smoother ride. Ideal for city traveling, by the 1570s they had become all the vogue in Rome.

In 1575, one irate bishop wrote a memorandum recommending that coaches be forbidden on account of the spirit of luxury and extravagance which the new fashion had introduced. Furthermore, he complained that the total number of such vehicles in Rome now amounted to more than 2,000 and routinely clogged the narrow twisting streets that had been built for foot and horse traffic. If all the coaches could be piled up in one enormous bonfire and burnt, it would be a good riddance, the bishop stated, as well as a most acceptable sacrifice to God. But Vittoria just had to have one. Importuned incessantly by his niece, Cardinal Montalto repeatedly agreed to buy her a coach, but it somehow failed to materialize.

Only two months after obtaining her vineyard, Vittoria wanted to sell it back to the cardinal uncle for 750 scudi more than he had paid for it. Evidently the fall harvest had been insubstantial as the trees and vines were too young to produce much fruit. Her plan was to invest the cash from the sale in annuities, which would bring greater income.

The fact that Vittoria was not alone in her importunities but was aided and abetted by her ambitious family is proven by a fascinating document which she, Francesco, her parents, and four brothers delivered to the cardinal. They had, evidently, held a family meeting on how to squeeze more money from him.

December 12, 1577

Memorandum of that which is requested by the grace of the most Illustrious Monsignor Padrone.

First, that the 2,000 scudi of the dowry that is called "of the vineyard" be put into annuities. In addition, we accept the offer of his most illustrious and reverend Holiness that assigns to Vittoria all the interest of the dowry for her food, clothing, salaries of her servants and other needs, and it is asked that as much be given to Signor Francesco for his food and needs.

But the Accorambonis were not content with simply reinvesting the dowry. Francesco had borrowed a great deal of money to satisfy his wife's creditors, and they wanted the old cardinal to loosen his purse strings and pay the bills.

And we must remember that Signor Francesco owes 600 scudi to the company of offices [evidently a lending institution], on which he has to pay interest. And there remain many scudi of old debts that he will be forced to satisfy if he stays in Rome and lives among men.

They then reminded the cardinal of his oft-repeated promise to buy Vittoria a coach and made a subtle threat if he did not comply:

And if his most Illustrious Sanctity cannot at the moment pay these, he is contented to assign him [Francesco] the interest only on the dowry, and to give him permission to go and stay a few years at Montalto, where it costs less to live than staying in Rome, where it is particularly necessary to have a coach. And his Holiness will deign to remember having promised this many times.

It would have reflected poorly on the cardinal if the coachless, indebted couple moved to Montalto because they could not pay their bills in Rome. People would murmur that he had been generous to his hometown but was evidently parsimonious with his closest relatives.

This is what is desired and humbly requested of your Holiness from all who have signed below:

Signor Claudio   Signor Francesco
Signora Tarquinia   Signora Vittoria
Mario
Marcello
Flaminio

To his credit, Vittoria's brother Ottavio, whom Montalto had made a bishop, drew up the document but refused to sign it.

> I, Ottavio, by their decree, holding myself as a man too interested
> in the affairs of your illustrious Holiness, abstain from voting."[†]

Montalto, taking a shrewd look at the situation, agreed to the request to reinvest the dowry on one condition: Vittoria would have to budget her personal expenses based on the investment income and not bounce back begging him for more. He even agreed to give Francesco the same amount of monthly income for his food, clothing, and servants.

The cardinal bought back the vineyard at the full appraisal price of 2,000 scudi, which Vittoria invested in bonds. Additionally, in February 1578, he gave her two annuities, one in the amount of 1,650 scudi and the other for 1,350 scudi, which yielded about eight percent interest a year. And so, Vittoria was now in complete control of her 5,000 scudi dowry and could do with it what she wanted. But if she were to live on the 400 scudi annual interest alone, she would have to reign in her shopping sprees.

The cardinal was delighted to possess once more his beloved vineyard. He immediately bought a neighboring piece of land and brought in bushes, trees, and flowers, which he personally planted and tended. A rich man, it is said, is not he who has the most, but he who needs the least. And Cardinal Montalto, requiring only the love of his family, his collection of theological books, and a place to make green things grow, felt rich indeed.

Curiously, despite the almost shameful moderation of his lifestyle, he was far richer than many other cardinals and Roman noblemen who lived in opulent palazzos on credit. When many such men died, and their relatives eagerly had their rings, crucifixes, and bejeweled altars appraised, they were often disgusted to learn that over the years all the gems had been replaced by glass.

Instead of throwing lavish banquets to impress others, Montalto bought little houses to rent out. Instead of buying furniture and horses on credit, he paid cash up front. If the household account books of the "richest" men in Rome could have been examined, it would have been

† Gnoli, pp. 34–35.

found that most of them were deeply in debt. Cardinal Montalto's account books, however, showed a gratifying balance.

He had worked hard all his life, living in monastic poverty. He had saved, and invested, and even if he died soon without ever becoming pope, Camilla and Francesco would have enough income from the rental properties (alone) to live comfortably. Now, as he approached his sixtieth birthday, he decided that it was time to own something truly lovely, paid, of course, with cash. He hired an architect named Domenico Fontana to design for him a princely palace on the hill overlooking his gardens. It would be called Villa Montalto.

But if, after all the family financial maneuverings, the cardinal was content with his growing plants and rising villa, Vittoria nevertheless remained dissatisfied with her life. The monthly income on her annuities was extremely limiting, and Cardinal Montalto had made clear she was not to ask him for any more.

It is likely that everything would have been quite different if Vittoria had had a child. Offspring would have made her a full member of the family, rather than an ornamental outsider siphoning off the patrimony to pay for her frivolities. Camilla would have forgiven her instantly for her bad temper and wasteful ways. The cardinal would have pried open his wallet, doling out money more generously to the mother of his great-nephew. Perhaps most importantly, children would have given Vittoria something useful to do.

There were many measures a woman could take to cure her infertility: drink a potion of pulverized snake skins, rabbit milk, and crayfish; have a virgin boy place a belt inscribed with prayers around her waist as she chanted three Our Fathers and three Ave Marias; inhale the fumes of crushed amber; contemplate a beautiful image of the Virgin and Child, and many more. The truly desperate could drink periwinkles pounded to powder and mixed with earthworms, or a brew made of the ashes of a frog mixed with the genitals of a wild boar. She could munch on the middle finger and anus of a fetus born two months early and wash it down with a glass of mule's urine. Or she could drink the blood of a freshly slaughtered hare, infused with the left hind paw of a weasel, steeped in vinegar. And if all else failed, an infertile wife could make a pilgrimage to Loreto, on the east coast of Italy, to the very house where Jesus had been miraculously conceived in Nazareth, and which, it was believed, had been flown to Italy by angels who rescued it from Muslim conquerors.

When these cures didn't work, Vittoria became a vicarious mother, a godmother to several neighborhood babies, according to the local parish registry. Holding the little bundle at the baptismal font, Vittoria must have enjoyed for a few minutes the feeling of squirmy warmth against her breast. But then she was forced to relinquish the child to the mother, and her arms were once again empty. Many of her goddaughters were named after her.

While Vittoria's brothers Mario, Giulio, and Ottavio were aided by the cardinal uncle in their careers, her favorite brother, Marcello, received assistance of a different kind, in this instance, saving his life. Marcello, a young man of devilish good looks, was a gambling, dueling, womanizing, hard-drinking rogue. At some point in the late 1570s, this swaggering sack of testosterone-enhanced bravado had brawled with a pharmacist's servant and ended up killing him. Fortunately for Marcello, little account was taken when a nobleman killed a servant, which meant that Marcello was not charged.

However, one hot summer night in 1580, Marcello stabbed the brother of Cardinal Pietro Pallavicino in the heart, killing him instantly. This time, the authorities were not prepared to take such a nonchalant view of murder. As soon as it became known that Marcello was the murderer, the governor of Rome issued an order for his arrest. Marcello took flight, galloping out of the city gates and finding refuge some twenty miles north of Rome, in the fortress of the Orsini family on Lake Bracciano. Fortunately for Marcello, the owner – Duke Paolo Giordano – was always happy to draft brave and reckless young men into his personal army of hoodlums.

For the sake of Vittoria, and of Francesco, who considered Marcello his best friend in the world, Cardinal Montalto used his connections once again to obtain a legal reprieve for Marcello. Little did the good cardinal know how dearly he would pay for his kindness.

But Cardinal Montalto could not prevent the servants of Cardinal Pallavicino from seeking bloody revenge on the man who had killed the cardinal's brother. When Marcello wanted to visit his family, he snuck into the city incognito and stayed quietly with Francesco and Vittoria. At night, Marcello and Francesco would walk the few blocks to the Accorambonis' palazzo, Marcello disguised in a wig, moustache, and borrowed cloak, and both men armed. Marcello's visits were always secretive, brief, and dangerous. The predicament of Vittoria's brother, along with her inability to have children and unhappy marriage, depressed her.

Worst of all, the one stroke of luck she had been counting on now seemed out of reach. Pope Gregory XIII had been seventy years old when he ascended the papal throne in 1572, in a century when most wealthy adult males died by their mid-fifties. And despite the fondest hopes of Vittoria, Tarquinia, and Cardinal Montalto, the years slipped by seemingly with no end in sight. The pope ate fruits and salads, avoided rich food and wine, and exercised regularly in the Vatican gardens, walking so briskly that his young secretaries, huffing and puffing, struggled to keep up with him. In January 1578, Gregory visited all of the seven main churches of Rome in freezing weather, a journey which didn't tire him at all but exhausted the twenty-year-olds in his suite.

During Easter week of 1579, the Mantuan ambassador reported that the pope seemed as vigorous as if he were only forty years of age. Many elderly popes required a chair during long ceremonies, but Gregory insisted on standing, even throughout the entire five-hour Easter service. "He is a very handsome old man," wrote the French traveler Michel de Montaigne in 1580, "of the middle height and upright, his face full of majesty, a long white beard. He is as healthy and vigorous as one could possibly wish, without gout, without colic, without stomach trouble."†

Gregory's predecessor, Pius V, had died at sixty-eight, and his own predecessor, Pius IV, at sixty-six. But it seemed that this pontiff was never going to die. Even worse for Vittoria, Cardinal Montalto

† Montaigne, p. 125.

had begun to lean on a stick and wheeze. If he died, all of his income from the church would disappear, as would her hopes of becoming the niece of a pontiff.

Frustrated on all sides, Vittoria's heart soared when at parties and feasts she was the object of attention of rich and powerful men. She danced gracefully in her silks and showed off the gems Camilla and Francesco had squeezed out of the family budget, or that she had bought on credit, or that Cardinal Montalto had donated to maintain family harmony instead of buying bread for the poor. And here were men who, unlike her bumbling husband, were worthy of her, men who could provide her with the things she wanted. Here for a few hours she was the center of attention, and her beauty was lauded as it always should have been, until she was forced to return to Camilla's meager home.

If written words could utter a sigh, Cardinal Maffei's do. "Finally," he wrote, "you could say this marriage would have been most happy if men knew to measure their happiness with the enjoyment of what they possess, not with the instability of what they hope, the only stumbling-block of true happiness. When we impetuously chase our hopes outside of secure and tangible things, they drag us to perilous precipices, and flee."[†]

Cardinal Santorio, who was no friend of the Accorambonis, believed that Vittoria stepped beyond the fatal boundary of flirting into the quagmire of adultery, and that her mother and brother Marcello encouraged it. "The name of marriage she abused with libertinism and voluptuousness," he wrote. "First a little bit and secretly, then openly, enticing her lovers, immoderate in her splendor, haughty of new conquests... She had a firm step, open eyes, and mouth always ready to laugh and charm." He added scornfully, "It seemed to the Accorambonis that vices and lust provided a clearer path to fortune."[‡] That much, at least, was true.

But there is no surviving evidence that Vittoria actually had sex with her admirers. Perhaps she was deterred by the punishment; to

---

[†] Strozzi, *Vita del Sommo*, folio 5b-6a.
[‡] Gnoli, p. 29.

maintain a noble family's honor, adulteresses were usually strangled with a red silk ribbon, thought to be worthy of the nobility, which inevitably broke and was replaced by a thick, knotted, low-class rope. If the adulteress remained unpunished, the honor of the entire family would tank and none of them would be able to hold up their heads in public. Unless the unfaithful female relative of a cardinal underwent punishment, the cardinal would not have been able to show his face in church. But we hear nothing of red silk wrapped around Vittoria's slender neck, only pearls and gold.

According to the ancient epic of the Trojan War, welcoming splendid beauty within one's doors could be a dangerous thing. Francesco was in some ways like the foolish shepherd, Paris, who stole the most beautiful woman in the world, Helen, and brought her to Troy. In stubbornly insisting on possessing a fabled beauty, both Paris and Francesco unwittingly unleashed a brutal war. For other, richer, more powerful men wanted her, too.

Chapter 4

THE LOVER

See how the faithful city has become a harlot! She once was full of justice; righteousness used to dwell in her – but now murderers!

– Isaiah 1:21

After eight years of waiting for Pope Gregory XIII to die, Vittoria and her family lost patience. After all, Cardinal Montalto's future pontifical glory was the only reason the most beautiful girl in Rome had married into the wretched Peretti family to begin with. In particular, her ambitious mother, Tarquinia, was considering Vittoria's options. In sixteenth-century Italy, divorce was not one of them.

Since the pope seemed to be immortal, Vittoria and Tarquinia began to hope that Francesco was not. Young, healthy men died all the time from malaria or dysentery. With no antibiotics, a simple cold could turn into bronchitis, and then pneumonia. With no means to stanch internal bleeding, riding and carriage accidents culled a few victims, particularly among young men who liked to race. Once relieved of her embarrassing husband, the charming young widow could make a better matrimonial choice and enjoy the rewards that her beauty so eminently deserved.

At the age of twenty-four, and having lost the first freshness of youth, Vittoria must have worried that her good looks might soon decay. Smallpox could ruin a woman's complexion overnight. And many women in their twenties started to lose teeth. Painful cavities were plentiful in a society fond of sweets but ignorant of hygiene, and a "dentist" was a big, burly man wielding a large pair of pliers. Once her looks were gone, she wouldn't be able to snag the kind of man she wanted, trading beauty for wealth and nobility. If Francesco were going to liberate her, it would have to be soon.

And then, a certain rich nobleman made it clear to Vittoria that he would be happy to marry her as soon as she was widowed. Paolo Giordano Orsini, the Duke of Bracciano, was the most powerful baron in Rome. Born in 1541, he was the scion of a great Roman family which dated back to the eighth century and was allied to the royal houses of Denmark, Sweden, Norway, Poland, Hungary, France, Spain, and Naples. The Spanish King Philip II called the duke his kinsman. Eleven European queens had been Orsinis, and no less than twelve sons of emperors and kings had married Orsini daughters. The clan boasted several cardinals in their family tree, along with two popes. They could thank the poet Dante for their eternal fame in literature; he gleefully consigned one corrupt Orsini pope – Nicholas III (reigned 1277-1280) – to hell.

Paolo Giordano was the proud owner of numerous palaces in Rome and of the frowning turreted fortress on Lake Bracciano, twenty miles to the north. Although he was the great-grandson of two popes – Julius II (reigned 1503-1512) on his father's side, and Paul III (reigned 1534-1549) on his mother's – Paolo Giordano's ancestors were not quite so great: one of them, Gentil Virginio, was an egomaniac who enjoyed prancing about in lavish costumes and switched loyalties whenever the wind changed direction. Another ancestor, Gian Giordano, was a megalomaniac afflicted by uncontrollable spending. His uncle Francesco was an arrogant spendthrift who murdered his brother in an ambush.

Paolo Giordano's father had died before he was born. His mother abandoned him to relatives to remarry when he was four and died six years later. Uncle Francesco, who by this time was thought to be mad, was put in charge of the estate until Paolo Giordano came of age, during which time he almost bankrupted the family. The boy was raised by another uncle, Cardinal Guid'Ascanio Sforza, who allowed him to roam Rome unsupervised, popping into taverns, gambling dens, and whorehouses at will. Raised so haphazardly, the child sustained himself with an unflagging certainty of his noble greatness and developed a shocking lack of self-discipline that would plague his entire life.

Now, at the age of forty, the duke offered any potential bride two enormous disadvantages. First of all, there was his appearance. Of a gigantic stature, he was so morbidly obese that he had difficulty finding a horse strong enough to hold him. He penned urgent letters to friends and cardinals begging them to locate colossal muscular steeds that wouldn't collapse as soon as he mounted them. On September 15, 1575, he wrote one such letter to Cardinal Antonio Caraffa. "Will your most Illustrious Sanctitude do me the favor of granting one of his bay mares for my person," he asked, "because of the weight and quality of my body, for which not every horse is good."†

His weight also served as a disadvantage in his military career. When the pope and several Catholic states declared war against the Ottoman Turks in 1571 for seizing Venetian vessels, Paolo Giordano insisted on commanding a galley in the upcoming naval battle. But Catholic military leaders were afraid that his ungainly bulk would roll around the deck like a loose barrel – hardly an inspiring sight in a naval commander. They yielded, as they always did, to his illustrious heritage, and Paolo Giordano waddled on board cheerfully. He returned from the victorious Battle of Lepanto gloriously wounded in the leg by a Turkish arrow. But reports filtered back that initial misgivings about his performance had proved correct; he had become the object of ridicule, "revealing himself to be so inept due to his excessive fatness."‡

Paolo Giordano had a scarlet face, bulging brown eyes, and wiry dark hair. He had a strange stiff moustache, which he must have waxed, that curled up at both ends, and a goatee so small it looked as if he had spilled some gravy on his chin. Though renowned as a man of noble tastes and exquisite manners – a contemporary wrote that he possessed "every supreme title of excellence; a noble soul, surpassing liberality, royal hospitality, largely charitable, gloriously magnificent, wise as a ruler, gentle and humane to his dependents, of incomparable

---

† Gnoli, p. 65, n.
‡ Murphy, p. 222.

courtesy" – his good breeding was only a coat of shellac over a rough and brutal soul. [†]

This savage passion was expressed in his second disadvantage: the little matter of his first wife's demise. In 1558, seventeen-year-old Paolo Giordano had married sixteen-year-old Isabella de Medici, the daughter of Duke Cosimo of Tuscany. A witty, talented beauty, Isabella spoke Spanish, French, and Latin, played several musical instruments, sang like an angel, and wrote beautiful poetry. Of Duke Cosimo's many children, Isabella was called "the fairest star of the de Medici."[‡] It was, of course, a marriage arranged for political reasons: Cosimo needed Orsini support to conquer Siena, as the extended family of the Orsinis owned several counties surrounding the city. A son born to the couple, uniting the blood of the Orsinis and de Medicis, would ensure political and military support in the future.

Unfortunately, Paolo Giordano could no more control his finances than his eating and seemed to have had what today we might call compulsive spending disorder. He bought horses, carriages, hunting dogs, falcons, furnishings, and fine clothing. He gave banquets, feasts, and lavish entertainments, including one in Rome in December 1563 to celebrate the visit of his in-laws, the ducal family of Tuscany. One of his servants wrote to his friends at Bracciano, "There are triumphal arches, jousts, hunts and such costumes that you could not imagine the money spent on them, but as for us courtiers we cannot touch any funds for household management or to put the palace in order."[§] By the tender age of sixteen, he was deeply in debt.

If the bride was disappointed in the groom, she must have been consoled by the dowry her father bestowed on her: 50,000 gold ducats and 5,000 ducats in jewels, the equivalent today of $20 million. Naturally, it was important that this sum did not find its way into the hands of the spendthrift groom. Duke Cosimo kept his daughter, and her dowry, firmly in Florence, where she arranged elegant entertainments for the court. Naturally, Paolo Giordano was free

---

† Martinengo-Cesaresco, p. 137.
‡ Langdon, p. 146.
§ Murphy, p. 129.

to visit her whenever he wished. But according to sixteenth-century tradition, it was a humiliating situation for a young man, who was expected to take his bride to *his* castle. The situation irked Paolo Giordano, who saw it as an insult to his Orsini pride. He took out his frustrations by frequenting the vilest whorehouses in Rome. Isabella, however, was delighted. She must have heaved an enormous sigh of relief as she waved her scented handkerchief from the palace balcony at his fat form and suffering horse riding off into the sunset. She used her freedom to take a lover, the lithe and handsome Troilo Orsini, a relative of Paolo Giordano, and gave birth to two of his children while her husband was out of town. Servants whisked them away to the local orphanage. Isabella also had several pregnancies she credited to Paolo Giordano, resulting in miscarriages and stillborn infants. Finally, the couple had two healthy children – Leonora, in 1571, and the heir, Virginio, in 1572.

Despite his inability to get his hands on his wife's dowry, Paolo Giordano continued his reckless high living. In 1567, the Venetian ambassador wrote, "The house of Orsini has as its head Paolo Giordano, Duke of Bracciano, and son-in-law of the Duke of Florence, young at about thirty years, of extreme size, but for all that strong enough and vigorous… He is greatly inclined and profuse in spending, and if he has 30,000 scudi a year income, he has debts of more than 150,000."[†]

In 1568, Paolo Giordano borrowed 40,000 scudi. He was in such desperate straits that he pawned three silver candlesticks, some silver plates and flasks, and some silk wall hangings. But the money obtained from these items didn't begin to cover his massive debts, so he resorted to selling off parcels of land.

By this time, the de Medicis had climbed the royal social ladder a good rung higher; in 1569, Pius V had raised the Duchy of Tuscany to a grand duchy. This stroke of fortune put Tuscany above and beyond the prestige of numerous Italian duchies squabbling for precedence at foreign courts. Given their sudden rise in the world, the de Medici

† Gnoli, p. 44, n.

family became more concerned about the unhappy, embarrassing marriage of Isabella and Paolo Giordano.

Isabella was safe as long as her powerful and devoted father was alive. But Cosimo died in 1574. The new grand duke, her somber brother Francesco, heartily disapproved of her adultery, despite having been unfaithful to his own wife for a decade with a married mistress. Francesco had never liked his sister, who was far more attractive, intelligent, and vivacious than he could ever hope to be. What's more, their father had preferred Isabella, often siding with her in family disputes.

Now the unpopular gloomy boy was a man with real power, and it was payback time. Isabella may have given birth to another illegitimate child in May 1576. Ambassador Ercole Cortile of the Duchy of Ferrara wrote that "Lady Isabella has been these past five days at Cafaggiolo [a country villa] and there are some saying that a previous time when she went, it was to let her body swell, and that it will be like that other time, when she was healthy again after nine months."[†] If true, Francesco would have been none too pleased.

In July that year, Paolo Giordano took his wife to the villa of Correto outside Florence on the pretext of going hunting. She never returned. That month, while washing her hair, or so it was reported, the thirty-three-year-old had a heart attack. But Ambassador Cortile heard differently. On July 29, he wrote his master a heart-wrenching account. "The Lady Isabella was strangled," he explained, "having been called by Lord Paolo when she, the poor woman, was in bed. She arose immediately, and as she was in a nightgown, drew a robe about her, and went to his room, passing through a room in which the priest known as Elicona was with several other servants. They say that her face and the set of her shoulders told that she may have known what was in store for her. Morgante [a servant] and his wife were in his chamber, and Lord Paolo hunted them out and bolted the door with great fury.

"Hidden under the bed was a Roman Knight of Malta, Massimo, who helped to kill the lady. He did not remain more than a quarter of

† Murphy, p. 312.

an hour locked in the room before Paolo called for a woman, Donna Lucrezia Frescobaldi, telling her to bring vinegar because the lady had fainted. Once she had entered, followed immediately by Morgante, she saw the poor lady on the ground propped against the bed and, overcome by her love for her, said, 'Oh, you have killed her! What need have you of vinegar or anything else?' Lord Paolo threatened her and urged her to hold her tongue or he would kill her."[†]

Isabella had reacted with contempt for everything her husband was and for everything he possessed. His blood was not as good as hers, his power was nothing compared to her family's, his debts were humiliating, his appearance grotesque. After eighteen years of her put-downs, and encouraged by her brother, it must have been with great joy that Paolo Giordano could finally spring upon her and squeeze the life out of her. That mouth would now be silenced forever.

Paolo Giordano had considerately prepared a coffin for his wife, which he whipped out after the job was done. He flung the body inside, threw the lid on it, and tossed the coffin upside down in a cart which took it to a church in Florence. There, in the ultimate insult to the vain Isabella, the dreadful cadaver was exposed to the curious who wanted to see what a woman looked like who had died while washing her hair. Even worse, they were permitted to touch the corpse and lift the skirts.

According to Ambassador Cortile, "It is said that there was never seen a more ugly monster. Her head was swollen beyond measure, the lips thickened and black like two sausages, the eyes open and bulging like two wounds, the breasts swollen and one completely split, it is said because of the weight of Lord Paolo who threw himself on her to kill her as quickly as possible. And the stench was so great that no one could go close." Sheer morbid fascination, however, propelled people to go close, holding their noses.

Because her body had been thrown upside down in the cart, the blood had rushed to her upper half. Cortile continued, "She was black from the middle up and completely white below, according to what Niccolo of Ferrara told me, who lifted the covers, as others had

† Langdon, pp. 165-166.

done to see her. She was buried the following night in the Basilica of San Lorenzo in Florence, in the Medici family crypt."[†] Then Paolo Giordano, who bought anything and everything he wanted despite his debts, regretfully announced he couldn't afford a proper tomb for her.

Adulterous strangled women disappeared from family records. Portraits that had proudly displayed their names had those names painted over and were sold as anonymous subjects in the flea markets. Family members weren't supposed to mention their dead dishonored relatives. And so Isabella, the fairest star of the de Medicis, disappeared. Her lover, the gallant Troilo, was assassinated soon after by the same assassin Paolo Giordano had used to kill Isabella.

After the murder, Paolo Giordano allowed his children – including the four-year-old Virginio Orsini – to continue residing in Florence at the court of their uncle, Grand Duke Francesco. He rarely visited and had to be badgered to send them money. "It has been said that Signor Paolo does not want them," the ambassador of Ferrara reported, "claiming that they are not his children."[‡] The grand duke fumed "about their father's irreparable shamelessness."[§]

A perennial fixture in the stews of Rome, for over four years the Orsini duke had no inclination to remarry. His first marriage hadn't gone so well, after all, and he must have enjoyed his freedom. When the de Medicis offered to arrange his marriage to one of several illustrious noblewomen with large dowries in tow, he turned them all down. The main reason for his single state seems to have been that he hadn't met a woman who had captured his heart. Until he saw Vittoria.

The elite of any cosmopolitan city is always limited in number. Rome had its great ancient families – the Orsinis, Colonnas, Savellis, and others – who had been at the pinnacle of society for centuries. These inbred clans were periodically rejuvenated by marrying into the new families of cardinals and popes. Whenever Rome had a papal event, a noble ball, or a grand feast, it was the same two or

---

† Ibid., p. 166.
‡ Murphy, p. 332.
§ Ibid., p. 294.

three hundred individuals who attended. Paolo Giordano, the most powerful Roman baron, and Vittoria Accoramboni, the niece of a cardinal with papal aspirations, must have come into contact at various festivities. Moreover, one of the duke's Roman palaces – the fortress-like Palazzo Orsini, built in 1450 – was near Camilla Peretti's corner house on the Via dei Leutari. Perhaps the duke had spotted Vittoria in the street.

Paolo Giordano had always been captivated by female beauty – except, of course, by that of his wife. He would have been entranced by Vittoria, possibly flattering and flirting with her. That might have been the end of it, had it not been for Vittoria's brother Marcello. When, in the summer of 1580, Marcello had stabbed the brother of Cardinal Pallavicino, he had fled to Bracciano Castle to enroll in Paolo Giordano's personal army of ruffians. He became friendly with the duke and, perhaps already aware of his attraction for Vittoria, began to interest him more and more in his lovely sister. His loyalty to Accoramboni family ambition proved far stronger than his loyalty to his brother-in-law Francesco, who was devoted to him.

Marcello explained to the duke that Vittoria was living a wretched existence among country oafs. Her nobility, delicacy, and beauty deserved more. She was terribly unhappy in Camilla's household, with her low-class laundress of a mother-in-law, her useless husband, and all of his noisy nieces and nephews. Meanwhile, Cardinal Montalto's health had become so bad there was no chance of him ever becoming pope. For the rest of her life, Vittoria would hardly be able to afford a decent dress, let alone the palatial luxury she desired. Vittoria, he pointed out, was worthy of being a duchess. And the duke agreed. It was, most likely, not only Vittoria's stunning looks that attracted him. Here, finally, was a woman who truly needed him, unlike the annoyingly independent Isabella. Here was a woman who stood in awe of him, instead of scorning him. Vittoria was a noble damsel in distress, and Paolo Giordano could play the part of valiant knight coming to the rescue.

We don't know the details of the courtship, but we do know that the duke introduced into Vittoria's service one Caterina of

Bologna, loyal to him and not to the Peretti family. It is likely that Caterina smuggled letters between the duke and Vittoria, or that she and her mistress pretended to go shopping but secretly met the duke somewhere in Rome. Unfortunately for Vittoria's reputation, Rome's gossip mill soon buzzed with the duke's infatuation for her. Perhaps society's elite had seen the two flirting at balls and banquets, and others had spotted them walking in the streets with Vittoria's maid, Caterina, trailing behind. No one could mistake the desire in Paolo Giordano's bulging eyes and Vittoria's coy body language that stated, *I am not yours, but how I wish I could be.*

Although gossip flew from person to person, it was aided and abetted by a statue named Pasquino after a papal tailor who, it was said, couldn't stop chattering about all the scandalous stories he overheard in the Vatican. A block behind the Piazza Navona, right behind the Palazzo Orsini, and across from Camilla's house, stood a mutilated statue fragment of Hercules. It had once adorned the first-century Stadium of Domitian which had stood on the spot, and at some point in the following centuries of earthquakes, pillaging, and neglect, had fallen and been buried by muddy Tiber floods. In 1501, Cardinal Giovanni Battista Orsini unearthed it when making repairs to the road behind his palace.

It was a ridiculous-looking statue, with a comical noseless face, and armless. Perhaps as a joke, the cardinal propped it on a pedestal against the rear wall of his house, right where it had been found. Local students took to dressing up the statue for holidays in classical or mythological garb. Soon they began hanging placards on it criticizing their professors. Others began to tack up nasty little epigrams about the pope and cardinals. In a country with no free press, the anonymous writings quickly became a means of venting popular discontent. Many of the stinging epigrams about sinful popes and cardinals were uncannily accurate and must have come from eavesdropping servants or Vatican employees. Pasquino was the Deep Throat of sixteenth-century Rome, the ultimate mouthpiece of government insiders aching to publicize their fascinating tales but terrified of revealing their identity.

And now Pasquino was chattering about Duke Paolo Giordano Orsini, whose first wife had mysteriously died while washing her hair, and Vittoria Accoramboni, the most beautiful woman in Rome, who was unhappily married to a cardinal's nephew. The Peretti family must have read the placards and epigrams about Vittoria, as the statue was just yards from their front door, but it is not known how they reacted to such slander. When a gangster like Paolo Giordano Orsini vowed that he would marry a woman as soon as her husband died, it was usually nothing less than a death sentence.

Perhaps Vittoria dismissed it as nonsense. Surely if Cardinal Montalto believed Francesco was in danger from the murderous duke who lusted after his wife, he would have sent him out of town. In all likelihood, the duke's repulsive appearance made Vittoria's protestations of innocence believable. Had he been a handsome, muscular stud, suspicion would have been greater. But Paolo Giordano was the kind of man more suited to moving a woman's stomach to convulsions than her heart.

Yet looks aside, and ignoring the fact that he had murdered his wife and was over his head in debt, he was quite a catch. If Vittoria ever married him, she would be the *Duchess* of Bracciano. And Marcello, who aided and abetted the affair, driving the impassioned duke into a frenzy, would be the duke's brother-in-law. Perhaps the most ambitious of the Accorambonis was Tarquinia, who had always hoped to use her daughter's beauty for family greatness. For centuries, scholars have debated exactly how much Vittoria knew about Paolo Giordano's plans to do away with Francesco. The more naïve among them have seen her as an innocent victim, a pitiful creature swept up in a whirlwind of events beyond her control. Others have portrayed her as a steely-eyed murderess, in on every detail of the plot.

Both theories are unlikely; the truth probably lies somewhere in between. If Vittoria had been completely innocent of any wish for an early widowhood, she would have been alarmed to hear Paolo Giordano's vow to marry her. She would have informed him that she would never marry him if Francesco were to meet an untimely end. She would have stopped seeing him and fired his accomplice, the waiting-woman Caterina. She would have warned Francesco that an ill-advised flirtation of hers might prove fatal for him, and that he should be armed and accompanied by bodyguards at all times. She might even have confessed her dangerous coquetry to the cardinal uncle and asked him to find ways to protect Francesco. But, as far as we know, she did nothing.

Yet it is also hard to believe that the duke would have burdened the delicate, tragic Vittoria with details of the time, place, and means of Francesco's death. It is likely that, having vowed to marry her, and hearing no protest, he took her silence as a tacit consent. And she must have known that something was afoot. It was strange to speak of Francesco's imminent demise when he was not in bed with malarial fever. He had neither shown signs of illness, nor had he been injured in a fall from a horse or crushed by a toppling carriage. On the contrary, Francesco Peretti was bouncing with youthful good health.

A sinister omen occurred in February 1581 during Carnival – that riotous anything-goes period before the austere forty days of Lent. Paolo Giordano and his brother-in-law, Cardinal Ferdinando de Medici, each sponsored a horse in a race, both decked out in beautiful long velvet trappings. The Orsini horse wore black trappings with huge tears embroidered in silver and the words, *Either tears or blood*, perhaps a coded message of some sort for Vittoria: *Either my tears will melt your resistance, and you will come into my arms, or I will take you with blood.*

If Vittoria understood the frightening message, she evidently decided to let the chips fall where they may. It is likely that the Lenten and Easter events of 1581 were stressful for her. Paolo Giordano's ardent expressions of love and insistence on marrying her must have been exciting, but also nerve-wracking. What if her husband, Camilla, or Cardinal Montalto found out? Was something really being planned to hurt Francesco? How could she smile and chat as normal with the family at the parades, services, and dinners which she, as the close relative of a cardinal, was expected to attend?

She must have known that Paolo Giordano could hasten her widowhood easily, if he were so inclined, and he would almost certainly never be punished for it. He was a powerful duke, and such men were rarely hauled before the law. Instead of facing justice for their misdeeds, the pope might chat with such people about mending their ways, and the malefactor might build an altar as penance before he went out to commit crimes afresh.

Paolo Giordano's power did not rest solely on his awe-inspiring ancestry or his numerous palaces. His personal army provided him with prestige, protection, and revenge. Such gangs were vestiges of the Middle Ages, when the lord of a castle commanded hundreds of men-at-arms necessary to protect his land from invasion. But Paolo Giordano's men were not courtly knights prepared to defend their lord's territories; they were violent gangsters ready to murder at their master's command.

Assassinations and duels occurred almost daily in Rome, and in most cases the murderers' names were made public immediately. Yet when it came to arresting them, the pope's hands were tied. Barons such as Paolo Giordano Orsini claimed legal immunity for their men. Tradition decreed that the pope could not arrest anyone protected by a powerful lord, not even the most notorious murderer. Authorities were not permitted to set foot on a nobleman's property, unless invited, and if they captured one of his men on the street, the baron would order the bailiff to set him free.

The popes allowed this claim of immunity because in earlier centuries Roman barons had kidnapped and murdered the Vicars of Christ to aid their own political aspirations. In 1303, members of the Colonna family had captured and severely beaten Pope Boniface VIII, who died several days later. They also probably poisoned his successor, Benedict XI, a year later. It comes as no surprise that the next pope, Clement X, packed his bags and moved the papal court to France. First in Avignon, then in various Italian towns, for nearly 140 years pontiffs enjoyed peace and quiet without being threatened daily by their own violent noblemen. Only in 1443 did the popes return to Rome for good, and an uneasy truce held sway as long as the pontiffs recognized the noblemen's claims of immunity. Although no pope had been harmed by a baron since their return, the fear remained, a fear the barons continued to exploit with their bandit gangs.

Certain European judicial systems helped swell the number of bandits because of the reluctance to execute young men. Indeed, the word *bandit* comes from the Italian *bandito*, meaning 'banished', as most of them were, instead of hanged, as they should have been. Though we think of historical justice as merciless, involving torture, disemboweling, and beheading for the slightest offenses, in some cases the courts were shockingly lenient. Burgundian law preferred to shame robbers instead of incarcerating or executing them – they were required to kneel and kiss a dog's anus in front of their fellow citizens. This person was doomed forevermore to be the butt, pardon the pun, of jokes.

Italians, loving melodrama, turned their courtrooms into stages for high theater. The young criminal, prostrate on the floor, begged the judge, the pope, and God on high to forgive him, vowing never to do it again. His aged mother, in sack cloth and ashes, wailed as she prayed the rosary. His lovely wife ripped her dress at the breast – just enough to let the judge see a nipple – tore her hair, and displayed her caterwauling infants, who would starve without a father. Such performances usually ended happily as Italians far prefer comedy to tragedy. The malefactor was exiled, the family saved, the nipple discreetly tucked away until needed again. The problem with such gratifying performances was that the criminal was now wandering the countryside, likely to join a gang of bandits and commit new crimes.

Many bandits were foolish noble youths such as Marcello who had killed someone in an ambush or drunken argument. Others were poor men seeking employment, or mercenary soldiers temporarily without a war to fight. Italian nations had very small standing armies and required an onrush of volunteers or mercenaries when war loomed. After the war, these soldiers, often far from home, discovered that the easiest way to earn a living was to rob travelers and pillage villages. As long as the robberies were kept within acceptable limits, the government didn't pursue the bandits with much diligence. These violent criminals made fearless soldiers; as such, they were priceless assets to the state in time of war.

Even when bandits went beyond the bounds of good taste – murdering families, burning entire villages, raping girls – Pope Gregory XIII, who hated harsh justice, was still reluctant to execute them. He invited them to Rome to publicly confess their sins, promise never to murder anybody again, and perform a penance – such as giving alms to the poor or making a pilgrimage to a holy site. The pope would issue a bill of absolution, proof on parchment that God had forgiven the assassin's sins. It was in keeping with the Catholic way of dealing with the problem.

Naturally, such leniency encouraged crime. One bandit priest, known as Father Guercini, asked the pope for a brief absolving him of the forty-four murders he had committed. Gregory XIII agreed, but a few days later received word from Guercini to write out the absolution for forty-eight murders, as he had just killed four more people. The pope obediently issued the dispensation for forty-eight murders.

Some of the worst bandits were in the retinues of the most highly respected cardinals. Cardinal Ferdinando de Medici, brother of Grand Duke Francesco and brother-in-law of Paolo Giordano, had a troop of bodyguards who should have been adorning the gallows rather than serving a prince of the Church. In early June 1580, Cardinal Luigi d'Este's men assaulted police officers but could not be arrested because of the cardinal's immunity. On June 15, the pope held a meeting with the entire Sacred College and complained bitterly that his cardinals were sheltering the most hardened criminals. But the pope's lecture did no good. A few days later, Cardinal Mark Altemps's men engaged the police in a violent fight.

When Michel de Montaigne visited Rome in 1581, he was advised to keep his cash in a bank, withdrawing only what he needed for each day. "Even the houses here are so insecure," he wrote in his travel diary, "that those who were rather amply provided with means were usually advised to give their purse in keeping with the bankers of the city, in order not to find their strong-box broken open, which has happened to many of them. Item, that to go about by night is hardly safe."[†]

When the people of Rome protested loudly about the crime, Gregory finally admitted he needed to do something. He tried to flush bandits out of the woods outside Rome. When that didn't work, he decided to cut down forests where they hid – an arduous, expensive job that produced no results as he could hardly cut down every tree in the Papal States; the bandits simply moved to other parts of the forest. At a complete loss about how to handle the bandit situation, the pope wrung his hands in desperation.

The most dangerous bandit of all was one Alfonso Piccolomini, the Duke of Montemarciano, whose castle Gregory XIII razed as punishment for his crimes. Piccolomini ordered his men to cut their victims' throats in the presence of their mothers and wives, while his followers danced and sang ribald songs. He declared his one goal was to kill the pope's son, Giacomo.

This threat deeply troubled Gregory. He had fathered the child in 1543, before he became a priest, and in 1577 made him the Duke of Sora, a small fiefdom near Naples. Likeable, though not terribly bright, Giacomo was the apple of his father's eye, and now the pope trembled for his son's safety. In a rare surge of decisiveness, Gregory tried to raise troops against Piccolomini, but locals refused to serve, fearing the bandit would retaliate by killing their families.

Though Gregory was a failure as a temporal ruler, he was a success as leader of the Catholic Church. Gregory gave generously to widows, orphans, and girls who needed dowries. During his first year in office, he personally visited Rome's hospitals to make sure the sick were being given good care. He decreed that traveling German princes could no longer force monasteries and convents to board their hunting dogs and horses or provide them with splendid banquets after the hunt. Gregory replaced drunken and illiterate priests with young ones recently graduated from the stellar new Jesuit seminaries.

The pope's rigor even extended to the Sacred College; in 1575 he severely chastised Cardinals de Medici and Maffei for gambling

† Montaigne, p. 120.

away 30,000 scudi each, a fortune they could have used for charitable works. Gregory's sincere piety put a new stamp on the College of Cardinals, at least on the surface. In 1576, the Spanish canonist Martino Azpilcueta wrote, "For many centuries past no Sacred College has been so eminently distinguished for its blamelessness, piety, prudence, righteousness, and continence, as well as for every kind of learning."[†] The Venetian ambassador, Mocenigo, added "No more feasts, no more games, no more hunting nor fine liveries, no luxury."[‡]

Despite Gregory's religious gains, his judicial leniency encouraged the roaming gangs of bandits inside and outside Rome to increase and thrive. Though we might wonder how one could estimate the number of bandits hiding in the woods, the nineteenth-century German historian Joseph Hübner reported that there were as many as 27,000 during Gregory's reign. And several dozen of the worst were in the pay of Duke Paolo Giordano Orsini, who wanted to make Vittoria Accoramboni a widow.

[†] Pastor, *Popes*, Vol. 19, p. 215.
[‡] Hubner, Vol. 1, p. 84.

Chapter 5

THE CARDINAL UNCLE

*O God, you are my God, earnestly I seek you; my soul thirsts for you,
my body longs for you, in a dry and weary land where there is no water.*

– *Psalm 63: 1-3*

Vittoria probably saw her cardinal uncle as a sweet, foolish old man, whom she milked frequently for silk gowns and pearl earrings and badgered for a coach. He was, after all, genuinely fond of her and sacrificed his own wishes to keep her happy.

The cardinal was congenial not only with his family, but also with his Church colleagues. He studiously distanced himself from Vatican politicking and backstabbing and wreathed his foreboding features in a smile when discoursing with other cardinals. He refused to join a political faction, as it would have prevented him from remaining on good terms with all. "In an admirable fashion he procured the favor of the cardinals," reported one early *relatione*, "honoring them, praising them, and showing himself desirous to grant them every satisfaction… He did not contend with any cardinal to impose his opinion, but preferred with sweetness to let them win."[†]

One frequent topic of business among the princes of the Church was European kings behaving badly, but whenever the topic came up, Cardinal Montalto excused their errors, pointing out how difficult it was to rule a realm. Word of his compassionate understanding winged its way to the kings of France and Spain, monarchs who played a role in electing a pope, and they took note.

Many blue-blooded cardinals were offended that a man of such shameful birth had joined the Sacred College. Loudest in his disdain

† Cicogna, *Conclave nel fu creato*, no page given.

was Cardinal Alessandro Farnese, the princely grandson of Pope Paul III. One day at a Vatican meeting of the entire Sacred College, Farnese referred to Montalto – loudly enough for him to hear – as "Cardinal Jackass of the Marches." Some cardinals laughed, but Montalto "pretended not to hear them, and turning with a happy face towards his calumniators, thanked them with great humility for the favors he had always received from them."[†] This was a mild, gentle soul, it was observed, who tried to please everyone and wouldn't dream of hurting a fly.

Vittoria and her family seem to have assumed that the easygoing cardinal would never make any trouble for them, even if they committed the most heinous acts against him in their quest for riches and power. But this assumption ignored two important clues – the cardinal's face, and his past. Cardinal Montalto did not have the kindly face one might expect from such a harmless old man. Indeed, his features were frightening, and he almost always looked angry. He resembled an Old Testament patriarch, with a long gray beard and small, flashing, dark eyes under wild unkempt eyebrows. He had – if there is such a thing – a low-class face that bespoke his humble origins, a visage without a single noble angle.

His forehead was deeply lined and strangely short, his eyes set too far north. He had a pudgy slab of a nose, as if a butcher had tossed aside a thumb-sized piece of unwanted beef and it had attached itself to the center of Montalto's face. Deep folds ran between his nose and his narrow slash of a mouth, and the loss of several teeth had shortened his jaw. Even when he was a young man, his fellow monks, laughing at the unprepossessing physiognomy of the man who aspired to the throne of Saint Peter, said, "You, Father Felice, have exactly the face of a pope!"[‡]

His thick bristly hair was clipped short. His huge boulder of a head was perched on wide shoulders without the benefit of a neck in between. He was barrel-chested, bandy-legged, and he had the odd

---

† Ibid.
‡ Anon., p. 61.

habit of listening to others with his eyes half-closed. It was generally admitted to be a pity that his sister Camilla looked just like him.

Appearance aside, the Accorambonis would have done well to consider Montalto's past before they started planning Vittoria's marriage to another man. The cardinal had not always been so congenial, and earlier in his Church career his reputation had been tarnished by rage and vengefulness.

He had entered a monastery at age ten to learn to read and write, as his parents could not afford to send him to school. There, the other monks were impressed by the bright, energetic boy, who volunteered to mop the floors and do whatever other grunt work they desired. They began instructing him in Italian first, then Latin, and finally Greek. He made tremendous progress. He memorized the entire Bible by heart, along with many works of the early Church fathers. At the tender age of twelve, on September 2, 1534, he took the vows of a Franciscan monk and became Fra, or Brother, Felice.

As a precocious child, Felice was no threat to the other monks. But by the time he reached his late teens, he had outstripped his colleagues in theological disputation. "All the other students in the monastery were extremely jealous of the progress that he made every day in his studies," wrote his chronicler, "and many more were jealous when they saw him advance in esteem. He was not only being spoken of in the monastery, but also in the city, and he had trampled all his adversaries in school."[†] If he had veiled his shining intellect with a gloss of modesty or self-deprecating good humor, perhaps he could have lived in peace. But Felice enjoyed letting his better-born colleagues know that he, despite his miserable birth, was smarter than them.

Felice's fellow students "tried to upset him, throwing water in his face, or pulling his hood over his face, or giving him a blow so that he would fall on the ground, and other insolences. They would then run to the regent and tell him that Fra Felice had done to them what they, in fact, had just done to him."[‡]

† Ibid., p. 19.
‡ Ibid., p. 20.

At first Fra Felice, knowing patience was a Christian virtue, suffered everything in silence. It was only when the other boys started making fun of his pig-farming past that he lost his temper. Again and again, when a group of five particularly bad boys saw him, they cried out *gru gru*, the call made to bring home rooting pigs. *Gru gru*, they squealed, even at night through the keyhole of his cell.

"For this persecution, Fra Felice decided to break the head of the first one who did this again, and in a rage he took a baton, which was usually kept next to the door of the monastery, and to which three keys were tied, and hid it under his tunic." And when the group of taunting boys came toward him, and the foremost cried out *gru gru*, "Fra Felice brought out the baton that he had kept hidden under his habit and hit his adversary two or three times on the neck saying to him, 'Truly I have made it clear that I was a pig keeper, and not a pig, but just as you have been a bad pig, I am a good pig keeper.' And he continued to beat him so that he fell unconscious to the ground without being able to raise himself, and moreover one of the keys carried off the earlobe of an ear, shedding much blood."[†]

Felice was lashed twenty-five times and kept in a dungeon for nine days on only bread and water. When he emerged, he was sent to another monastery. It was a scenario that would be repeated often throughout his long ecclesiastical career – talent and brilliance contrasted with angry bad behavior and his annoying insistence that he was the future pope.

Tortured as he was by his fellow monks, Felice started carrying in his pocket a little book in which he wrote the names of those who had trespassed against him, and the exact nature of their sins. He also noted down the names of those who had treated him with kindness, with details of the favors given. When he was pope, he declared, he would bring out his little book to reward and punish accordingly. Hearing this, his fellow monks roared with laughter.

In 1543, Felice was ordained a priest and took the name of Father Montalto. At nineteen he had started preaching and delivered rousing sermons without using notes. Whenever Father Montalto preached,

† Ibid., pp. 22–23.

the church was packed, and even better, the usually parsimonious congregations were moved to make generous donations. Some sermons, however, were designed specially to insult the illustrious officials sitting in the front row, men whose behavior the preacher did not approve of. These gentlemen complained bitterly to Rome.

Despite the periodic protests trickling into the Vatican about Father Montalto's insolent sermons and frequent arguments with fellow monks, high-level Church officials heard of the young preacher's success with his parishioners and summoned him to Rome. Having spent his life in Italian villages and towns, Montalto must have been shocked by the international nature of the capital. There was the prickly Spaniard, wrapped in his black cloak, casting looks of scorn all around him and doing battle with pride as his weapon of choice. Over there, the smooth, silky Frenchman rustled in puffed pastel silk, conquering with charm.

Even the different Italian nationalities wore distinctive clothes and spoke with strong regional accents. Here were the somber-robed Venetians, Europe's best listeners, nonchalantly worming the most dangerous secrets out of the powerful. The courtly Florentine, frugal and talkative, chatted with the Genoan, his pockets stuffed with coins to buy power and information. Neapolitans were easy to spot; their dark good looks were spiced with Arab blood, and they were even flashier and rowdier than the Romans.

In 1552, Montalto preached twice a week, and his sermons attracted great crowds, including cardinals and noblemen. In Rome, the young priest lived in the Franciscan Monastery of the Holy Apostles, where his superiority and arrogance once more aroused the ire of his fellow monks. The esteemed preacher, who had by now received his doctorate in theology, was no longer in a position to beat nasty monks over the head with a baton, but he continued to note down their transgressions against him in his little book. Worse, he wrote up lists of their sins on large sheets of paper and posted them on the dining hall door for all to see.

It became clear to Church officials that Montalto's genius was wasted among the petty jealousies of the monastery. He was indefatigable in his efforts for the Church, studying, writing sermons, preaching to large crowds, and formulating briefs and theological opinions for the cardinals. His doctrine was sound, his way of life strict. He required hardly any sleep and spent all his waking hours working. In 1556, his powerful mentors, Cardinal Rodolfo Pio Carpi, Protector of the Franciscans, and Monsignor Michele Ghislieri, Commissary General of the Roman Inquisition, decided to send him into the world as a Vatican representative. They were supported by the strict new pope, Paul IV, who greatly admired Montalto.

Cardinal Carpi arranged a mouthwatering banquet of honorable opportunities for Felice to choose from, far away from the Franciscan monastery in Rome. Felice opted for the most challenging position, that of papal inquisitor to the Republic of Venice. If he could bring the independent-minded Venetians firmly under the Vatican thumb, he would win great honor in Rome and perhaps be made a cardinal.

The unique history of Venice shaped its fierce independence. A collection of islands and lagoons, it had hosted small fishing communities going back to time immemorial. But when the Roman Empire began to topple, and hordes of Huns, Lombards, Goths, and other barbarians attacked Roman cities for booty, many of the inhabitants of Aquilea, Verona, and Padua fled to the Venetian islands. No barbarians in their right mind would besiege a pitiful swamp. Those few who tried found themselves lost in the zigzagging natural waterways or stuck in the sand when the tide went out.

Living on stilts in the sea, the Venetians never felt truly Italian. While the Florentines, Romans, and Milanese sat solidly on the earth and fretted over earthly things, Venice built the most successful merchant marine fleet in the world and a powerful navy to protect her ships and trade routes. Each year their ruler, the doge, who was elected for life, married the sea in an elaborate ceremony, throwing a solid gold wedding band into the Grand Canal.

As a Catholic nation, Venice was duty-bound to support the pope. Yet Venetian trading interests involved not only Catholic countries, but also heretics to the north and the Ottoman Empire in the eastern Mediterranean. To avoid offending a valuable trading partner or, heaven forbid, becoming enmeshed in a costly war that would block the shipping lanes, Venice often refused to take a hard political stance and blithely ignored papal decrees to do so. When frustrated pontiffs placed the entire republic under interdict – banning the Sacraments and the burial of the dead in sanctified soil – Venice shrugged and its priests continued business as usual. "We are Venetians, then Christians" was their motto.[†]

By the sixteenth century, as Venetian firepower diminished, its diplomacy intensified; it was, after all, far cheaper to send ambassadors than gunships. Venice fielded the most talented diplomatic corps in Europe, and Venetian ambassadors, who listened compassionately and reported far more than they spoke, became the chief confidantes of many popes and kings. Venetian diplomacy was like a sinuous acrobat, sliding into impossible contortions with a shining smile on her face. Venice sympathized, temporized, offered advice, and made polite excuses, but rarely committed herself.

Because Venice took an elastic approach to politics, the republic expected that foreign politicians adopt the same tractable manner when dealing with Venice. The ambassadors of other European states knew better than to stomp into the Senate and make threats or demands. Even a Vatican inquisitor, in his pious efforts to root out heresy, was expected to have a gracious, conciliatory manner, working hand in hand with the Venetian government, granting favors and making concessions when requested.

Having received reports of Father Montalto's irascible nature, the Venetian Senate politely requested the Vatican to send them another inquisitor, but to no avail. On January 17, 1557, Father Felice Montalto arrived in the Grand Lagoon to take up his duties.

He was shocked by the physical differences between Rome and Venice. Rome was a city of somnambulant majesty, upon which history weighed heavily. Rome took itself very seriously; it was the center of two world empires – the ancient Roman and the modern Catholic – and neither was a laughing matter. The old empire was found in the huge monuments, heavy chunks of Roman baths, broken

† Wiel, p. 273.

aqueducts, and tumbling temples; the new empire was manifested in solid churches and stately palaces. And in between the stones of the old and new empires, goats grazed, and sheep nibbled, and cows chewed their cud.

But Venice was as glittering and improbable as a mermaid splayed out on the crest of a wave. Its glories shocked first-time visitors. The English writer Thomas Coryat, visiting in 1608, wrote that Venice, "yeeldeth the most glorious and heavenly shew upon the water that ever any mortal eye beheld, such a shew as did even ravish me both with delight and admiration."† He called Venice "that Diamond set in the ring of the Adriatique gulfe, and the most resplendent mirrour of Europe."‡

In the right light, Venice was almost youthful, although she was already a thousand years old when Father Montalto arrived. When the sun shone, the city sparkled beneath a turquoise sky, a lady of venerable age still possessed of splendid beauty and youthful humor despite a few cracks in her façade. She gloried in her antiquity, if only for the memories of her thousands of lovers. Kissed by a Byzantine breeze, Venice was a city of delicate pastel palaces with keyhole-shaped windows. But when the sky turned gray, she suddenly aged, her marble monuments reminiscent of the tomb. She hunkered down, crouched disconsolately on the lagoon, waiting breathlessly for another transparent sky.

For all its architectural grandeur, Venice was a city of merchants. Crime was frowned upon because it interfered with making money. When residents felt safe to wander the streets and canals, they invariably spent money, which was taxed. If they were too afraid to leave their houses, they wouldn't spend money, and the Venetian economy and taxation would stagnate. Feeling safe in its shimmering embrace, traders and visitors from all over the world came in droves to the city and dropped huge sums purchasing merchandise and souvenirs.

One of the republic's most profitable ventures was printing. Venice was the heart of Europe's printing industry, hundreds of printers

---

† Coryat, Vol. 1, p. 157.
‡ Ibid., dedication.

producing hundreds of thousands of books in a variety of languages, which were shipped throughout the world. And the Venetians, always good merchants at heart, sometimes printed heretical works – omitting the name of the printer or using a false one – and smuggled them out to Protestant countries where they fetched high prices. Venetian printers couldn't understand why religion should interfere with good business practice.

Unfortunately for Venice, one of the new inquisitor's main responsibilities was to enforce the Vatican's Index of Prohibited Books. The suppression of heretical books had been initiated in 1543 by Pope Paul III, and the first index was published in 1557. Heresy was thought to be a kind of infection, spreading from one individual to the next, or one community to the next. Because of their wider audience, books were considered more dangerous than individuals. Bad books, Paul III said, were a pestilence, which at a single blow could infect whole cities and provinces. They had certainly been the breeze which carried Martin Luther's ideas around Europe, making him the world's first international bestselling author.

Books with any hint of heresy were forbidden, as well as books not of a heretical nature, but written by heretical authors. No anonymous books on any subject whatsoever were to be printed, nor any pornographic books, or those that made fun of the Church. Since the most revered comedies in the Italian language had a corrupt monk or drunken priest somewhere in the story, almost all comedies were forbidden. There were so many books listed on the first index, among them well-read works on philosophy and history used in schools, that it seemed there was nothing left to read. While many Catholics quarreled with the decree, the Venetians merely shrugged and ignored it.

Venice was, therefore, horrified to learn that the new inquisitor brought with him a list of sixty-one condemned printers and editors, along with forty-eight banned editions of the Bible, and the condemnation of hundreds of other popular books. Father Montalto had his servants deliver orders for each bookseller to hand over a list of his entire inventory in stores and warehouses. Those who refused to do so were excommunicated.

Montalto's servant tacked up decrees of excommunication on the front of the bookstores; the Senate's bailiff yanked them down, and Montalto's servant nailed them up again. Montalto barged into bookstores and even private homes, pulling books off the shelves and throwing the forbidden ones on the floor. On Palm Sunday 1559, he burned 10,000 forbidden books in Saint Mark's Square to the horror of the Venetian people and Senate; those books could have been sold for a fine sum.

Although the Venetians had no wish to insult the pope – who could prevail upon other Catholic nations to stop trading with them – the Senate seriously debated whether they should throw Father Montalto into a dungeon or at least into the sewage-filled Grand Canal, where he and his list of forbidden books and briefs of excommunication could float serenely among the turds out to sea. It was a tempting thought, and only the frantic apologies of the Vatican nuncio, Rome's ambassador to Venice, prevented the inquisitor from doing the breaststroke in the lagoon.

One of Montalto's responsibilities was to instruct the Franciscans of Venice in Church doctrine. But the monks "complained of the rude and haughty manner in which he taught theology."† He enforced strict discipline, placing disobedient monks in prison on bread and water, or sending them to row the pope's galleys. His fellow monks spied on him and slipped messages to the Senate of his bad behavior. When plague hit Venice, and monks were not allowed to leave the monastery for food, they hid their rations from Montalto in an effort to starve him to death.

When that didn't work, in 1560, the Franciscan monks of Venice denounced him to the Senate as an enemy of the republic, and the Senate petitioned Rome for his recall. After three years fighting the Venetians, Montalto, too, had had enough. He wanted to return to Rome to advance his career. His mentor, Michele Ghislieri, who in

† Leti, *Sixte V*, Vol. 1, p. 134.

the meantime had been named a cardinal and taken the name of Cardinal Alessandrino, granted his request.

But before he left, Father Montalto had one more statement to make. When the senators protected a certain renegade priest who had turned heretic, late one night Montalto tacked up a huge degree of excommunication against the entire Venetian Senate in Saint Mark's Square. Then, knowing they would try to arrest him, he quickly paddled out of town with his baggage in a gondola. The Venetians and the Franciscan monks thanked God for Montalto's departure, crying, "God guard us from the government of Montalto, God free us from his operations, and God protect us from his return."[†]

Despite his disastrous tenure in Venice, Montalto's cardinal friends in Rome were proud of his efforts to enforce Church laws and improve morals in the monastery. They appointed him a consultant to the Roman Inquisition. Back in Rome, he found exciting changes afoot to reform the Church. Although the new pope, Pius IV, had a wild past (twenty years earlier he had fathered three children and contracted syphilis), he had changed his ways by the time he became pontiff and realized that the Church, too, was in urgent need of reform. He reopened the Council of Trent, that belated Vatican response to Luther's heresies, which had stalled years earlier without accomplishing anything. When the council finally closed in 1563, it had sat on and off for 18 years.

The council tightened rules on clerical behavior; prelates were forbidden to marry, despite pleas from numerous European rulers who thought that married clergy would be less likely to seduce other men's wives and daughters, and the omnipresent altar boys. Nor could priests live openly with mistresses and enjoy gluttonous feasts and orgies with prostitutes. Monks designated to care for the sick in hospitals were no longer permitted to spend most of their time gambling in taverns.

The conclave of 1565 was a fortunate one for Father Montalto. His protector and best friend, Cardinal Alessandrino, was elected Pope Pius V. Montalto's heart must have soared when he heard the

[†] Anon., p. 83.

exciting news. Alessandrino had often promised Montalto that if he ever became pope, he would make him a cardinal.

In 1566, Pius V made Montalto general of the Franciscan order, a position that required he visit monasteries to look over their finances, confirm good Catholic doctrine, and establish discipline. He initiated efficient new measures for putting the monasteries' finances in order, saving a great deal of money.

As Felice Montalto rose in power and favor, many of his enemies feared he would seek revenge on them for ancient slights. Everyone knew he had the creepy habit of writing them down in that little book of his so that he would never forget. But Montalto realized that a man with a reputation for vendetta would never be elected cardinal, let alone pope. In the late 1560s, he completely changed his demeanor from angry and gruff to harmless and agreeable. He adopted a forgiving manner and even did favors for those who had slighted him. "Montalto is a truly good man," they said, "to have forgotten that we were previously his enemies."[†]

Had he truly mellowed with age, or was it merely a stratagem to win Church advancement? Whatever it was, it worked. On May 17, 1570, Felice Montalto was given the red hat, as it was called; he was made a cardinal along with thirteen others. In the presence of some forty cardinals, who must have been pea-green with envy, Pius V told him, "We have made you cardinal because of your merit, and your merit will lead to the papacy."[‡]

It was with the greatest joy that Cardinal Montalto suddenly found himself in the financial position to bring Camilla, now widowed, and her two children to Rome. Throughout the 1550s and 1560s, he had sent her fifteen scudi a month, which was barely enough to keep her family fed. Now, although he couldn't offer them luxury, he could certainly provide food, as well as a decent dwelling with a few servants. In later years, it would be recalled with great mirth that Camilla had plodded into Rome astride a mangy ass, led by a ragged Francesco.

[†] Leti, *Sixte V*, Vol. 1, p. 335.
[‡] Anon., p. 111.

Pius V died on May 5, 1572. Cardinal Montalto stood by his side during his final illness, gave the dying pontiff extreme unction, and closed his eyes. He lost the best friend he would ever have. But the pope's many kindnesses over the course of two decades had been recorded in the little book, and even years after Pius's death Montalto would find a way to reward him.

It must have been with a heavy heart that Montalto prepared to elect a successor. But he used the opportunity to win friends in the Sacred College. According to his chronicler, "He showed no interest in any faction, and when someone tried to win him over to one, he pretended to be ignorant of any sort of intrigue, and replied with words full of simplicity, saying, 'That never having been in a conclave, he did not want to make a mistake, and that those with experience should decide.' The most that came out of his mouth was that in conscience he did not know whom to vote for, considering all capable, and he wished he had enough votes to give one to each cardinal."[†]

It was a stroke of bad luck for Cardinal Montalto when the Sacred College elected Ugo Boncompagni, who took the name Gregory XIII. An able churchman, Cardinal Boncompagni had led a mission to Spain several years earlier, with Father Montalto among his assistants. The cardinal had so disliked Montalto's rude manners and blunt speech that he had placed him in the baggage cart, bouncing up and down for hundreds of miles each way in between leather trunks.

But "Montalto showed great happiness at this election, assuring everyone later in secret discussions that his preference had always been directed toward this individual, founding all this on the honor he had received from his kindness on the voyage to Spain."[‡] Many marveled at these comments, having heard the baggage cart story. But Montalto took note that Gregory won the election not because he had been the most powerful, noble, or intelligent cardinal, but because he was a man without enemies, an affable soul whom everyone liked.

Cardinal Montalto "armed himself with an incredible humility and unheard-of patience. He pretended to not stir up the water

[†] Ibid., pp. 114-116.
[‡] Ibid., p. 116.

entombed in his guts or show that weakness of spirit that he naturally possessed, and in short, he seemed another Montalto in his dress, his gestures, words, and actions."[†]

Gregory XIII was not fooled by Montalto's sudden docile demeanor and actually thought less of him for it. "Pope Gregory knew that Montalto was a bizarre spirit who had suddenly changed nature," the chronicler reported. "He firmly believed that this appearance of humility, which he showed to everyone, was full of deceit, whereupon the pope, who hated deceitful men, could not like him, and this reconfirmed his initial opinion."[‡] The pope told his inner circle to "beware of that great charnel-box of a grey friar" and took away his important Church positions.[§]

One day in February 1581, as Gregory left a religious function at Saint Mary Major, he saw the nearly finished villa of Cardinal Montalto rising three stories, each one decorated by magnificent Ionic, Doric, or Corinthian columns. The pope remarked, "Poor cardinals do not build palaces."[¶] As soon as he reached the Vatican, he yanked Montalto's annual "poor cardinal" pension of 1,200 scudi.

The cardinal immediately took down the arms of Gregory XIII, which he had posted above his gate, and put up instead those of his deceased friend, Pius V. Nor did he actually lose a dime. Grand Duke Francesco of Tuscany, eager to win Montalto's vote for his candidate in the next conclave, bestowed on him an annual pension of 1,200 scudi.

If Cardinal Montalto could not win over the pope, he could work on the other cardinals who were, naturally, more important in the next conclave than Gregory, who would not be voting. He visited them often and invited them to the breezy delights of his vineyard, complimenting them on their wisdom and noble families. And, to appear to be less of a threat as a potential future pope, he took to leaning on a stick and coughing. A sick old man would never be able to rule the patrimony of Saint Peter by himself. He would have to rely on diligent cardinals, giving them most of the power so he could rest

† Ibid., pp. 113-114.
‡ Ibid., p. 116.
§ Ranke, Vol.1, p. 338, n.
¶ Pastor, *Popes*, Vol. 21, p. 41.

in bed and pray. Even Montalto's servants believed in his infirmities. They told their friends on the streets of Rome, "At the moment our master lives, but soon we will be without him."[†]

The cardinal enjoyed spending time with Camilla's family, where an inordinate amount of his energy was expended in trying to keep Vittoria happy. In good weather he spent his days in his vineyard. Gazing out over Rome, he made future pontifical plans for the city, and here his three years in Venice came to his aid. Not all that time had been spent in bickering with monks, booksellers, and politicians. For the first time ever, he had seen what a beautiful, orderly, and well-planned city looked like. Saint Mark's Square was the most gorgeous sight in Europe at the time. Rome had nothing like it.

Even Saint Peter's Square, the center of the Christian world, was half its modern size, surrounded by barracks and tiny dark streets. The front of Saint Peter's Basilica comprised five buildings of different heights and architectural styles, cobbled together over time. Montalto decided that when he was pope, he would have to do something about that hodgepodge of a square. And then there was the nagging problem of the dome. The original basilica, built by Emperor Constantine in the fourth century, had been mostly razed as a much larger church was going up around it in fits and starts, but mostly in fits. For decades in the sixteenth century, the great dome, which was to serve as a shining beacon to all Christianity, had remained half-built, with trees growing out of crumbling piers.

Montalto tasked Domenico Fontana, the architect of his villa, to come up with engineering solutions to Rome's daunting problems. Born on the shores of Lake Lugano in 1543, Fontana, too, was a man of humble origins, hard work, and the stubborn courage required to tackle the most formidable challenges. Together they made plans so that on the first day of Montalto's papacy – whenever that might be – they would be ready to start making changes.

Once the home of more than a million people, Rome now had barely 80,000. Trees and shrubs covered two-thirds of the city, mostly on the ancient Seven Hills, where the lack of water prevented human

† Anon., p. 147.

habitation. The aqueducts would have to be repaired to irrigate the parched earth, opening up huge new sections of the city for shops and residences. And the maze of undulating medieval streets in the center, choked as they were with the newfangled coaches, would have to be widened, even if it meant tearing down the most revered structures.

By early spring 1581, Cardinal Montalto's villa was finished enough for him to move in. With a glad heart, he packed up his trunk loads of religious books destined for the new library he had built, and his few other possessions, and left the hot, riotous Via dei Leutari for the cool serenity of the vineyard. He could be immensely proud of himself. Through his brilliance, hard work, and more recently, his good nature, Felice Peretti had risen from a pig sty to a cardinal's palace. Now he was poised to fulfill the childhood prophecy and become the next Vicar of Christ.

True, Pope Gregory, who hated him, was taking an unconscionably long time to die. And the Accorambonis were chomping at the bit to become the rich and honored relatives of the next pope. But Cardinal Montalto had made plans not only for Rome, but for his entire family. Those who would benefit most, of course, would be Camilla, Francesco, and Vittoria, but Francesco's sister Maria, her husband, and her four children would also reap rewards, as well as all of Vittoria's relatives. They only needed to have a little more patience.

Chapter 6

MURDER IN THE GARDEN OF GOD

A prudent man foreseeth the evil, and hideth himself: but the simple pass on, and are punished.

– *Proverbs 22:3*

On the night of Sunday, April 16, 1581, Camilla Peretti's house on the Via dei Leutari was entombed in darkness. The day was long over, the candles snuffed out. After supper, the embers in the kitchen hearth had glowed briefly, then cooled to gray ash. The noises of the day had trailed off into silence. Gone was the thudding of footsteps on wooden floors, the creaking open and slamming shut of doors. Gone were the measured notes of conversation of the Peretti adults, the cries and squeals of children, the gossip and yelling of servants. Perhaps, as midnight approached, there was only the sound of mice nesting in the walls or scuttling across the floor in search of a crumb.

Outside, the street so teeming with life during the day was also mostly mute. The constant clattering of horses and carriages, the shouts of coachmen, the curses of suppliers pushing heavy carts, the lilting greetings of neighbors – all had vanished into the night. Perhaps now and then a horseman galloped past or a carriage rattled by, hurrying home to safety after late-night revelry.

Francesco and Vittoria were asleep when her maid Caterina knocked loudly on their bedroom door. It was unusual to be disturbed at such an hour unless a family member was ill, or there was news that the pope had died. Surely, something of great moment was happening. Francesco opened the door, and Caterina gave him a note which, she said, had just been delivered by Domenico Acquaviva, known as Mancino, a friend of Marcello who was well known to Francesco.

The note was from Marcello, begging Francesco to meet him in the Sforza garden on Monte Cavallo, one of the hills of Rome. Marcello was in great danger and urgently needed Francesco's help. Francesco must have believed that Pallavicino henchmen were hot on his trail, hoping to avenge Marcello's stabbing of the cardinal's brother the summer before. And that Marcello, concealed in the garden, was too terrified to move. When Francesco asked Caterina where Mancino was, as he wanted to find out more about Marcello's situation, she said that Mancino had handed her the note and departed.

As Francesco pulled on his hose and doublet, he told Vittoria that her brother was in trouble and needed his help. He grabbed his sword – only a fool walked out at night in Rome without a weapon – and roused a servant to accompany him holding a lantern. Vittoria followed him down the winding stone stairs and into the courtyard, and right behind them came his mother, his sister, and other women of the household who had been awakened by the messenger banging on the street door. In robes and nightcaps, holding candles high and squinting in the darkness, they asked what was going on.

When Francesco told Camilla that he must go immediately to help Marcello, she begged him not to go on such a dangerous mission. It was the middle of the night. The messenger had run off as soon as he had delivered the note, which was suspicious. And they lived in violent times. Vittoria, too, chimed in, imploring Francesco not to go. It was one thing to dream of being the Duchess of Bracciano, but it was quite another to send young Francesco off to a brutal death in a garden. Perhaps she was suddenly afraid. The women began to cry and got on their knees in front of Francesco, begging him to at least wait a few hours until dawn and then go out with a company of armed servants to find Marcello. Perhaps he wasn't even in Rome, and this was some trick to ambush Francesco. Why hadn't Mancino waited to speak to him and lead him to the spot on Monte Cavallo where Marcello was hiding? The story didn't make sense.

But at no point did Vittoria tell her husband why she, in particular, feared for his life. She neglected to mention that both Paolo Giordano Orsini and Marcello wanted her to become a widow, and this note was an invitation to certain death. She should have confessed her foolish flirtation, barred the door with her body, thrown her arms around his knees. Camilla could have ordered her male servants to hold Francesco until she could send for Cardinal Montalto to sort out the mess. But Vittoria, other than joining with the others in asking him not to go, said nothing.

Francesco, loyal to Marcello, and boosted by that feeling of immortality that propels the young to heroism and idiocy, "scorned all these reasons ... He left then armed only with his sword, leaving in his mother's heart the dolorous presage of misfortune at hand."[†]

The women, kneeling with outstretched hands, saw Francesco and his servant disappear down the domed passageway that led to the street, the lantern casting monstrous shadows on the walls. The heavy door thudded shut behind them. And at this moment, if not before, Vittoria's guilt was made manifest. She let Francesco walk out the door without telling him the truth. In that moment, all the pain that was to come was conceived.

It is hard for us today to understand the unutterable darkness of a city without electricity after sunset. With no moon, the traveler was sunk in blindness, wrapped in the black velvet embrace of night. It was almost impossible to make out the streets and the outlines of buildings. The light of a single lantern was almost swallowed in the darkness.

But on that cool spring night, Rome was partially lit by a moon three-quarters full. Francesco picked his way through the silent silver streets, between the looming buildings, following his servant holding the lantern high. It was a long walk to the Sforza garden, through narrow twisting roads with many turns. For Rome had few long, straight streets, but many little ones that dead-ended into palaces or gardens.

---

† Ibid., p. 611.

Even if there had been no murderers waiting for him at his destination as Camilla feared, the journey itself was dangerous. Bandits, lying in wait for foolish late-night passersby, could have robbed and knifed him. But Francesco arrived safely at Monte Cavallo. He climbed a twisting path up the hill around Pope Gregory's summer palace, the Quirinal, and its extensive gardens. He skirted the Grimani vineyard and finally approached the gate of the Sforza garden.

Three guns went off, and Francesco fell to the ground, his sword untouched in its sheath. Numerous assassins raced out of the bushes and stabbed him repeatedly in the neck and chest to make sure the deed was done, and there would be no lingering recovery. The servant with the lantern raced screaming back to the Peretti house, and the assassins melted into the night, leaving Francesco's bloody body in the dirt.

The servant banged on the door, sobbing and babbling wildly. Camilla and Vittoria, who had been waiting anxiously, opened it, and the servant announced to Camilla that she no longer had a son. The women began to wail. The entire household was roused, the family, the servants, all running to and fro crying, praying, screaming. Camilla sent a messenger to Cardinal Montalto with the news.

Cardinal Montalto had not been more than a few weeks in his new villa. On spring nights a calming breeze swept through his rooms, whispering ancient wordless secrets to help him sleep. But this night his sleep was broken by a servant standing by his bed with a candle. *Your Reverence must rouse yourself. Your nephew Francesco has been murdered in a garden. Signora Camilla needs you.*

There are transformational moments in certain human lives when grim reality comes hurtling down at us like the heavy metal cleaver of a guillotine. Life is forever sliced cleanly in two – the before, and the after. Nothing will ever be the same again. Crushed by loss and injustice, hope is shattered and joy vanished. Should healing ever come, it will leave deep thick scars, and any happiness will be of the muted variety. And this was just such a moment in the life of Cardinal Felice Montalto.

All churchmen, and indeed, most Catholics, kept an altar in or near the bedroom, and now Cardinal Montalto availed himself of his. Silently, the cardinal threw himself in front of the crucifix and prayed. He must surely have prayed for the repose of his beloved nephew's soul. But perhaps he uttered another prayer. A prayer that God would grant him the means for vengeance.

The cardinal got dressed and rode to the house on the Via dei Leutari. The wails of the women could be heard on the street. With great composure, he calmed them, offering what consolation he could. The cardinal then ordered servants to fetch Francesco's body to his villa, which was not far from the murder scene. Camilla must have gone with him, carrying a bundle of hastily gathered burial clothes for her son. Probably Vittoria and Maria went as well. We can imagine Cardinal Montalto looking at the corpse before the women washed it. Francesco's torso had been blasted with gunshots, his neck and chest covered with blood and gore. And, behind his stoic mask, perhaps the cardinal remembered Jesus's words, *I am come not to bring peace but a sword.* Would that time come?

We can see Camilla, throwing herself on her son's corpse, salty tears on her lips as she kissed the cold flesh. And Vittoria, where was she? Did she cry and fling herself on the body, or was she weeping silently in the corner, riven by guilt?

An hour before the sun rose, Rome started to wake. Calling gruff greetings to one another, tradesmen pulled their heavy creaking carts through the streets of pewter-colored light. As the light brightened to silver, donkeys laden with produce brayed in protest at their owners coaxing them to market on the nearby square. The footsteps of servants on their way to work clicked on the stones, their voices rising even as the silver light warmed to rose gold.

The Italian love of drama ensured that news of a tragic midnight murder flew through town on the wings of dawn. Francesco's was not the only murder that night, but his was the most interesting. He was, after all, the nephew of a cardinal with papal aspirations. And all Rome knew that Paolo Giordano Orsini, the Duke of Bracciano, wanted Francesco's wife for himself.

That this poor young man was, quite possibly, murdered by the powerful duke, was the most horrible, delicious gossip. Servants told their masters, masters told their friends, and the friends who went out for early morning shopping told shop owners who told their families living upstairs. Some people sent notes around to their acquaintances: *Have you heard...?* And by the time the sun was starting to warm the city, just about everyone knew.

There is a fleeting moment in the early morning when the shadows of houses, still clutching the coolness of night, are forced to relinquish their grip as light and warmth conquer them. At this moment on the morning of April 17, 1581, the body of Francesco Peretti, cleaned up and dressed in his best slashed doublet and hose, was carried on a bier to the Church of Saint Mary of the Angels right across from the Villa Montalto. Cardinal Montalto said the funeral Mass with no pomp, and oddly enough, no tears, and buried his only nephew.

That morning the pope was going to hold a consistory, an important meeting of all the cardinals. It was the only official Vatican business that remained on Cardinal Montalto's calendar since Gregory had taken away all his positions. Naturally, everyone assumed the poor old man, coughing, leaning on his stick, would stay home, sobbing over his bitter loss.

But a loss that requires vengeance also requires calculation. Even if Paolo Giordano's guilt became painfully clear, it would be ridiculous to suppose that Pope Gregory, who had a hard time executing the most heinous serial killer of low birth, would ever punish a Roman duke. This particular duke was closely allied with the ruler of Tuscany, Francesco de Medici, who still considered himself Paolo Giordano's brother-in-law even though poor Isabella had been strangled five years earlier. The Italian concept of family firmly embraced in-laws and former in-laws, and a stain upon the Orsini name would discolor the de Medici name. Tuscany, which shared its southern border with the Papal States, would never permit scandal, let alone punishment, to harm Paolo Giordano, even if his in-laws loathed him.

Men like Paolo Giordano were above the law, a fact that had always grated on Cardinal Montalto, but now the injustice had landed in his own lap. Moreover, Grand Duke Francesco de Medici was Cardinal Montalto's patron, paying him an annual subsidy to make up for the poor cardinal's pension that Pope Gregory had withdrawn two months earlier. The grand duke's brother, the powerful Cardinal Ferdinando de Medici, was Montalto's supporter and friend, and a pope-maker in the next conclave. Montalto could hardly shriek for their brother-in-law to be punished.

As a distant relative of Paolo Giordano, King Philip II of Spain also had a say in the matter. If Gregory made any noise about punishing Paolo Giordano, both King Philip and Grand Duke Francesco could hold up trade agreements with the Papal States or neglect to hand over Church rents. The Duke of Bracciano was just too politically connected for the pope to do anything to him. And, with his close connection to monarchs and influential cardinals, Paolo Giordano could prevent Montalto from ever becoming pope if he believed any vengeance whatsoever might be in store.

Cardinal Montalto also had to consider his fellow members of the Sacred College, men who would vote for the next pope whenever Gregory finally kicked the bucket. It was well known that cardinals would not elect a vindictive man to rule over them. Such a pope would surely take revenge on his cardinals if they irritated him. Cardinals wanted to elect a kindly, easygoing pope, who would let them have their own way, a man who would quickly forgive their misdeeds and generously give them money and power.

If Cardinal Montalto, within hours of his nephew's assassination, could show himself to be calm and forgiving, this opportunity might eventually propel him onto the papal throne. Such an impressive display of Christian forgiveness could not be overlooked. Once pope, he would be able to wreak vengeance any way he wanted.

While a cardinal usually wore a red robe called a sottana, under a knee-length white linen shirt called a rochet, his mourning dress was a fuchsia sottana with no rochet. Those who thought they might see Cardinal Montalto that morning surely expected him to wear mourning. But Montalto put on his usual red robes and rochet and stepped into his carriage to clatter to Saint Peter's as if nothing untoward had occurred in the night.

"Montalto appeared as usual in consistory," reported the chronicler, "and was among the first to arrive, and in him no disturbance was apparent. And the cardinals who, because of the bitterness of the situation, wanted to give him some words of consolation, marveled at his calm response... When Pope Gregory XIII, who had learned everything, entered in consistory and rested his eyes on the face of Cardinal Montalto, he was seen to cry for compassion, without the cardinal even changing color in appearance. The marvel grew when, at the beginning of the consistory, Montalto went to an audience with the pope, as usual, to talk of much business, and his Holiness, before the cardinal spoke, was seen to cry copious tears from his eyes, and consoling him, promised him the most severe justice."

And now came the cardinal's papal moment. "Cardinal Montalto gave him many thanks for the very kind affection of his Holiness and begged him insistently not to make any inquiry of any kind about this crime, pardoning with good will whoever had been the author, and said it would never have occurred if it weren't the will of God. Then he immediately changed the subject to discuss business."[†]

Some of the spectators of this astonishing scene had a hard time believing Montalto's sentiments were genuine. A *relatione* reported, "While this discussion was going on between the pope and Montalto, the courtiers were studying the faces of both of them, and the eye of the courtier is only with difficulty deceived. They did not exaggerate when affirming that Montalto was not at all moved by the pope's tears, and had great serenity of expression, and seeing the signs of the pope's true compassion, he maintained the same composure the entire time that they spoke. This self-discipline was shocking to the others as well as the pope."[‡]

His strategy worked. "His faith obtained the infinite admiration not only of the pope but also of the cardinals present. And his Holiness

† Ibid., pp. 612-613.
‡ Strozzi, *Vita del Sommo*, folio 8a.

after the consistory said to Cardinal Buoncompagni, his nephew, 'He was a learned monk, and now he is a good cardinal, and if he doesn't die he will be a great pope.'"[†]

Monsignor Alessandro de Medici, ambassador of the Grand Duke of Tuscany to Rome, sat down that morning and wrote his master about the events, though he got a few facts wrong. "Last night about two hours after sunset," he wrote, "an unknown person went to the house of Signor Francesco, nephew of Cardinal Montalto and husband of the Corambona, under the pretext of giving him a certain note. And he was taken outside his house and conducted to a place where he was killed by guns and many other wounds and was found spread out on the ground at the gate of Cardinal Sforza's garden at Monte Cavallo. As of now the authorities do not know who committed this crime, though much invented gossip is being spread. And Montalto his uncle, despite all this, went to the consistory this morning, perhaps wanting to show how few family affections he had."[‡]

According to time-honored tradition, upon the death of a cardinal's close relative, the Sacred College, prelates, and nobles of Rome rendered condolence visits. Cardinal Montalto sat on his cardinalatial throne in his long audience chamber, receiving his guests. When someone asked him if he knew where this horrible blow had come from – meaning, the Duke of Bracciano – he said, "From God, and He takes from me all human consolation so that I rely on celestial ones."[§] Others urged him to investigate the criminals and punish them. He replied calmly, "I am not so tender with my relatives that I will sin through a vendetta. Everything is God's will,"[¶] and, "God will punish the criminals."[**]

The cardinals and nobles of Rome were not certain if his forgiveness stemmed from saintliness or cowardice; considering his vile birth, perhaps he had no sense of family honor. Others believed

† Anon., p. 613.
‡ Gnoli, p. 85, n.
§ Ibid., p. 86.
¶ Ibid.
** Ibid.

the cardinal's forbearance was deceit designed to help him ascend the papal throne, "resentment being a clear killer to the future pontificate."[†]

Rome was most astonished when the reputed murderer himself rolled up to Villa Montalto. Certainly it would have made Paolo Giordano look guilty if he had been the only Roman nobleman *not* to offer condolences; still, people were shocked at his audacity. The fat duke climbed down from his carriage and ambled into the villa to lament the atrocious crime. Those visitors who had been dawdling in the courtyard immediately ran inside to witness what was about to unfold. Surely the cardinal would have to show some sign of anger or repulsion. But studying Cardinal Montalto's face as he spoke with Paolo Giordano, they "could not see any sign whatsoever that Montalto suspected him. He accepted the polite compliments of Signor Paolo with an extraordinary serenity of expression and an affability of conversation."[‡]

Finally, the duke took his leave, and the cardinal did him the honor of walking with him downstairs to the threshold of the house, all the while thanking him for his graciousness. In mounting his coach, the duke smiled and said to one of his servants, "Truly he is a great monk."[§] Paolo Giordano must have believed that either Cardinal Montalto did not suspect him, or that he was too afraid of him to seek justice. So far, the duke's plan was going perfectly.

But Cardinal Montalto's plan was also going perfectly, and the irony could not have been lost on him that Paolo Giordano's despicable murder of his nephew could pluck him out of the Sacred College and place him on the papal throne. Montalto's dignity in the face of horror "won the admiration of all Rome which expected different demonstrations from a cardinal so gravely offended."[¶]

Now there remained the question of what to do with Vittoria. Because she had had no children with Francesco, she had no remaining ties to the Peretti family, and she certainly didn't want to

† Ibid., p. 121.
‡ Strozzi, *Vita del Sommo*, p. 8b.
§ Ibid.
¶ Anon., p. 612.

stay there with the children and the chickens. Tarquinia wanted her daughter back home where this time around she could arrange a truly splendid marriage for her that would boost all of the family's fortunes. Tarquinia had recently engineered another rise in the world, moving to a larger, newer palazzo on the Via de Scrofa, just a block away from their old house and in between the Pantheon and the Piazza Navona. Such a home would be a more suitable place for a duke to woo his future duchess.

Cardinal Montalto allowed Vittoria to return to her parents with all her clothing, gold, jewels, and other gifts from the Peretti family. This was a generous gesture, as legally the cardinal was required only to return the dowry, which he had already done years earlier. He could have sent her home with only the clothes on her back.

On April 25, Vittoria's brother Mario galloped into town with more tragic news. Her brother Scipione, who had been in the service of Cardinal Sforza, had died of an illness in the town of Macerata. The condolence visits started up afresh at the Accoramboni palace, though Vittoria spent most of the time bedridden, emotionally exhausted from having lost her husband and her brother in the space of a week. Though Tarquinia was deeply saddened by the loss of her son, she couldn't afford to languish in bed; she had work to do. She must get Vittoria on her feet and married to the duke as soon as possible.

The dead are usually quickly forgotten because the living are too busy to mourn them for long. But not so Cardinal Montalto. He would never forget. He wrote down Francesco's death in his little book of debts owed. Leafing through it, perhaps he remembered Jesus's words from the book of John: "I am the true vine, and my Father is the gardener. He cuts off every branch in me that bears no fruit, while every branch that does bear fruit he prunes so that it will be even more fruitful."

Like a good gardener, he would prune and cut, mercilessly eradicating the weeds by the roots.

Chapter 7

THE GRIEVING WIDOW

Give her as much torture and grief as the glory and luxury she gave herself. In her heart she boasts, 'I sit as queen; I am not a widow, and I will never mourn.'

– Revelation 18:7

It is odd to think of a statue with psychic abilities, but the talking statue Pasquino often had an eerily correct foreknowledge of Roman events. This is likely because those who tacked up their poems on the wall behind him, leaned their cartoons against his base or hung their witticisms from his neck were servants in the homes of Rome's movers and shakers. Waiting silently in the shadows of a room for instructions to deliver a message or fetch some wine, servants overheard the most scurrilous conversations of those in the know.

No sooner was Francesco buried than placards were placed around Pasquino's neck accusing Tarquinia and Marcello of planning Francesco's murder so that the entire family could become rich when Vittoria married the duke. According to the chronicler, "It is certain that some of Vittoria's relatives were suspected of helping to liberate her from her first husband out of ambition to achieve a greater fortune. But how much wiser would it have been to advise her to be content with her duty and her present situation, which would soon have reached the apex of greatness."† Unfortunately, the apex of greatness did not come quickly enough to save Francesco Peretti.

That April of 1581, Paolo Giordano spent most of his time in his family palace in the Campo de' Fiori, in the heart of Rome. Periodically, he bounced out to his villa of Magnanapoli just outside the city. On the evening of Thursday, April 27, he sent a servant

† Anon., p. 610.

from Magnanapoli to Father Paolo Maletta, a priest at a little Roman church, San Biagio dell'Anello, who at some point in the past had heard the duke's confession. The servant instructed Father Paolo to come out to the villa for an important discussion. The priest, wondering what on earth would make such an important lord send for him, immediately stopped what he was doing and stepped outside to find the duke's carriage waiting for him.

At Magnanapoli, the duke informed Father Paolo that he was concerned for his eternal soul, though the reason for this concern was not that he had just ordered the assassination of an innocent young man; he was worried, he said, because he had made a vow to God that he would marry a certain young woman as soon as she became a widow. According to the priest's later testimony, the duke said he had chosen Vittoria Accoramboni because he "had known her as a very chaste woman, most faithful to her husband, and God-fearing."[†] Her husband having recently died as a result of God's will, Paolo Giordano now needed to fulfill his vow immediately or face divine punishment. The priest must unite Paolo Giordano in holy matrimony with Vittoria Accoramboni.

Paolo Giordano instructed the priest to visit Vittoria, tell her of his vow, and ask her to be his wife. The wedding would be held before a priest, two witnesses, and a notary, as required by the Council of Trent. However, because of the unsavory circumstances of the marriage, the duke would not have the banns published, in violation of the council's edicts.

In 1563, the Council of Trent had been called upon to address the perplexing issue of what made a marriage legal. Before the council, the Vatican stated that a legal marriage did not require a sacramental ceremony in a church. It was enough if the two parties promised themselves to each other, and the groom gave the bride a ring. Such a marriage was clandestine (secret) but also valid. Sometimes when parents announced they had found a perfect match for their daughter in the elderly widower next door, the girl replied curtly that

† Gnoli, p. 89.

she was already married, thank you very much, having contracted a clandestine union with the cute boy down the street.

Since divorce was not possible, people who were miserably married suddenly remembered they had made a clandestine marriage as teenagers, which rendered the current marriage null and void. With the absence of witnesses and no written registry of the event, no one could be sure *what* had happened. Bishops were appealed to, lawsuits were initiated, and the status of the children's legitimacy came into question as well as their inheritances. To prevent these multi-generational messes from occurring with such harrowing frequency, the council refused to recognize as legal any clandestine marriages made from 1563 onwards. Every wedding must include a priest to perform the Tridentine marriage rite, two witnesses, and the registration of the marriage in the parish book.

The Council of Trent also required that marriages be publicly announced from the pulpit for three Sundays before the event. Before or after the sermon, the parish priest was to state in a loud voice the names of the bride and groom, the names of their parents, their places of birth, residence, age, and whether they had ever been married before, including the name of the woman's deceased husband. If anyone knew of any impediment to the marriage, they had time to come forward and inform Church authorities.

The most common impediment was a legal one: that one of the parties was already married. Perhaps the groom had an unloved wife in another town. Before the three weeks were up, a relative having heard of the banns would come to speak to the parish priest about the impossibility of the new marriage. It was the priest's responsibility to hold off on the wedding until he had fully investigated the claims. If he was uncertain of their validity, he would refer the matter to his bishop. There were also impediments of blood, called consanguinity: the bride and groom should not be more closely related than third cousins. This was a problem in some Italian towns where everyone was third cousins or less, but Church dispensations for such marriages were usually easy to obtain for a price.

A moral impediment might be that one of the parties had made a vow of celibacy, that the couple had conducted a notorious adultery or lived in sin, or that the groom had murdered the husband of the bride in order to marry her himself. In the case of Paolo Giordano and Vittoria, if the parish priest were to read the name of the bride's dead husband, Francesco Peretti, murdered days earlier under mysterious circumstances, there was sure to be an outcry against the marriage because of the impediment. At that moment, it looked as if there would be no murder investigation at all, given Cardinal Montalto's Christian resignation to Francesco's demise, and Paolo Giordano didn't want to stir up police interest by the reading of the banns.

But any announcement of the upcoming marriage would have involved a far more serious problem than a police investigation. The noble house of de Medici would simply not have stood for their relative, who had previously married the ruling grand duke's sister, demeaning the entire family by wedding a woman of inferior rank. They would surely have complained vociferously to the pope and threatened every parish priest in Rome, until no one dared marry the couple.

The Council of Trent stated that if the contracting parties refused to publish the banns, the parish priest could not assist at their marriage except in certain cases. Deathbed marriages, for instance, did not require banns. And if the bride and groom convinced the local bishop that their families might try to thwart a valid union with violence, he might agree to dispense with the banns and allow the marriage to go forward. Perhaps Paolo Giordano might have justified his case with this clause.

Father Paolo could not have been happy to get involved in such a case. If he did not comply, the duke and his henchmen could make his life miserable or snuff it out altogether. If he did comply, his bishop, Cardinal de Medici, Grand Duke Francesco of Tuscany, the pope, and the King of Spain could punish him severely. According to his later testimony, he pointed out to the duke that Vittoria was not of sufficient birth and quality to be the bride of an Orsini duke and a near relation of the de Medicis. Moreover, it was dangerous to go against the decrees of the holy Council of Trent.

Then the priest delicately asked him if "there were not some impediment that would cause the marriage to be declared void."[†] The duke angrily replied that there was no impediment, that he had made a vow and would fulfill it or bring God's wrath upon himself. According to the priest, Paolo Giordano added "that he would do in this case what his conscience dictated what he was obliged to do, and that I should not intend to give him advice."[‡] Father Paolo reluctantly agreed to speak to Vittoria.

The following day, April 28, he went to the Accoramboni palazzo. The duke's coach was idling in front of the building. Inside, the priest was led upstairs to wait in an antechamber outside Vittoria's room, where he found her brother, the abbot Mario, who was also waiting. Paolo Giordano was with the Lady Vittoria, a servant explained, consoling her for the loss of her brother, Scipione. As the duke strode out of Vittoria's room with her father, he summoned Mario.

"Signor Paolo Giordano came to my house to offer his condolences for our travails," Mario would later testify, "and after this had been discharged, he told me that since it had pleased God to leave Signora Vittoria, my sister, a widow, that he had resolved to marry her, and I replied that this was too great a favor because we were not worthy to be his servants, let alone his relatives. And since I was not the head of the house, I didn't have the authority to resolve it, and his Excellency replied that this was not worth worrying about, since it was for the honor and utility of our family. He said that he had sent for his confessor, who was already at our house, to speak to Lady Vittoria, and then Lord Signor Paolo immediately left."[§]

Father Paolo was ushered into Vittoria's chamber, Mario beside him. She was crying, wearing black mourning weeds and a white veil. The priest began to console her on the death of her brother, but she

† Gnoli, p. 89.
‡ Ibid., pp. 89-90.
§ Ibid., p. 425.

made it clear that she was still mourning her husband, "and she said that she had loved him dearly."[†]

There must have been an uncomfortable silence before the priest broached the subject of the grieving widow's immediate remarriage. Father Paolo said that as the duke's confessor, he was responsible for his conscience, and Paolo Giordano "had made a vow to God, for the good that he has received, to take her as his wife." Vittoria "replied only that she was not worthy of such favor, and that she would leave her honor and her soul in the hands of his Excellency."[‡] It was a passive, tragic *yes*. The priest suggested that he return the following day to hear Vittoria's confession and obtain from her a definite reply.

On Saturday, April 29, Father Paolo returned to take Vittoria's confession and obtained from her a solemn vow of taking Signor Paulo as her consort. On April 30, only thirteen days after Francesco's murder, a wedding ceremony was held – sort of. Paolo Giordano did not fulfill his earlier promise of having a priest perform the ceremony, with numerous witnesses attending and a notary standing nearby, scratching the information on a sheet of parchment. Father Paolo had easily been bullied by the duke to take messages to Vittoria and render advice, but it seems he finally put his foot down when it came to performing the marriage itself, a ceremony that would surely have landed him in a dungeon with a resounding thud. He stayed resolutely in his church that day.

Mario, too, avoided the ceremony like the plague, but he later testified that Vittoria told him about it. A ring was an indispensable part of a clandestine marriage, helping to shore up its shaky foundation. Paolo Giordano, she said, put a ring on her finger, and with her Bolognese maid, Caterina, as a witness, said, "Now I marry Signora Vittoria." And Vittoria, "receiving it, consented to marry Orsini."[§] This would have been enough to ensure a legal marriage before 1563, but now, in 1581, the validity was dubious. In the

† Ibid., p. 90.
‡ Ibid., p. 91.
§ Ibid., p. 92.

eyes of the Church, it would have been more like a legally binding engagement to be married.

Mario stated that according to Vittoria, "Everything had happened with the knowledge of Father Paolo, and that he had assured her and the signor that because of the vow and the ring it was an indissoluble sacrament, and that they could live together without sex."[†] Father Paolo himself testified that he had informed Vittoria that she "must not consent to sleep with him if first the marriage was not done solemnly because otherwise their souls would be in damnation."[‡]

But the duke was not pleased with the last condition. The whole point of the murder and the marriage was to finally have sex with the delectable Vittoria. Either they were married, or they weren't. Crushed between fear of papal authorities and fear of Paolo Giordano, Father Paolo and Abbot Mario had placed the couple in the legal limbo of the maybe-married, and the duke was having none of it.

Now Paolo Giordano wanted to conduct another ceremony more in line with the Council of Trent, a ceremony which would allow consummation but, given the interfering relatives, would not include the banns. The duke instructed Father Paolo to meet with Monsignor Pirro Taro, vice regent of the vicariate, to see if it was possible to have a wedding with a priest, two witnesses and a notary but without the banns. The duke instructed Taro not to mention the names of the bride and groom. Taro did as he was asked, and Monsignor Pirro said that both of them should give the matter some thought.

But here Father Paolo took the opportunity to hop on a horse and ride to Spoleto, a hundred miles north of Rome, where he was supposed to visit the churches and monasteries with the bishop's assistant, Pietro Orsini, a distant relative of the duke. The poor priest was in a terrible position, caught between the proverbial rock and a hard place, and he must have hoped that somehow the whole thing would pass over in his absence.

He must have been horrified when he arrived in the town of Borghetto and found a servant of Paolo Giordano's waiting for him,

† Ibid.
‡ Ibid., p. 424.

who "presented me with a letter of his Excellency's all in his own hand, in which he wrote me that he marveled much that I had left without saying a word, and that he had remained in great suspense. In the same letter I replied to him that I had to leave at the request of Don Signor Pietro, and that he should have patience until my return."[†]

And patience would most likely have obtained for Paolo Giordano everything he wanted. In a major metropolitan city like Rome, rife with murders, duels, rapes, arsons, Church scandals, excommunications, malaria, famine, floods, and plagues, the tragic murder of a cardinal's unremarkable nephew would have soon been forgotten. If instead of rushing to marry Vittoria, the duke had seen fit to travel abroad that summer, suspicions of his guilt would have faded. As a grandee of Spain, he could have taken the opportunity to visit his kinsman, King Philip II, at his nearly completed Escorial Palace in Madrid. He could have stayed with his de Medici in-laws in Tuscany, visiting his neglected children, or journeyed to the Republic of Venice, where his family had served honorably in many military campaigns. Or he could have stayed at Lake Bracciano with his bandits and gone hunting. But Paolo Giordano simply couldn't help himself. He stayed in Rome.

Meanwhile, Vittoria could have lived quietly in her parents' house, or taken her grieving self, wrapped in copious widow's weeds, to retirement in a convent for a year. Once she had returned to the Palazzo Accoramboni, after a year of sober behavior on both their parts, the duke could have begun to call on her and ask for her hand. Such a marriage would not have caused the firestorm of protest and suspicion created by vows made only days after Francesco's murder. Unfortunately, patience had never been Paolo Giordano's strong suit. He had never been able to deny himself a glass of wine, a pork chop, a new coach, or a pretty prostitute, let alone the love of his life.

It is interesting to speculate whether Vittoria tried to dissuade him from his haste. Perhaps she suggested they wait a few months, and he dismissed this suggestion, given the heat of his ardor. Or perhaps she didn't try at all, given the heat of her own ardor for position and

† Ibid.

wealth. She may have worried that he might change his mind if she angered him by insisting on waiting. Worse, in the meantime the duke might clutch his chest at the banquet table and keel over stone dead into a custard pudding. Then she would never become a duchess, and Francesco's death would have been in vain.

Fearing that the blame attached to him for Francesco's murder would create a clear impediment to the marriage, Paolo Giordano instructed an acquaintance of his to pretend to be the assassin. The fall guy was a certain Cesare Pallantieri, a Renaissance rebel-without-a-cause banished to Florence several months earlier for brawling. Pallantieri wrote the governor of Rome that he had snuck into the city on April 16, ambushed Francesco Peretti, and shot him for having tried to poison him the year before. He was making the truth known, the letter continued, so that innocent people (and here he meant Paolo Giordano) would not be blamed for the crime.

Investigations showed, however, that Cesare Pallantieri was seen in Florence the night of April 16 and the morning of April 17. And in a city where the flimsiest piece of gossip flew high and low in a matter of hours, no one in Rome had ever heard even the slightest rumor of the ridiculous poisoning story. The Pallantieri letter made Paolo Giordano look guiltier than ever.

The sight of the Orsini carriage parked daily in front of the Accoramboni house within days of the assassination had already sparked speculation. *Now that he has killed the husband*, people said, *he is going to marry the widow immediately*. Camilla fidgeted uncomfortably. In the days after Francesco's murder, before Vittoria returned to her parents, the women had mourned together and consoled each other. Camilla had not believed the reports that her daughter-in-law had had a hand in the murder. Perhaps Paolo Giordano had indeed killed Francesco to marry Vittoria, but if Vittoria were innocent, she would repulse his advances with horror. Why was she receiving daily hours-long visits from the man who had most likely murdered her husband?

Camilla would undoubtedly have complained to her brother. *Vittoria must have been in on it. She's going to marry the duke. We didn't*

give her enough silk dresses. You never came through with the carriage.
That's why Francesco is dead. We couldn't give her enough things.

Cardinal Montalto loved Vittoria as a daughter. Though he had, in his past, been extremely harsh with men, he usually had a soft spot for the fairer sex, and he was closer to his sister than anyone on earth. Perhaps he said to Camilla, *Surely Vittoria hadn't known of Paolo Giordano's plans to murder Francesco. Hadn't she thrown herself on her knees that night and begged him not to go out? And the Accoramboni family was hardly in a position to bar the duke from visiting them. Vittoria would surely reject any suitor so soon, but especially the presumed murderer, who will eventually waddle away in frustration. Perhaps nothing will come of it, after all.*

Pope Gregory, too, was upset about the perpetual parking place of the duke's carriage. He called in Cardinal Montalto and told him he was going to investigate the duke's involvement in Francesco's murder. And Cardinal Montalto once more made known his Christian forgiveness. An *avvisi* of April 30 reported, "Cardinal Montalto supplicated his Holiness not to investigate this murder anymore, as he had pardoned the murderer."[†]

Through his spy network, Cardinal de Medici knew more than Camilla, Montalto, and Pope Gregory put together. He learned that either the duke had already married Vittoria without publishing the banns or was planning to do so. Oddly, the duke's murder of Francesco was not at all troubling; duels and assassinations burnished a family's reputation, proving its men were courageous and honorable. But marrying beneath oneself was an unforgivable crime.

In addition to the nagging question of a dishonorable marriage, the cardinal and his brother were concerned for the financial interests of their nephew, Virginio, who was now nine, and their niece, Leonora, ten. Paolo Giordano, sixteen years older than Vittoria and plagued by obesity and its attending ailments, would almost certainly die before her. As his widow, just how much of the estate would she inherit?

[†] Ibid., p. 100, n.

Despite the duke's lavish lifestyle and numerous palaces, there would be little left for the children once they paid their father's crushing debts. If a widow grabbed a chunk of the estate, the children would be forced to sell their land and castles and be left with a pittance. Poor little Leonora would be dowerless, possibly crammed into a convent for life. Virginio would be the duke of absolutely nothing. The great Orsinis, who for centuries had made Rome ring with the clash of arms, had ruled Christ's Church as popes, and had married into the highest echelons of royalty, would come to a shameful end.

Cardinal Ferdinando de Medici had never liked his embarrassing brother-in-law. The coldly calculating churchman saw him as wildly spendthrift, emotionally unstable, and physically repulsive. For twenty-three years the de Medicis had dutifully trudged behind Paolo Giordano with a broom and dustpan cleaning up his messes. They had loaned him money, smoothed over his brushes with the law, and put the brakes on his frequent sale of land. But he was, after all, a close relative, and his dishonor would dishonor them all. They looked out for him not because they cared for him, but to prevent him from harming their own interests.

Now, with the out-of-control duke threatening his most embarrassing antics yet, Cardinal de Medici pulled in the big guns. He convinced the grand duke, the Spanish ambassador, and numerous other cardinals to implore Pope Gregory to annul any marriage that might have already occurred and to forbid any future marriage. Scandal and disgrace would taint them all if something weren't done about it immediately.

The pope agreed. Unsure what to do about the murder investigation, he was at least certain that he would not permit the suspected murderer to marry the victim's wife. On May 5, Monsignor Mario Marzio, lieutenant of the vicariate of Rome, called Vittoria to his palazzo in the Piazza di Trevi. She arrived accompanied by some lady friends to find a notary and five witnesses waiting for her. The Monsignor informed her that Gregory had forbidden her to contract marriage without the written permission of the pope himself, and that without such permission any marriage would be null and void.

Out of respect for Paolo Giordano's nobility, and probably out of fear of his army, the decree mentioned neither the duke nor Francesco's murder. The Monsignor read it to her first in the official Latin version and then in Italian so that she could understand. The notary wrote down that Vittoria was present and had heard the decree. And the five witnesses signed their names.

Vittoria, who had remarried five days earlier, managed to look shocked. She replied that the recent deaths of her husband and brother made it unlikely that she would remarry any time soon. But when she decided to do so, she was convinced that his Holiness, as a just prince, would not take away this legal right from her, nor as head of the Church would he deny her this sacrament. Stunned, she and her ladies rustled out of the chamber.

When Paolo Giordano heard the news of the papal decree, he was incandescent with rage. He was also aware of the very real possibility that the de Medicis, expert in administering poison and dagger thrusts themselves, might murder Vittoria to prevent him from marrying her. One evening a few days after the decree was issued, his coach pulled into the Accoramboni courtyard and, a while later, departed. Inside were Vittoria, her mother, and her maid Caterina, secretly dashing out of Rome to the duke's villa of Magnanapoli, where they would be safe from de Medici murder.

According to Mario Accoramboni's testimony, the duke "saw this business disturbed, and he feared worse to come if he stayed far away from my sister. Being informed that because of the vow and the ring my sister was already his wife, for worthy reasons he resolved to take her to his villa, which he did. There he wrote a document in his own hand declaring that his Excellency led my sister to his house as his wife because she was not safe in our house, and promising to hold her intact [no sex] until he had permission from the pope."[†] It is unlikely, however, that the duke kept Vittoria intact.

Vittoria's father stayed in Rome and spread the word that she was so sick with grief from her recent tragedies that she was near the point of death, unable to see a single visitor. Those who came by to

† Ibid., p. 426.

comfort the dying woman had no idea she was feasting with the Duke of Bracciano at his country estate.

At Magnanapoli, Paolo Giordano bestowed items of great value on Vittoria. And now, finally, she possessed the luxury goods she had always dreamed of. According to an inventory, she received silverware: two silver basins worked with reliefs; twenty silver place settings; two silver candlesticks; two silver trays; a silver jug attached to a basin with a chain, used for hand washing; and a mirror set in a silver etching.

She also received jewelry: a chain of thirty gold links; an enameled gold chain with a gold pinecone pendant; and a box edged in diamonds and rubies, containing twenty pieces of jewelry of diamonds and pearls. He gave her four brooches: a gold unicorn with a body of mother-of-pearl; a gold galley studded with rubies; another, smaller ship also adorned with rubies; and a gold pin in the shape of tree branch bedecked with pearls and other jewels. Perhaps best of all, he gave her two spectacular gowns, one made of real gold thread and the other of silver.

Though Vittoria was currently relishing a palatial lifestyle – waited on hand and foot by servants and proudly wearing a gold chain of thirty links – her situation was precarious. She was not recognized as the Duchess of Bracciano and was considered to be living in sin. If Paolo Giordano died suddenly, she would trundle home with nothing, not even the jewelry he had given her. His heirs would wrest it from her by force, if they had to, and the law would not intervene. If the duke tired of her, he could throw her out in the street where, given her scurrilous reputation as a murderess and a slut, no one would pick her up and dust her off. She must have prodded the duke to do something to remedy a situation so difficult for a woman of her refinement and sensitivity.

Paolo Giordano requested an audience with Pope Gregory, during which he boldly asked for permission to marry Vittoria. Gregory replied that under the circumstances he would never grant permission. The duke protested that even the pope had no right to unjustly prevent a marriage, and besides, Vittoria already was his wife, living with him at Magnanapoli.

For once in his life, the usually complacent Gregory flew into a rage. He ordered the duke to return Vittoria to her father's house immediately and forbade him to see her, speak to her, write to her, or communicate with her in any way. The duke barreled out of the audience chamber without the requisite farewell courtesies. But he knew he had lost that round and sent word to Magnanapoli that Vittoria must return to Rome. Then he went to bed overcome by frustration.

Word of the marriage raced through Rome like wildfire. Camilla ranted and raved, and Cardinal Montalto felt sick at heart. Was Vittoria innocent of the murder, yet unable to withstand the duke's tempting offer? As his wife, she could live in palaces and have all the jewels, dresses, and carriages she wanted. Beautiful girls wanted beautiful things, after all. Very few beautiful girls were born to be saints or nuns; that seemed to be reserved for the plain ones.

Vittoria was back with her family, but this was not enough for the enraged pope. On May 21, Gregory sent her a decree that as of the following day she should not dare to set foot out of her father's house, not even to hear Mass, and that she should not speak to the duke nor to any person sent by him, nor receive his letters or send any to him, under pain of imprisonment in a convent for life and severe financial penalties. The same morning another decree commanded Vittoria's father, Claudio, and her brother, Mario, under pain of a fine of 2,000 ducats and the loss of all ecclesiastical pensions, not to permit the duke to enter their house, nor to speak or write to Vittoria. On May 23, the duke himself received a decree that if he contacted Vittoria in any way, either personally or through intermediaries, or if he even walked past her house, he would be fined 10,000 gold ducats and be proclaimed a traitor.

Meanwhile, Monsignor Pirro Taro had been waiting for Father Paolo to return from Spoleto. He remembered their conversation earlier in the month, when Father Paolo had asked him about performing a marriage according to the Council of Trent but without publishing the banns. Given the subsequent uproar over Paolo Giordano's marriage, it became immediately clear to him whom the priest had been talking about. The day after Father Paolo's return, Monsignor Taro sent his bailiff, Monsignor Bernardino Cotta, to the Church of San Biagio dell'Anello to haul him off to jail.

Monsignor Cotta then summoned Abbot Mario for interrogation and had him thrown in prison, too. For the next several days the two were interrogated, their testimony recorded by a scribe. Abbot Mario confirmed that Father Paolo had advised Vittoria to make the vow to marry the duke, and that based on his advice the duke had placed the ring on her finger. The terrified Father Paolo, on the other hand, denied having advised her to make the vow and said he knew nothing of any ring.

From his sick bed, Paolo Giordano raged like a madman. Many of Rome's elite, including the pope's son, the Duke of Sora, rode out to visit him. They pointed out to him how dangerous it would be to fall into disgrace with King Philip of Spain, Grand Duke Francesco of Tuscany, Pope Gregory, and even the extended Orsini family who honored him as their head. He must give up this dangerous passion and return to an honorable and tranquil life. His brother-in-law, Cardinal de Medici, was particularly concerned. The duke threatened to stain the family honor by his ignominious marriage to Vittoria and reduce his children's inheritance.

But Paulo Giordano never gave a thought to his children, whom he believed might not even be his, given their mother's indiscretions. Yet outright resistance was clearly getting him nowhere. Eventually, he seemed to be moved by the arguments of his friends and agreed to give up Vittoria. As he calmed down, his health improved, and he was able to go out for carriage rides.

By June 1, Monsignor Taro had completed his investigation into the marriage of Paolo Giordano and Vittoria, and went personally to visit the duke. The marriage was known, the Monsignor said, and had been declared null and void because it was clandestine. Both parties were free to contract marriage, as long as it wasn't to each other. The duke seemed resigned to this decree and left Rome for Bracciano, where he wrote a letter to the pope, thanking him for reminding him of his honor. But the sentiments were probably not sincere. The following month, when a group of audacious bandits attacked Rome, it was said that they had come from Bracciano.

Within a matter of five weeks, Vittoria had been widowed, moved back in with her family, lost her brother Scipione, secretly married the duke, eloped with him to his country estate, and finally, having had her marriage declared null and void, returned to her father's house. The emotional agitation affected her health, too, and the illness was perhaps boosted by a generous helping of guilt. She became so gravely ill that at one point that her family feared she would die.

By July, as Vittoria was recovering, her former sister-in-law Maria suddenly became ill and died. Maria had been in her early thirties, and though the deaths of the young were not unusual given the rampant malaria and dysentery, the Roman rumor mill attributed her demise to something else entirely. The Accorambonis, it was said, had poisoned her through a Greek sorceress in the service of Paolo Giordano, a woman known to be proficient in concocting fatal brews. Camilla was almost wild with grief, having lost both her children in the space of three months, and possibly both deaths had occurred because of Vittoria's unbridled ambition. Surely the evil woman had murdered again.

Camilla badgered her brother to seek vengeance. His "God's will" lecture, though it had impressed many, certainly didn't sit very well with her. But Cardinal Montalto waved her protests away. He adopted Maria's four children, giving them the surname of Peretti, and made them and Camilla his heirs. He spent his days cultivating his vines, fruit and olive trees, growing asparagus, cabbage, and cauliflower, and shoveling manure onto the roots of fragrant blooming plants. He asked friends and family members to help him dig, prune and harvest, and carry the buckets of precious water that his thirsty plants so desperately needed. It seemed to many that he was no longer a highly educated prince of the Church with papal aspirations, but a common gardener who loved his work.

Periodically, he took a little book out of his pocket and opened it.

Chapter 8

BEAUTY BEHIND BARS

If I am guilty — woe to me! Even if I am innocent, I cannot lift my head, for I am full of shame and drowned in my affliction.

– Job 10:15

In September 1581, Paolo Giordano went twice to the pope's summer villa of Mondragone outside Rome to beg for an audience. According to the *avvisi*, the pope would not grant him one. He had made his wishes quite clear about the duke and Vittoria and did not want to be bothered by any more annoying pleas.

In early October, the duke traveled with Cardinal de Medici to visit Cardinal d'Este at his fabulous villa near Tivoli. Many other cardinals, too, had been invited to enjoy the extensive gardens with their unique fountains and waterfalls. During this visit, Paolo Giordano confessed that he no longer thought about Vittoria and was glad the marriage had fallen through. He had, he admitted, been briefly bewitched, but that was now over. Such a statement made in front of so many cardinals was designed to wing its way immediately back to the pope, and Gregory must have been glad to hear it.

Soon after, the duke petitioned Gregory to nullify the decree forbidding him to speak or write to Vittoria. He had no interest in her any more, he wrote, so the decree was unnecessary. Moreover, it was dishonorable for an Orsini duke to have such an embarrassing edict hanging over his head, and the shame extended to the de Medicis, as they were so closely allied with him. The pope, aware of the increasing audacity of Bracciano bandits plundering Rome, agreed to revoke the edict.

But Paolo Giordano willfully misinterpreted the pope's favor. If the edict were revoked, he reasoned, then that part of the edict that forbade him to marry Vittoria was also revoked. Therefore, he was now legally permitted to marry her. And within days of the revocation, Vittoria was lodged once more at Magnanapoli, wearing her real gold gown and eating off her very own silver platters.

In November, it seemed as if the duke were planning a huge wedding celebration to be held the following February, during Carnival. He was contracting with bakers, butchers, and musicians for a magnificent multi-day banquet and ball. Alarmed at the preparations, Grand Duke Francesco begged King Philip of Spain to do something. In response, the king wrote Paolo Giordano that he was amazed that he, his relative and principal cavalier, would create such humiliating scandal with a shameful marriage. However, in the meantime he would assign him the taxes on the silk coming into Naples. It was a bribe, thinly veiling a threat. If he did not comply, the duke would lose his Spanish revenues.

But Grand Duke Francesco and Cardinal de Medici knew this would not be enough. They convinced the pope to issue another edict to prevent a new marriage. On December 4, 1581, Gregory decreed that Paolo Giordano would be fined 25,000 ducats if he did not immediately return Vittoria to her father and if he had any communication with her again.

The duke, who was broke, obediently shuttled Vittoria back to her father's house a second time. But he continued to visit her. The Accorambonis, also threatened by an enormous fine if they permitted the duke to walk through their doors, were in quite a quandary. They couldn't exactly tell Paolo Giordano Orsini, who had so greatly honored their family, that he wasn't welcome. But neither could they afford the fine.

One of the Accoramboni men (the *avvisi* don't say which one) obtained a private audience with the pope. He begged Gregory to let Vittoria remarry the duke, this time legally. Things had advanced to the point, he confessed, that otherwise she would be deprived of her honor. This was a polite indication that Vittoria was no longer intact. The pope asked if the duke still met with Vittoria, and her relative said yes. Gregory dismissed him saying that he would take care of the situation.

The pope was furious that his decrees had not been heeded. Obviously, he needed to take more drastic measures to prevent the two of them from seeing each other and remarrying. Moreover, though he was in no position to interrogate Paolo Giordano about the murder of Francesco Peretti, there was nothing to prevent him from questioning Vittoria. The Accorambonis had no immunity from arrest as they were not noble enough.

Gregory sent instructions to the bailiff, Monsignor Cotta, instructing him to arrest Vittoria for the murder of her husband. On December 9, Cotta and his guards surrounded the Accoramboni house. Dozens of passersby stopped to gawk. Neighbors leaned out of windows to watch the show. Within minutes, the guards led a tragically pale Vittoria out of the house and into a waiting coach.

An *avvisi* reported, "Accompanied by the entire guard of Rome with a great crowd of people, the execution of the warrant was made in her own house, and not in that of Signor Paolo, but with such a concourse of din and people, that it has given much talk because of the quality of the person involved."[†] It was indeed rare for even a minor noblewoman to be imprisoned.

Vittoria, along with her entire family, was under grave suspicion in Francesco's murder because of her hasty marriage to the duke. The desire of any widow to remarry was viewed negatively as it indicated a taint of unseemly sensuality. But remarrying while the husband's corpse was still cooling in the grave was insulting to the dead and defied all traditions of proper behavior. In this case, it seemed as if it had been part of a plan, an agreement she had made before Francesco's death.

Once she was in custody, the authorities weren't quite sure what to do with her. They took her first to the Savelli prison, a filthy, dreadful place. Then there came an order to imprison her in the comfortable Convent of Saint Cecilia in Trastevere, a more suitable abode for a gentlewoman. But authorities apparently feared that

† Gnoli, p. 115, n.

Paolo Giordano and his thugs could easily break into the convent and rescue her. It was, after all, only defended by the Mother Superior wielding a crucifix.

It was therefore decided to move Vittoria to Castel Sant'Angelo, an impregnable bastion that overlooked the bend of the Tiber River near Saint Peter's, in the less populated part of Rome west of the Tiber. The building had not originally been constructed as a stronghold but as the imperial tomb for Emperor Hadrian's family around AD 130 and had undergone numerous changes over the years. Towers had been built around it and luxurious frescoed papal apartments on top of it. The Vatican treasury was stored inside as the place was impossible to rob. And the worst dungeons in the world were located deep in the heart of the rock: tiny, freezing, windowless closets that had once housed imperial corpses.

Vittoria was interrogated daily about what she knew of Francesco's death. How far had her relationship gone with Paolo Giordano before the murder? Had he made it known that he was planning to kill her husband? Hadn't she thought it strange he promised to marry her as soon as she was a widow when her husband was still young and healthy?

But Vittoria divulged nothing, and it was difficult for the most hardened prosecutors to proceed with great rigor for long when confronted with her sobs, sighs, heaving bosom, and lovely face. Moreover, Vittoria declared that she was pregnant and bewailed the cruel fate that had taken two husbands away from her in such a short space of time. What would happen to her poor innocent child? Instead of formulating a criminal case against her, the prosecutors told the pope she was clearly innocent and petitioned him to release her. But Gregory kept her in Castel Sant'Angelo as the only place with walls stout enough to keep her apart from Paolo Giordano.

From Bracciano, the duke wrote to the pope's son, the Duke of Sora, to the governor of Rome, and to various cardinals complaining that the Accoramboni family was under his protection, and therefore Vittoria should have had immunity from arrest. But the object of his affections stayed where she was.

If Vittoria truly did know nothing, Gregory was still resolved to find the men responsible for the murder. Safely ensconced at Bracciano, Marcello received a notice that he should come to Rome to defend himself against the suspicion of murdering Francesco. Marcello didn't come, and there was no possibility of sending guards to bring him to Rome. Paolo Giordano's gang of Bracciano bandits would simply massacre the pope's men.

But Domenico Acquaviva, known as Mancino, was living quietly in the Papal States and was easier to arrest. Everyone knew that he had handed Vittoria's maid Caterina the note for Francesco the night of the murder. Mancino was arrested in January 1582 and taken to Rome. On February 24, he was interrogated and spilled the beans without torture.

He said that Vittoria's mother, Tarquinia, was deeply involved in the murder, salivating to have her daughter become a duchess. Mancino added that two of those who had shot and stabbed Francesco were a certain Melchiore of Gubbio and Paolo Basca of Bracciano, "both in the service," reported the chronicler, "of a signor whose name we will keep silent out of respect."[†]

As the investigation zeroed in on Paolo Giordano, Cardinal de Medici became frantic. There was talk that if the duke was found guilty, Castle Bracciano would be confiscated from the Orsinis and given to the family of Cardinal Farnese, de Medici's hated archrival for the papacy. Cardinal de Medici informed his friend Cardinal Montalto that he urgently needed his help. And Cardinal Montalto, who would need Cardinal de Medici's support in the next conclave, agreed. Montalto petitioned the pope to drop the investigation, which he did. Mancino was released from prison, and Tarquinia Accoramboni was never brought in for questioning.

Meanwhile, the bandit problem continued to get worse. Caravans carrying Church taxes to Rome were attacked and plundered. Trade goods could barely make it into Rome because the roads were so infested with robbers. When merchants began sending their goods by ship, the bandits boarded boats and became pirates. The entire

† Anon., p. 615

Roman economy was on the brink of ruin. Criminals even threatened to murder cardinals in Rome itself. One day, fearing they would be attacked, twenty-four out of forty cardinals refused to attend a cardinals' Mass in the church of Santa Maria del Popolo. The sixteen who dared attend had armed guards like Secret Service agents, hands on pistol holsters, constantly scanning the church for threats.

Cardinal Montalto was quick to point out the weakness of Pope Gregory. The country, he often said, was tottering toward disaster. The wise and venerable Sacred College, he continued, smiling at his fellow cardinals, would have to help the next pope create an orderly society for the public benefit. The people deserved a better administration, a safer environment, and less tolerance of bandits.

The biggest bandit of all was once again having money problems. Paolo Giordano returned to Rome to sell Formello, a little area in his duchy, to the nobleman Paolo Sforza. But the duke couldn't sell the land without the permission of Cardinal de Medici, who had loaned him 14,000 scudi with Formello as security. And the cardinal, who wanted him to feel the pinch, refused to agree to the sale. Paolo Giordano had to learn that his powerful relatives could make his life miserable if he didn't follow their advice and dump Vittoria for good.

Apart from his financial issues, the duke's prestige was taking a battering. At Bracciano, Paolo Giordano was supposed to receive King Philip II's new ambassador to the Papal States, Juan Enrique de Gusman, Count Olivares, on his journey to Rome. All the preparations were made, and the duke waited for his honored visitor, but the king had ordered the count to bypass Bracciano. This very purposeful insult shocked the duke. When he called on the ambassador in Rome, the count gave him a message from the king. Philip could not tolerate a grandee of Spain wanting to marry a woman of such greatly inferior status. The entire Orsini clan, the de Medicis, and the Spanish royal family would be tainted by the shame of it, and no one would have anything more to do with Paolo Giordano if he married her again.

The duke was, temporarily, beaten once more. According to an *avvisi* of July 18, he wrote letters to the pope, the Grand Duke of Tuscany, Cardinal de Medici, and the pope's son, the Duke of Sora, stating that he no longer wanted Vittoria as his wife. He also addressed a letter to Vittoria.

Vittoria was still firmly lodged in the Castel Sant'Angelo, though she had charmed her jailer, Napoleone Malvagia, into moving her to nice breezy rooms upstairs. When the jailer's wife gave birth to a daughter, Vittoria, whose own pregnancy had disappeared, acted as her godmother at the baptism, and the child was named after her. Vittoria was allowed to walk freely around the fortress, enjoying the view of Rome and the unfinished dome of Saint Peter's from the windy battlements. She was a delightful prisoner and made only one difficulty: she insisted that she be addressed as the Duchess of Bracciano. She had in her possession letters of Paolo Giordano, in which he called her his duchess. And she refused to part with the wedding ring.

But one day in the middle of July, a letter addressed to her arrived from Paolo Giordano. She trembled as she opened it. In the letter, the duke declared their marriage null and void. He was now giving her the freedom to marry someone else. Vittoria seemed shocked. She raced to a window and started to throw herself out. A serving woman was right behind her and grabbed her leg and the thick folds of her gown. She tried with difficulty to pull her in, but for a while Vittoria's life seemed literally to hang in the balance.

Meanwhile, on the ramparts below, soldiers heard Vittoria's shrill screams and looked up to see her flailing out of the window. They raced upstairs and helped her servant bring her in. When they carefully placed her on the floor, she appeared to be unconscious. Given the manipulative tactics of the thwarted pair, it is possible that the duke's renunciation, which resulted in a suicide attempt witnessed by hundreds of Romans in the streets below the fortress, was nothing more than a bit of theater.

If so, the duke achieved his goal. Having renounced Vittoria, he was immediately taken back into the good graces of the King of Spain, the grand duke, Cardinal de Medici, and the pope. There was no more talk of investigating Francesco's murder, and the duke was once again living high on the hog with borrowed money.

Clearly, the suicide act had a second goal, which was Vittoria's release from prison. The pope and Cardinal de Medici feared, however, that the moment Vittoria was free the duke would forget his promises, swoop into Rome, and grab her. Gregory didn't want to keep her imprisoned forever and tried to come up with another means of preventing a marriage. Perhaps Vittoria wanted to enter a convent? He could arrange the most prestigious convent for her, a beautiful, peaceful place. However, she steadfastly refused to become a nun.

The other option was to marry her to someone else. That way, clearly, Paolo Giordano couldn't marry her because then it would be bigamy. The pope spread the word that a lovely noble bride was up for grabs. Considering that the duke had killed her first husband and would likely kill her second one to get his hands on her, very few expressed an interest. A man named Iocovacci said that he would like to take Vittoria away as his bride, which raised the pope's hopes. But looking into the matter, Gregory discovered that Iocovacci lived at Bracciano and was a servant of the duke's.

Having wrapped her jailer around her little finger, Vittoria believed that if she could only have an audience with the pope, she might have the same luck with him and convince him to spring her from prison. She sent her mother, Tarquinia, to beg the pope for an audience, which occurred on August 10, 1582. It was a long conversation, but Vittoria was granted neither an audience nor her release.

But then Cardinal Carlo Borromeo, the saintly archbishop of Milan, weighed in on her side. The nephew of Pius V, Borromeo was perhaps the most devout cardinal who ever lived. Highly respected by the pope and the entire Sacred College, in 1610 he would be proclaimed a saint. If Vittoria was guilty of murder, he said, punish her. If she was not guilty, she must be released from prison. The pope had to agree and decided to release Vittoria as long as she promised not to marry the duke again.

He also insisted that she not remain in Rome; that would be like leaving a raw steak out for a slavering bulldog whenever Paolo Giordano came to town. She must sign a document drawn up by a notary that within three days of her release she would leave for Gubbio, where her parents still owned a little palazzo. If she left Gubbio without papal permission, her father would be fined 10,000 ducats, part of which sum he had to put up in advance as security.

On the night of November 8, two hours past sunset, Vittoria was escorted from prison into her mother's waiting coach and returned to her family's home. The following day, a notary of the vicar called on her to remind her of the continued validity of the papal decree of May 5, 1581, which prohibited her from contracting marriage without the pope's permission and declaring null and void the one she had already contracted.

Vittoria was perturbed that although she had, evidently, been found innocent of Francesco's murder, there were still conditions attached to her release. She asked for a private audience with the pope, hoping her charms could win him over as they had Cardinal Montalto, Paolo Giordano, and her jailer. The pope agreed to hear her.

According to an *avvisi* dated November 10, Vittoria and several relatives met with the pope in his audience chamber. "Prostrate on the ground and with a faint voice and tearful eyes and hands on her breast," the *avvisi* stated, Vittoria said, "Holy and Sainted Father, I have suffered long travails, the loss of my husband, imprisonment, and many other mockeries, which for a long time have enslaved me, not for my fault so much as for my lack of shrewdness. If I did not have an innocent conscience and did not hope for blessing from your Holiness, the soft heart of a woman of such a tender age would not be capable of enduring such calamity."

She then spoke bitterly of Paolo Giordano. "I have been oppressed and violated by the shrewdness and greatness of a cavalier well known to your Holiness," she continued. "I dare now to demand and confidently hope not just for pardon, but to awaken in the most clement heart of Your Beatitude pity for a young and noble woman, deceived and tormented. I implore your compassion, even more because I was born of blood ... I implore the clemency of you my lord and father to remove the exile and not insist that I remain deprived of my country, my relatives, and those of my blood, which would add wounds to the death, making the world doubt my innocence and honesty."

The *avvisi* continued, "The pope, listening to the affected prayers of this afflicted nymph, accompanied by rivers of tears and with a commotion to soften the hardest stone, as a prince full of clemency and piety, and seeing a great error, with blessings and promises of paternal love, promised to grant her what she had asked, but that in the meantime she had to go to Gubbio to render obedience."[†] Despite her piteous sobs about innocent honesty, the pope knew she couldn't be anywhere near Paolo Giordano.

As Vittoria was packing to go to Gubbio, she decided she would, oddly enough, call on Cardinal Montalto. She swept into the audience chamber of his villa, her lovely face wreathed in sad smiles, her eyes shining with tears, and knelt before him to kiss his hand. An *avvisi* of November 17 reported, "Cardinal Montalto welcomed her and embraced her with incredible signs of tenderness, as if she were a daughter instead of a niece."[‡]

Vittoria then asked his advice on how she should dress: in the black full mourning of a grieving widow, or in the drab beige color a widow wore in the intermediate stage of mourning before returning to her normal wardrobe. Considering the fact that she had already tried to remarry within days of the murder, "The cardinal advised her to wear the tawny habit, which she had taken, to be a color appropriate to her present state."[§] She knelt once more and fervidly kissed his hand, then rose to depart. We can picture him, watching her slender form and wide skirts rustling out of his audience chamber, wondering what role she had played in his nephew's murder.

The day before her departure for Gubbio, Vittoria bade the pope farewell, once more flinging herself at his feet and sobbing. Finally, on November 24, she left Rome accompanied by a cortege of her relatives' carriages, with all the servants armed to prevent robbery on the road.

---

† Ibid., pp. 132–134.
‡ Ibid., p. 135.
§ Ibid.

Vittoria did not like being stuck in Gubbio. On January 3, 1583, she wrote the pope:

Most Holy Father:

Your Holiness, having found me worthy in leaving Rome to kiss your most holy feet, I now dare, assured in the great goodness and kindness of Your Beatitude, to come to you to remind you how you granted me mercy. I petitioned you not to force me to stay in Gubbio, and your Holiness replied that I should obey. Since then I have arrived and rendered obedience. Now my honor and reputation are weighed down by being condemned like a criminal. I race to the holy feet, imploring you for the mercy of Jesus Christ to grant me the favor that it be canceled because I desire nothing more than honor, assuring you that having received this boon, I will obey or pay with my life. Receiving this from your most holy and benign nature, I will pray for the long and most happy life of Your Beatitude.

Your most humble and devoted Servant
Vittoria Accoramboni[†]

On January 23, the pope sent word to Vittoria that she was permitted to leave Gubbio. However, he expressly stated that the May 5, 1581, decree remained in effect, which prohibited Vittoria from marrying anyone without express papal permission, and if she disobeyed, the marriage would be null and void.

Vittoria was not satisfied with this. The one decree still in effect was precisely the one she wanted revoked. She must have had reason to believe that another wedding with the duke was in the offing, and it was urgent to obtain a document of some sort that seemed to revoke the decree prohibiting their marriage.

She wrote to Monsignor Lodovico Bianchetti, the pope's master of the chamber, that such a decree hanging over her head stained her honor and reputation and disturbed the tranquility of her soul. She swore that she would never marry "you know who."[‡]

† Ibid., pp. 137–138.
‡ Ibid., p.139.

The Monsignor took her request to the pope, and on February 11, 1583, Gregory revoked the earlier decree, with one stipulation: "His Holiness has given permission to Signora Vittoria Accoramboni to contract marriage with whomsoever she wants, except with that person whom his Holiness has forbidden."[†]

Monsignor Bianchetti was delighted that he had obtained the favor for Vittoria and on February 12, he wrote gleefully:

Most Illustrious and Respected Sister,

… God has conceded this favor. I went to Our Lord [the pope], explaining to him as best I could that I know the desire of your ladyship, which would not move you to do anything if not for the tranquility of soul and honor and reputation, assuring him that you promised never to marry you know who, and that you had written me this and given me your word. He was content at hearing this and on Thursday ordered Monsignor Pirro Taro to revoke the decree so that nothing would be left against you. I rejoice with you with all my heart…

From your most illustrious ladyship's most devoted servant, Lodovico Bianchetti[‡]

That day, February 19, Vittoria received another letter, this one from Monsignor Pirro Taro, the vice regent.

Illustrious lady, honored as a sister:

This is to advise you that Our Lord is content to annul all the decrees and warnings that he has made up until now… With regards to the future, it is up to your ladyship to observe inviolably that which his Holiness has written. I am certain that now that he has shown himself favorable, you can hope for much more in the future if you follow the same path, and you can rely on me.

Rome, February 12, 1583.
Your most illustrious ladyship's affectionate servant, Pirro Taro[§]

† Ibid.
‡ Ibid., pp. 139-140.
§ Ibid., p. 141.

Although the pope had revoked the decrees with the express stipulation that she not marry Paolo Giordano, Vittoria now had in her hands an official letter from one of the pope's top officials declaring that *all* decrees had been revoked. And Monsignor Bianchetti's letter did not forbid her from marrying Paolo Giordano Orsini, only "you know who." Legally, such a vague term had no meaning. These were exactly the documents she wanted.

Chapter 9

DISOBEDIENCE

"This is what God says: 'Why do you disobey the Lord's commands? You will not prosper. Because you have forsaken the Lord, he has forsaken you."

– *2 Chronicles 24:20*

Vittoria had ardently pushed for papal permission to return to Rome. Oddly, once she had obtained it, she lingered in Gubbio, for Paolo Giordano had let her know he would be traveling to Venice and would swing by Gubbio to pick her up on the way. If he married her in the republic instead of in the Papal States, the pope would have less authority over the legitimacy of the marriage. The independent Venetians enjoyed ignoring edicts from Rome. Some of them got lost, and the pope had to resend them. Others were held up in lengthy senatorial debates that went on for years. The very characteristics that had so irked Felice Montalto as inquisitor could now help Vittoria be recognized as the Duchess of Bracciano.

But just as his baggage was packed and loaded, the duke learned he had to stay in Rome to attend to a major legal mess. Unbeknownst to him, all Orsini property had been entangled by a recently discovered decree made in 1477 by Napoleone Orsini, which was "as narrow," according to the *avvisi*, "as his Excellency's waist is large, by which all the sales that he had made up until now, which are many, are rendered invalid."[†] And Paolo Giordano, always hemorrhaging money, had sold a great deal of land.

The decree stated that to prevent the loss of Orsini lands, any properties sold starting in 1477 by Orsinis who were now deceased must be returned by the purchasers to the Orsini family without

† Ibid., p. 147.

any compensation. Any sales made by the current duke would have to be revoked, with the duke returning the purchase price. Several cardinals who had bought property from Paolo Giordano's father were threatened with financial ruin by the decree and resolved to fight it in court. And Paolo Giordano certainly didn't have the money to buy back properties he had sold in recent years to pay his exorbitant debts. Reluctantly, the duke unpacked his bags and remained in Rome, consulting his legal advisors.

Pope Gregory's weakness with regards to the bandits sunk to a new low on March 30 when he permitted the most vicious criminal in Italy, Alfonso Piccolomini, the Duke of Montemarciano, to enter Rome accompanied by thirty noble cavaliers, ten of them exiled from Rome for murder. The cortege rode into the courtyard of Cardinal de Medici's palace where Piccolomini was welcomed like royalty.

Piccolomini had come to Rome to request the pope's spiritual and legal absolution for his many murders. Fearing the bandit king would renew his earlier threat of murdering his son if he didn't comply, the pope agreed. When asked how many murders he had committed, Piccolomini blithely replied three hundred and seventy. The pope duly filled in the number and sent back the dispensation.

In May, Piccolomini and his men rode to Bracciano as guests of the duke. The pope, fearing he might join with Paolo Giordano's men and attack Rome, agreed to give Piccolomini back his confiscated lands on the condition that he not return to the Papal States. The bandit duly left the country, settling into a Florentine palace as a guest of the grand duke.

But even as Piccolomini's brutality was being neutralized, violence erupted in Rome from another bold and reckless young man. One of Paolo Giordano's most faithful adherents was a young cousin named Lodovico Orsini, who had been born around 1560. Known for jealously guarding what he called his honor, he had recently returned from the battlefields of Portugal, which he had helped conquer for Spain.

In April 1583, the bailiff of Rome ignored the tradition of respecting the immunity of a noble house from police interference and forced his way into the Orsini palace known as Monte Giordano, located near Castel Sant'Angelo. While the Orsinis and their servants were taking part in a religious procession, the guards arrested two wanted criminals living there. Upon his return, Lodovico roused the other men to find and punish the bailiff and his guards. Racing through the streets of Rome, they found them in a piazza, and a free-for-all took place. Shots rang out, swords were drawn, and the cries of the dying and wounded resounded in the square. Three noble thugs, including Lodovico's half-brother, seventeen-year-old Raimondo Orsini, died.

It so happened that an old man and his beloved servant were walking home on a nearby street when they heard the fracas. A stray bullet wounded the servant, and the old man had to drag him to the house of a church canon and bang on the door, begging for help. There they stayed the night, too afraid of continuing street violence to send for a doctor. The servant died the next day. The old man was Cardinal Montalto, who once again had been caught up in the violence of the lawless young men of Rome. He had to send word to the Sacred College requesting troops to guard him on his way home.

Goaded by Lodovico Orsini, the families of the dead noblemen swore vengeance and led hundreds of their followers rioting through the streets. For four days, shops and government offices were closed, and only the foolish went outside the safety of their homes. When asked what should be done to quell the violence, the pope replied that the grand fury must be allowed to burn itself out. Then, fearing for his own safety and that of his son, he complied with the families' requests to hunt down and execute the bailiff and his guards, though they had just been following his orders. Five of the guards found hiding in the Vatican were murdered on the spot.

The pope's weakness in the face of violence encouraged further crimes. The Venetian ambassador wrote, "This incident will serve as an impediment for a long time to the future execution of justice."[†] The new bailiff, seeing his predecessor's head on a pike, refused to arrest anyone protected by a nobleman. On June 25, the Mantuan

† Ibid..

ambassador reported that there was so much violence in the Papal States, right up to the city gates, that no one dared to venture outside them. Even inside the city, crime was rampant. Bandits took to breaking into stables and wounding helpless animals, threatening to return and kill them unless the owners sent them protection money.

Hunger began to take its toll. The bandits had burned large sections of farmland, and floods had ruined many others. Those crops that had been salvaged could not reach Rome because of muddy roads and lurking bandits. The pope's family bought what grain there was and sold it outside the city at double the price. Bread was no longer sold in the piazzas, but grass mixed with parsley at ridiculously high prices. The hungry banged on the doors of the wealthy who turned them away as they barely had enough grain to feed their servants. Famished citizens rioted outside bakeries. Starving people broke into homes and stole food or, if they couldn't find any, stole furniture and clothing that they sold on the street to buy food. In broad daylight, pedestrians were mugged, and coaches were held up by the desperate.

Of all the cardinals, Montalto gave the greatest help to the people. When he ran out of money he borrowed it to feed them, and the cry went up that the most saintly man in Rome was Cardinal Montalto. "He acquired great fame as a good man," the chronicler reported, "so that the poor gushed over him as the true father of the country in giving alms to his children. Others said, 'Cardinal Montalto himself lives on alms, and gives alms to others, and the cardinals who manage the goods of the Church merely point the way to the hospital.'"[†]

Although the pope was useless in dealing with the famine, crime had reached the point where even he realized the chaos could not continue. His bailiffs had recently arrested some thirty murderers, and his advisor, the nobleman Vincenzo Vitelli, pushed the pope to execute them rather than letting them off scot-free with a promise to mend their ways. Some of these men were in the service of Paolo Giordano and Lodovico Orsini, who both begged for their release and promised to be responsible for their actions. Fed up with street violence, on August 27 the pope executed three of Lodovico's grooms,

† Anon., p. 122.

along with Paolo Giordano's favorite servant. Then Vitelli proposed that the violent Lodovico Orsini himself be arrested for disturbing the peace.

On the evening of September 4, 1583, Lodovico Orsini obtained his revenge. Vitelli was returning home from having dinner with the pope's son when his coach was surrounded by men who fired guns at him. One horse fell dead, three servants were wounded, and Vitelli was shot in the thigh. He stumbled out of his coach, sword in hand, but was cut down by an assassin with a sword. The attackers tried to cut off Vitelli's head, but his servants fended them off. Vitelli was carried home alive, but died from his grievous wounds two days later, and Lodovico escaped from Rome. When Vitelli's widow, the mother of thirteen children, and his wealthy family pushed the pope for justice, he confiscated Lodovico's properties and sent guards to despoil Lodovico's palace of Monte Giordano. But all his expensive furnishings had already been cleared out.

Though Paolo Giordano had been at Bracciano when Vitelli was killed, no one doubted that he had ordered the assassination. After all, his favorite servant had been hanged at Vitelli's instigation; his honorable name had been besmirched; his power doubted, and his cousin Lodovico threatened with arrest.

Three days after the murder, the duke announced his intention to leave Rome immediately on a pilgrimage to the holy house of Loreto. Given the uproar over Vitelli's death, he asked the pope for assurance that he would not seize Bracciano during his absence. As a sign of good will, he sent the pope some wanted murderers and ordered others out of the Papal States. Not only did the pope agree to Paolo Giordano's request, but he gave him a paid commission to look into the fortifications of Ancona, seventeen miles from Loreto, to determine whether they were up to withstanding a Turkish siege.

From Loreto, the duke sent word to Vittoria, who had been vegetating in Gubbio for ten months, to pack up her household and ride the twenty-five miles to the town of Trevi. There she would stay at the home of his friend, Cavalier Lelio Valenti. Finally, after twenty-one months of vicissitudes, the two lovers were to be reunited.

The papal decrees, her imprisonment, and the enforced separation had only served to strengthen their stubborn insistence on being together. Vittoria remained at Trevi while her lover fulfilled his mission to Ancona. Paolo Giordano picked her up, took her to Bracciano, and left her in the care of her brother, Marcello, while he went to give the pope his report on the fortifications.

During the duke's absence, Vittoria had a chance to explore the castle that Paolo Giordano's first wife had scorned as a drafty pile of rocks. The structure was much like Paolo Giordano himself: brooding, dominating, enormous, and violent. It was a sacred site for the Orsinis, the manifestation of their power, the symbol in stone of domination. The high crenellated walls were interspersed with five turrets bristling with anger. Built in the 1470s, it was the last hurrah of the medieval fortress, which would soon develop into the Renaissance palace designed not for defense but for pleasure.

Early in her marriage, Isabella had spent one horrifying winter at Bracciano and never returned. She cooked up every excuse possible to avoid going there. She had to stay in Florence due to problems with her feet, a dysfunctional liver, a possible pregnancy that never materialized, a troubled head, intermittent fever, the pregnancy of her sister-in-law, and her father's ill health.

Vittoria, on the other hand, almost swooned with delight at the palatial rooms with magnificent furniture and attentive servants. The castle was situated on a circular lake formed by a volcanic crater. Teeming with pike, perch, eel, and whitefish, the lake was a sparkling, silvery-sapphire mirror, its shores dotted by three equidistant, sand-colored villages. The surrounding emerald, gently rolling hills were full of wildlife – boar, fox, pheasant, quail, and partridge. Gazing from the windswept battlements of the castle, Vittoria's gaze took in the richness of the land. She would be duchess of all this. She had come a long way from living with Camilla and the chickens in Rome.

While Vittoria explored her castle, the duke called on the pope who now gave him such a warm welcome that it gave rise to rumors that he had finally agreed to let him marry Vittoria. Some ambassadors believed the marriage had already taken place during his trip to Ancona. Others thought he would marry her quietly in Rome. Word leaked out that Paolo Giordano had been conferring with theologians about the legality of marrying Vittoria again. He had showed them Monsignor Pirro Taro's letter to Vittoria stating that all decrees had been removed. Fortunately for the duke, Taro had died and was, therefore, in no position to rebut the strange interpretation of his letter. The theologians responded not only that Paolo Giordano *could* marry her, but marry her he *must* for the health of his soul.

In the castle of Bracciano on the morning of October 10, 1583, Paolo Giordano married Vittoria again, this time more officially, with a priest, a notary, and numerous witnesses. However, he had not had the banns read for three Sundays, so the wedding was not completely in compliance with the Council of Trent. And then there was that little matter of the pope's written prohibition.

Vittoria brought as dowry the 5,000 scudi given by her father when she had married Francesco and later returned by Cardinal Montalto. But because her father and brothers could not give her a dowry "which was suitable to the quality and preeminence and dignity of the most illustrious and excellent signor duke, her future husband," Paolo Giordano himself dowered her with 20,000 scudi in the form of various properties.[†] It seems the duke wanted Vittoria to live comfortably if he predeceased her.

A few days later he returned to Rome and seemed to be fitting up his palace to receive his new duchess. Some thought that the pope had agreed to the wedding in order to upset the Grand Duke of Tuscany, who had irritated him on various diplomatic matters. Or perhaps, as Vicar of Christ, he realized he could not put asunder what God had joined together. But such speculation was absolutely false. Gregory had no idea that Paolo Giordano had married Vittoria again, and if he had, he would not have treated him so generously.

In the fall of 1583, the pope began to pull together a long list of new cardinals. Numerous recent deaths had reduced the ranks of the Sacred College, and Gregory was searching for moral, educated churchmen who would be assets not only as cardinals, but as potential

† Ibid., p.191.

popes. It was common for kings, princes, and noblemen to push hard for their own candidates. Finally, on December 12, he announced the creation of nineteen new princes of the Church.

According to tradition, new cardinals visited every other member of the Sacred College resident in Rome, after which the older cardinals visited the new ones. Cardinal Montalto used this opportunity to showcase his age and infirmities. According to his chronicler, the cardinal didn't make several visits each day, briskly trotting about Rome in his carriage as the other cardinals did, but only one every two or three days, complaining about the weakness in his legs. When asked his age, he reportedly added seven years to it.

He often invited the other cardinals to visit him but rarely went out himself, and when he did so, "pretended to lean on a stick, and now on the arm of another prelate or on a cardinal, whom he grabbed when he wanted to walk up or down stairs... When he coughed, people were afraid that he might crack his heart in his chest, and it took him a quarter of an hour to ascend every staircase... And they said to him, Good old fellow, you have run your course, God give you strength."[†]

Many of the new cardinals told him that he shouldn't risk his health by visiting them because at his age it was excusable to stay home. One day while calling on Cardinal Michele della Torre, Montalto had great difficulty mounting the stairs, huffing asthmatically. The younger cardinal was alarmed, afraid his colleague might drop dead on his steps before his very eyes. "Monsignor," he cautioned, "you are killing yourself in trying to be generous to others."[‡] Cardinal Andrew of Austria was less kind; he called Montalto *Lazarus*, as one who was alive but also in the grave.

Montalto used his poor health as an excuse to avoid choosing to champion either the faction of France or that of Spain. Europe's two greatest powers were bitter rivals all over the continent, but particularly in Rome, where they tried to buy cardinals and influence papal elections to get a friend in Saint Peter's chair. Joining one party

† Ibid., pp. 129–130.
‡ Ibid., p. 131.

would ensure financial and political support from that king and like-minded cardinals, but it would also ensure the enmity of the other party, which would try to prevent the cardinal from becoming pope in the next conclave. Refusing to join either party often resulted in arousing the anger of both. But in Montalto's case, those who had hoped for his support were not angry at him, having "concluded that he was on his last legs and incapable of joining a party because from moment to moment his age was calling him to heaven."

While Montalto was advertising his illnesses, Vittoria continued to live the good life at Bracciano. Many speculated whether the duke's unending fascination with Vittoria had been caused by witchcraft. Perhaps the ambitious Vittoria had employed the duke's Greek enchantress to concoct love potions, causing him to recklessly risk his reputation and standing. Society was always eager to blame women's witchcraft for the uncontrollable yearnings of men's private parts. Some Roman gossips began calling Paolo Giordano the Duke of Accorambono.

Vittoria had only to snap her fingers to have the most exquisite jewelry, gowns, and furniture appear. It didn't concern her that it wasn't paid for, or that little Virginio would have to find the funds to pay for it after his father died. The lovely stuff was hers, and that was all that mattered.

Paolo Giordano took Vittoria on a tour of his extensive duchy, showing her all his lands, farms, villages, and castles, as far as the Tyrrhenian Sea. Peasants and villagers knelt before her, as if she were a queen. In warm weather she was rowed out on Lake Bracciano in a barge draped with a velvet awning, underneath which she sat on silken pillows.

It was good to be the duchess.

Chapter 10

ANNULMENT

Not a word from their mouth can be trusted; their heart is filled with destruction. Their throat is an open grave; with their tongue they speak deceit.

– Psalm 5:9

Cardinal de Medici was confused to see Vittoria living openly with Paolo Giordano as his wife. He hoped the two had come to an agreement whereby Vittoria agreed to be the duke's mistress. There was nothing wrong with a man having a mistress – the cardinal had had several himself, as well as children by them – and a noble, beautiful mistress burnished a man's image. But there would be great disgrace if the duke had married her. He candidly asked his brother-in-law if the rumors of marriage were true.

On January 31, 1584, the duke replied from Bracciano:

Most Illustrious and Reverend Signor In-Law and Most Respected Padrone,

Having learned that many are talking and trying to make the world believe that I have married Signora Vittoria, I know that your Reverence, as one who has heard the truth, will not let himself be persuaded by this. Nonetheless, for the greater repose of your soul, I don't want you to believe such vanity, and give you my pledge that the lady is not my wife, and I could not ignore the wish of his Holiness, who has prohibited a marriage between her and me.

I remember very clearly the declaration and promise that I made in writing to his Majesty the Catholic king [King Philip II of Spain], to his Highness the grand duke, and to your most illustrious self, not to marry her. Therefore, I assure you with every certainty that these are false and malign voices and, knowing your Reverence quite

> well, I will not say more, except that I am your most sincere and
> affectionate servant, and I kiss your hands with great reverence.†

Cardinal de Medici couldn't imagine that the duke would put such a
blatant lie in writing. He concluded that Paolo Giordano and Vittoria
had worked out an agreement for a mistress position and not a wife
position. He accepted Paolo Giordano's word. Perhaps the situation
had, indeed, been resolved.

Just as the duke was finally enjoying Vittoria as his wife, his
health took a turn for the worse. The old arrow wound on his thigh
from the Battle of Lepanto became infected. Some doctors thought
it was gangrenous, others cancerous, and yet others believed it was
leprous. The wound spread to his knee, and the flesh swelled with pus
and stank like rancid meat. At Bracciano, the church bells pealed out
urgently to signal people to pray for the duke.

Though Vittoria nursed him devotedly, his illness worsened. On
the night of July 3, 1584, Cardinal de Medici sent his own doctor
to Bracciano and Cardinal d'Este sent his surgeon, though they held
out little hope. The duke agreed to amputation if there was no other
way to save his life. The doctors decided to wait a while and, over the
course of the next few days, the wound began to heal.

Paolo Giordano had another problem on his hands beside that
of poor health: his violent, arrogant young cousin, Lodovico Orsini.
Having been banished from the Papal States for murdering Vincenzo
Vitelli the previous September, Lodovico had been bouncing around
Italy, settling first in Tuscany, ricocheting up to Venice and then back
to the Papal States, where he terrorized the countryside with hundreds
of other bandits. Paolo Giordano pulled some strings and in April
1584 obtained for Lodovico a Venetian military commission. But
cash-strapped Lodovico didn't have enough money to travel there in a
befitting state, and went to Bracciano to see whether Paolo Giordano
could raise some for his voyage.

Lodovico brought with him his usual entourage of ruffians and
outlaws, as well as his secretary, Francesco Filelfo, whose gripping

† Gnoli, p. 190.

account of the family tragedy will be detailed later. In sixteenth-century Italy, secretaries were refined gentlemen, often better educated than their employers. Many secretaries were the younger sons of noble families with no prospects of inheritance; they used their excellent manners and thorough education to support themselves. Secretaries were required to be fluent in several languages, ancient and modern. Their penmanship had to be exquisite. Discretion was an important requirement; secretary does have the word *secret* in it, after all. Secretaries knew everything about their masters, from hemorrhoids to sexual escapades to embezzlement and murder. But the most important quality of a secretary was loyalty until death, a quality that Filelfo, as we shall see, possessed.

Oddly, Lodovico's secretary had been in the employ of Cardinal Felice Montalto in the 1570s and passed into the service of Vittoria's brother, Ottavio, bishop of Fossombrone. It is possible that Paolo Giordano hired Filelfo away from Ottavio to work for Lodovico; it is not known how long he had been in his employ when the family congregated at Bracciano in the spring of 1584.

Filelfo later wrote of that meeting, "I visited Signora Vittoria at Bracciano and received many courtesies from her." He didn't seem to care much for Vittoria's brother, Marcello, however; few people did. "Between Signor Marcello and me at Bracciano, if there was not much closeness, there passed between us courteous words and compliments."[†]

There, in the castle, Lodovico and Vittoria had the opportunity to size each other up. They didn't like what they saw. An avid defender of Orsini family honor – amply demonstrated by his brutal murder of Vitelli – Lodovico saw Vittoria as a cunning, social-climbing, money-hungry slut. She had bewitched Paolo Giordano into marrying her and was now perched to swoop in the moment he breathed his last and take as much money as possible from his beleaguered estate, leaving his young heir a pauper. The duke's besotted love for her had already besmirched the family name, dragging it through the mud with the pope, the Grand Duke of Tuscany, and the King of Spain.

† Cicogna, *Filelfo*, p. 54.

And now his second marriage, though still secret, would surely get out and dishonor the Orsinis all over again.

According to one contemporary historian, Lodovico was "no friend of Accoramboni. He had always cursed the marriage Paolo had contracted with her due to his love, a love which, in truth, would have been pardonable at any other age than his, as he was nearing fifty. Lodovico went from cursing this deed of Paolo's, to contempt for her who occasioned it, with the heated bitterness of youth, and ridiculing and vituperating the person of Vittoria and her brothers."[†]

Lodovico made his feelings clear to Vittoria by treating her with little respect, and Vittoria complained to the duke. Paolo Giordano, in turn, argued openly with Lodovico about his treatment of the new duchess. Clearly, it was necessary for the duke to separate the two of them. Fortunately, at around that time he was able to settle a property dispute that resulted in the sum of 16,000 scudi. The duke gave a portion of the proceeds to Lodovico and promised him an annual stipend. Armed with cash, in the winter of 1584-1585, Lodovico set out for Venice in princely state with thirty bandits riding beside him.

*   *   *

In late December 1584, Paolo Giordano came to Rome with Vittoria to test the waters. He decided he would tell people he wanted to marry her and then sit back and gage the reaction. If it was really bad, he would drop the subject. If it wasn't too bad, he could let them know he had already married her.

Like criminals returning to the scene of their crime, the duke and Vittoria had the audacity to call on Cardinal Montalto, who welcomed them with open arms, and professed that he believed their innocence in his nephew's murder. It is likely that during this visit, Paolo Giordano studied the cardinal carefully. Despite Montalto's kindness, the duke still did not trust him. He knew how much the old man had loved his nephew. And he knew the cardinal was aware that the murder had been committed to enable him to marry Vittoria. Was there such forgiveness in any man's heart, even the holiest saint?

[†] Strozzi, *Vita del Sommo*, folio 13b.

Paolo Giordano, a liar himself, must have debated how much of a liar Cardinal Montalto was.

Despite the cardinal's joyous welcome, Paolo Giordano lost his nerve when it came to announcing plans to marry Vittoria. Members of the extended Orsini family were murmuring about the rumors of his already having married her again. The Spanish ambassador was shifting uneasily, as the duke was a relative of the King of Spain, and the Grand Duke of Tuscany kept asking questions. Nor would the pope be happy to learn that the duke had ignored his edict. In early February 1585, he took Vittoria back to Bracciano.

But the visit had stirred the pope's suspicions. He talked of issuing another edict prohibiting their marriage and annulling all previous marriages. To avoid the scandal, Cardinal de Medici advised the duke to send Vittoria back to her parents' house yet again. The duke replied heatedly that de Medici should liberate him from this travail "because living in such an unsettled manner afflicts me enough, and is the cause of many of my disorders."[†]

Unwilling to separate from Vittoria again, Paolo Giordano decided to throw himself on the mercy of the pope and reveal his marriage. On February 26, he commissioned Orazio Morone, bishop of Sutri and Nepi, whose diocese included Bracciano, to visit the pope and read him a letter. In the papal audience chamber, with the white-robed pontiff sitting stiffly on his throne, the poor bishop must have gulped nervously before starting to read:

Most blessed Father,

Signor Paolo, fearing that your Holiness might have a bad opinion of him, believing that he did not live in marriage as a good Christian, has sent me to notify your Holiness that since October of the year 1583, after the orders of your Holiness had removed the impediments placed by you and your ministers, he married Signora Vittoria Corramboni according to the solemnities of the Holy Church.

† Ibid., pp. 204-205.

> This marriage he has kept secret until now to avoid various
> disturbances, and now he makes it known for the great zeal he
> holds for the favor of your Holiness, to whom he wants to be the
> most obsequious and to serve you perpetually in his profession,
> living as a good Christian.†

The duke then made known his intention to build a monastery outside
Bracciano for the brothers of Saints John and Paul and a hospital for
the poor. Gaping in shock, the pope asked Bishop Morone if Cardinal
de Medici had been informed of the marriage. The bishop replied
that Paolo Giordano did not wish the cardinal to be informed as yet,
and we can assume that the duke didn't have the heart to admit to his
brother-in-law that he had told him so many bold-faced lies.

Gregory ordered Bishop Morone to tell the cardinal immediately
about the duke's new marriage. On the same day, February 26,
Morone wrote Cardinal de Medici a full account. And finally, the
cardinal realized that Paolo Giordano had played him for a fool. His
favor and protection were gone forever, something which would
weigh heavily in the next conclave.

Gregory also told Morone that he would create a papal
commission of three or four learned theologians to examine all
pertaining documents: his edict against the first marriage, the letter
of Pirro Taro mentioning the removal of all impediments, Vittoria's
written promise to obey the pope, the documents from the second
marriage, and the decisions of Paolo Giordano's theologians supporting
the marriage. The commission would then render a verdict. In the
meantime, Morone should return to Bracciano and inform the couple
that the pope had serious doubts about the legality of their union.

On March 15, Paolo Giordano sent his secretary Fiorello to
give Cardinal de Medici the theologians' document supporting his
marriage:

> I have commissioned Fiorello to give a document to your most
> illustrious Holiness so that you can see my reasons and understand
> how this was done for my conscience. I pray your Holiness to
> quiet down this business because everything was done by me out

† Ibid., p. 205.

of pure conscience and to be worthy of the favor of his Holiness the pope. There was no reason why we couldn't contract marriage, and the sacraments were performed with all convenience, and the only thought is to live a Christian life… Now that it is done, and done merely to live as a Christian, your Illustrious Reverence must beg his Holiness to give his most holy blessing, and if there was any error in it, that we do not pay, but that we be esteemed by his Holiness. We beg it most humbly, and for the trouble of his Holiness we ask pardon.†

Paolo Giordano let Cardinal de Medici know he would be coming to Rome on March 17 to discuss the matter, but his brother-in-law instructed him to wait a while at Bracciano. Given Gregory's anger, it would be a terrible mistake if the duke barged into the papal audience chamber and started yelling about his good Christian life.

This sensible advice only served to outrage the duke. He peppered his cardinal friends with letters, lamenting that his honor was ruined when he was forbidden to enter the city. Such a situation was intolerable. He begged Cardinal de Medici "to work so that this business be calmed, because going further it is bound to cause my ruin, and I don't believe that my ruin would be useful or good to your most illustrious Holiness."‡

On March 30, Cardinal de Medici responded resentfully:

I was always of the opinion that this business of your Excellency's would calm down, and I am displeased to see you roused up and peeved and exasperated… As I have done in the past, I can once again try to accomplish your desires, but it is good to remember that I can ask but not command him who rules.

Don't deceive yourself at all by believing that your ruin weighs on me… Your remedy will be found in proceeding prudently, and postponing so much ardor, telling yourself that you must not be so impatient. You almost want to be thanked for the trouble you have made for everyone. A large part of the remedy can be found in waiting, and I don't think that my work will be enough unless combined with time. I cannot be entirely certain of success in what

† Ibid., pp. 208–209.
‡ Ibid., p. 210.

> you have asked of me because your haste has ruined much of what
> I have done. I am doing and will do a great deal to help you out
> of this… At any rate I am content that I have done my duty, and I
> remind you of yours.[†]

According to an *avvisi*, the desperate duke wrote the pope a letter begging him to be allowed "to enjoy in peace his dear wife destined for him by heaven as his eternal companion", and closed by adding, "At the end, it is better to disappoint men than God."[‡]

Finally, the theologians' response arrived, declaring the duke's second marriage to Vittoria invalid. It proved that the decrees prohibiting the two from marrying were still in effect as the pope had never officially revoked them. It listed impediments to the marriage: the suspicion of adultery between Paolo Giordano and Vittoria when Francesco was still alive, the daily contact the duke had had with Vittoria as soon as her husband was dead, the scandalous elopement to Magnanapoli within days of the murder, and, finally, the very grave suspicion that Vittoria had been mixed up in her husband's death, or at least had promised the duke she would marry him if Francesco died. The theologians also took very seriously Vittoria's written promise to the pope "assuring him that I will obey or pay with my life."[§]

When the duke heard that his marriage had been declared void, he wanted to race to Rome to fight the judgment himself. His cardinal friends advised him against such a rash step. Paolo Giordano then sent the pope ten notorious bandits in chains whom he had captured in his duchy. The pope sent his thanks, but that was all. Unwilling to have yet another decree issued against him, the duke declared that he was ready to separate from Vittoria.

But this, of course, was another lie. Paolo Giordano was playing for time until Lodovico could obtain for him a paid position as governor general of Venice; the former governor, Sforza Pallavicino, had recently died. Lodovico wrote the duke on April 6, "All these lords of office confess that in the person of your Excellency they recognize

† Ibid., pp. 439-440.
‡ Ibid., p. 213.
§ Ibid., p. 211.

all the qualities that they would want in their governor general, but they are very slow to make a resolution.... Your Excellency will be made governor without doubt because no one is above you."[†]

But Lodovico's influence on the Venetian Senate was doubtful. Due to his money problems, he had arrived nine months late to take up his position, which the Venetians found insulting. Shortly after his arrival, he and his gangsters presented themselves in the Senate hall, where no weapons of any kind were allowed, bristling with guns, swords, and daggers. It was a sign of things to come.

Lodovico and his men had numerous scuffles amongst themselves and with Venetian citizens. Venice, the Senate informed him, was not Rome. Fights, duels, and murders did not take place routinely on Venetian streets. The republic prided itself on its safety and was not going to put up with Lodovico Orsini's gang attacking good Venetians.

In particular, the Council of Ten, a feared and secretive committee responsible for upholding law and order in the republic, was not amused. For a while, the gang returned to attacking one another instead of the locals, but one day, three of Lodovico's men tried to enter a prostitute's house in Murano. When a friend of hers tried to keep them out at her request, the men forced their way in and killed him. The secretary of the Venetian Senate, Patavino, made it known that criminals would be hunted down and punished. In was a prescient comment.

† Ibid., p. 213.

Chapter 11

THE VACANT SEE

He hath put down the mighty from their seat and exalted them of low degree.

– Luke 1:52

There was an old Vatican saying, *the pope is not sick until dead,* which meant that it was inappropriate to discuss a pontiff's illness until death had ended it. Yet in the case of Gregory XIII, the saying was almost literally true. On April 5, 1585, he caught a cold, and on April 10 he was dead from a throat so swollen that it asphyxiated him. Finally, the moment Vittoria had waited for so long had arrived, albeit four years too late to save Francesco.

Still, it was welcome news. Paolo Giordano believed that the pope's decree against their marriage had died with him. To weigh in on this theory, even before Gregory's illness he had hired several theologians whom he paid generously to render the desired verdict. There was no canonical impediment, they agreed, and the prohibition had existed only at the wishes of Pope Gregory. Such decrees died with the pope, unless they were renewed by his successor.

Having heard these heartening conclusions, Paolo Giordano decided he would marry Vittoria again. He would patiently wait out the ten days of mourning rituals for the dead pope, and the moment the cardinals were locked inside the womb of the Vatican in conclave to elect the next pope, he would have the banns read.

Officially, cardinals in conclave were incommunicado from the outside world, and Cardinal de Medici would not have heard about the marriage until after a new pope had been elected. Conclaves, however, leaked like sieves, and many electors received news hidden inside the food platters brought to them twice a day by their servants.

Yet even if de Medici had received the news, trapped in conclave he would not have been in a position to stop the wedding.

Immediately after Gregory's death, the cardinals met to enforce law and order during the Vacant See, as the time between popes was called. For centuries, the death of a pope had unleashed horrific violence in Rome which only died down upon the election of his successor. Traditionally, those who harbored grudges waited years for the pope to die before seeking revenge. In this period of chaos, police were hard put to investigate murders, spending all their time trying to prevent new ones. Decapitated bodies were found daily in the streets, the heads bobbing up and down like buoys in the Tiber River.

Fearing that hordes of bandits might invade the city for plunder and rapine while the seat of Saint Peter lay empty, the cardinals ordered six of the sixteen city gates closed and guarded. The major Roman families promised to maintain law and order during the conclave, and Paolo Giordano was quick to place his brave armed men at the service of Church to maintain civil order so that the conclave could operate in peace.

The cardinals knew that Paolo Giordano was a liar and a murderer, and despite his pretty promises, they did not want hundreds of his criminals riding roughshod through the streets of Rome fomenting disturbances. As dean of the Sacred College, Cardinal Farnese thanked him for his good intentions but requested that he take his bandits to Bracciano, especially Marcello Accoramboni, a known murderer who had been exiled from Rome. If Marcello were found inside the city, Farnese said, he would be arrested, imprisoned, and heavily fined.

To general surprise, the duke swore his obedience. Not only did he send his bandits back to Bracciano, but he rode through the streets of Rome with several upstanding soldiers to quell disturbances caused by others. He threatened anyone breaking the law with his personal anger, as he had sworn to uphold law and order. There was, of course, an ulterior motive for the duke's submissiveness. He wanted to show the Sacred College and whichever cardinal became the next pope that he would do whatever they asked of him, as long as they allowed him to marry Vittoria.

Back at Bracciano, Marcello followed Paolo Giordano's orders and wrote him on April 17:

Most illustrious and excellent lord and eternal patron:

… As soon as I arrived I sent to various places for bandits as your Excellency commanded me. This morning I found Tasso, Acitello, and Luchitto with ten companions… I said to them in your Excellency's name that I wanted them to stay here in the state [Bracciano] for their own benefit where they will remain safe."†

It was four years to the day since Marcello had drawn Francesco Peretti out of bed at midnight to be brutally murdered in a garden. Perhaps the date meant nothing to him as he closed the letter with his new seal, a mingling of the arms of the Accoramboni and Orsini families. The murder had, no doubt, been worth it to him. Marcello was now the right-hand man of his brother-in-law, the Duke of Bracciano, and a kind of prime minister of his extensive territories. Paolo Giordano, in Rome busily making preparations for his upcoming wedding, probably never thought about the date, either. But it is certain that Cardinal Montalto, preparing for the conclave, was painfully aware of it.

Marcello was not the only one of Paolo Giordano's bandit friends that the Sacred College wanted at all costs to keep outside Rome during the conclave. Soon after Gregory died, on behalf of the Sacred College Cardinal Farnese met with the Venetian ambassador and requested that the Most Serene Republic prevent Lodovico Orsini from coming to Rome, "foreseeing that from his arrival there would arise great scandal," according to the ambassador, and "great expense."‡ The Vitelli family, expecting Lodovico to come bouncing back during the chaos of the Vacant See, had been busy hiring assassins. The cardinals feared the Vitellis would ambush Lodovico on his way into Rome, creating uproar inside the city as the two factions faced off in the streets.

---

† Gnoli, pp. 230–231.
‡ Ibid., p. 224.

But this request came too late. As soon as Lodovico had heard of Gregory's death, he had gone to the Venetian Senate and obtained permission to return to Rome. Now, having given permission, the Senate did not want to withdraw it and look like Vatican puppets. Lodovico sent his secretary Filelfo ahead of him on a fast horse "to make known his good intentions to the Sacred College, the Roman people, and his family, assuring them that he did not come to make trouble."[†] The cardinals were horrified to hear of his imminent arrival. Only the Vitellis were happy, gleefully sharpening their knives as they hid in bushes outside Rome.

As for the conclave, it rapidly became apparent that Montalto had a good chance of becoming pope. The Mantuan envoy, Camillo Capilupi, reported only two days after Gregory's death that Cardinal Montalto "has every prospect of success; he is behaving with the greatest prudence and circumspection; not even the Spaniards reject him."[‡] Philip II had sent a message that he would approve of Montalto "due to the inclination he had for repose and tranquility."[§]

While many cardinals canvassed for themselves or their friends, Cardinal Montalto adopted a different strategy. He declared himself incapable of being pope and praised all the other cardinals as being well suited for the difficult job. According to his chronicler, "Before entering into conclave he made many visits, as was customary, to the other cardinals, and it was pleasing to see him going on his cane, spitting, and at every step breathing heavily because of the pains, that he said were bad, and every two steps resting for weariness."[¶]

The most important cardinal to win over was Farnese. Since the death of his grandfather, Paul III, in 1549, Farnese had witnessed the election, reign, and death of six popes. Like a perennial spinster bridesmaid, Farnese was always the pope-maker but never the pope. Now, aged sixty-five, he knew this might be his last chance to win the papal tiara. A highly intelligent and capable statesman, he was beloved by the people of Rome for his magnificent lifestyle and his charity.

†   Ibid., pp. 229-230.
‡   Pastor, *Popes*, Vol. 21, p. 15.
§   Leti, *Sixte V*, Vol. 1, p. 356.
¶   Anon., p. 136.

It was not generally held against him that he had fathered several children in his younger years. The stricter regulations of the Council of Trent and his own advancing age had helped him morph into a sober churchman, quite suitable to become pope.

The cardinal had never liked Montalto for two reasons. First of all, he came from a disgracefully poor family, unlike the noble family of Farnese. Secondly, Montalto had had little to do with Church business the past thirteen years. Instead of wheeling and dealing with foreign diplomats, he had spent most of his time planting vines and harvesting olives, spreading manure, and toting water buckets, actions that were beneath the dignity of a cardinal. Farnese's disdain was a problem for Montalto's papal aspirations. But if Montalto couldn't make his colleague admire him, at least he could show Farnese that he was not to be feared.

The chronicler reported that Montalto "visited Cardinal Farnese the second time ... praising the merits of his family ... and showing nicely the imperfection of his health. Cardinal Farnese showed compassion for his illness, saying, 'You don't have to go into a conclave that might last a long time. Because of your age and indispositions, you would not live to see the election of a new pope.' And while Cardinal Farnese was saying this, he was looking at Montalto, who coughed even harder... He replied, 'The hope that I have of aiding your Reverence with my vote gives me the spirit to place myself voluntarily against death itself.'"

When Cardinal Farnese mumbled that he had no papal aspirations, Montalto said, "All the cardinals would be willing to raise to the papacy such a person of merit and experience, and to give it to one who is incapable of unworthiness." He added that since he was not possessed of the requisite qualities to be pope, he could at least show good will by serving his friends. His protestations of affection seemed to soften Cardinal Farnese.

Wheezing and limping, Cardinal Montalto visited most of the other cardinals in Rome, especially the pope-makers d'Este, de Medici, and Altemps. He assured them of his support in the conclave and his eternal gratitude and devotion for their friendship over the years. He clearly did a good job, as by the time the conclave started, every cardinal thought that if Montalto became pope, *he* would be his favorite cardinal, and would be richly rewarded with large pensions and important positions.

For several days preceding the opening of the conclave, the Sistine Chapel and its neighboring halls were abuzz with the sound of carpenters sawing boards to cover the windows. The conclave was supposed to be sealed off from the outside world, a dark womb, lit only by candles and the glow of the Holy Spirit, which was thought to direct the voting.

In the hall next to the Sistine Chapel, carpenters were also busy constructing the cardinals' cells, flimsily built chambers ranging from about fifteen feet to twenty-two feet square. Living in a cell was much like camping. Each cardinal had a bed, table, chamber pot chair, washbasin, and a little stove to reheat cold food. He generally had two servants, called *conclavistas*, to look after his needs and, if necessary, spy on the other cardinals to ferret out what they were plotting.

While the cardinals were getting ready for the conclave, which would begin on Sunday, April 21, Paolo Giordano was gleefully preparing for his wedding. The Council of Trent had decreed that the banns be read on three successive Sundays. But Paolo Giordano feared the conclave wouldn't last the requisite two weeks. When the conclave opened, the new pope, whoever he was, might hear about the banns and, caving into the protests of the grand duke, the King of Spain, Cardinal de Medici, and the Orsini family, prohibit the marriage with a new decree. And so Paolo Giordano arranged to have the banns read on three successive *days*: that Sunday, Monday, and Tuesday. The wedding would take place on Wednesday, April 24.

He wanted his marriage to be a fait accompli by the time the conclave was over, reasoning that the new pope would be loath to annul this one. For Paolo Giordano would be marrying Vittoria with Gregory's decree no longer in effect, as he believed, and would have had the banns read as required by the Council of Trent, sort of.

The duke threw himself into planning his wedding feast. In the sixteenth century, a host did not invite guests to such an expensive event with the sole purpose of feeding them. There was a script hidden behind every feast. The servants were actors, the food and vessels props, the host the director, and the guests the spectators. The theme of the play might be piety, and a clergyman might offer simple dishes as evidence of his restrained sobriety.

Paolo Giordano probably had another script in mind for his feasts, however. Given the brutal society of sixteenth-century Rome, there was perhaps a veiled threat behind the jolliest banquet. "I have the power and wealth to crush you," the host was saying. "Do not offend me, or you will be sorry." This was certainly the message when his *trinciante*, or carver, gave a brilliant performance slicing and slashing with his knives. It became fashionable for the *trinciante* to hoist a heavy roast in the air spitted on a giant fork with one hand, while the other hand sliced away rapidly, and slabs of meat fell gracefully on a plate below. But the display was not just about food. If Paolo Giordano's carver sliced a roast so dexterously, he could do the same to you.

This particular banquet had a unique script. Paolo Giordano was publicly declaring that although Gregory XIII might have stymied him for a time, now that the pope was dead he was flexing his muscles again. He was Paolo Giordano Orsini, and he could do whatever he wanted. This banquet was clearly a message for the next pope, as long as it wasn't Cardinal Montalto, of course.

As he joyously worked with butlers, cooks, and huntsmen for his fabulous wedding feast, there was one possibility that dampened his happiness – the slim chance that Cardinal Montalto would be elected pope. Yes, he had become popular with the people of Rome by giving them food during the famine. And he looked harmless enough, leaning on a stick and coughing. But with so many noble, stellar cardinals, would the Sacred College elect a dying pig keeper from the Marches?

In between his banquet preparations, Paolo Giordano made the rounds, begging the cardinals *not* to vote for Montalto. He was even willing to get down on his knees while imploring them. Paolo Giordano must have realized that his marriage, his wealth, and even his life depended on the cardinals not electing Montalto.

Chapter 12

DUPLICITY

Your tongue plots destruction; it is like a sharpened razor, you who practice deceit.

— Psalm 52:2

On April 20, the electors settled into their cells in the Vatican. Soon thereafter, the ambassadors of Spain, France, and the Holy Roman Emperor met with them, pushing their favorite candidates, and excluding certain others. At two hours past sunset, the master of ceremonies cried, "*Omnes extra!*" which meant that everyone who was not a cardinal, or a *conclavista*, needed to leave.

On Easter Sunday, April 21, after celebrating Mass, thirty-eight cardinals processed into the Sistine Chapel to officially open the conclave. The Sacred College at the time consisted of sixty cardinals, but many were out of town. Over the next few days, four more would arrive, bringing the total number of electors to forty-two. Several others would come too late to vote. All were Italian except three Germans, three Frenchmen, and one Spaniard.

And now Paolo Giordano was ready to pounce. As soon as the conclave began, with Cardinal de Medici firmly entombed inside, the duke had the banns read. Everyone knew of an impediment, but no one wanted to get stabbed that night. On the mornings of April 22 and 23, banns were read again, and again met by an uncomfortable silence.

In conclave, the major factions had already created a deadlock. Tuscany was deeply mired in a boundary dispute with the Duke of Parma, who happened to be Cardinal Farnese's brother. If the popular Cardinal Farnese became pope, he would certainly resolve the disagreement to the satisfaction of Parma. Naturally, if Cardinal de

Medici were elected, he would give the land to Tuscany. But even if he weren't chosen, de Medici needed at all costs to prevent the election of Farnese.

If de Medici worked assiduously against Farnese, Farnese worked just as hard against de Medici. The mutual hatred was fueled by the regrettable fact that Cardinal de Medici had taken as his latest mistress Cardinal Farnese's gorgeous married daughter, twenty-five-year-old Clelia. Cardinal Farnese fumed, and Cardinal de Medici laughed, and Clelia batted her long black eyelashes at both. And so, at the outset, the electors fell into two main factions – Farnese and de Medici.

Romans were wild about betting, and bookies made good livings. People bet on the gender of an unborn child (though that bet wasn't terribly interesting as there were only two possibilities). They bet on which prelates would be created cardinals. They bet on the weather. But the most exciting betting centered on the election of a new pontiff. Bets were accepted even when the current pope was alive and well. Twenty years earlier, Pope Pius IV had issued a bull prohibiting betting on papal elections as undignified, but no one paid any attention. People recorded their bets with notaries and bought tickets with the names of the chosen cardinals, which they would cash in if they won. Cardinal Farnese had been the hot favorite before Gregory's death.

Each vote in conclave has a special name: a scrutiny. Twice a day, beginning April 21, morning and afternoon, cardinals disguised their handwriting when scribbling the name of their candidate on a slip of paper. They then folded the paper several times, walked to the chalice in front of Michelangelo's daunting Last Judgment, and placed it inside. When all had voted, the names were read and tallied. A two-thirds majority was required for the winning candidate.

In the first scrutinies, numerous cardinals were proposed by their friends. The worthy Cardinal Gugliemo Sirleto, a great scholar of irreproachable morals, was opposed by several because he was beloved by Spain. Many cardinals feared that Sirleto would govern the Church as the "chaplain of the Catholic king," and make life difficult for those cardinals belonging to the French faction.[†] Cardinal Giambattista Castagna was proposed, but the older cardinals were reluctant to vote for someone who had received his red hat only in the last promotion. Cardinal Giacomo Savelli, though he had been well liked by Gregory XIII and came from one of the principal families of Rome, was annoying and unpopular with his colleagues. He had the advantage of ill health – which would likely mean cardinals acquiring more power under his reign and an earlier chance to become pope themselves – but this was offset by his brood of greedy bastards who would plunder the papal treasury, leaving little for the cardinals.

Agostino Valerio, Cardinal of Verona, was too young at fifty. He might reign for decades, outliving several worthy cardinals who would never have another chance to become pope. As the Venetian envoy wrote, "The Roman courtiers like the wheel to turn often, because each man hopes to win in the lottery. They give each Pope five years to live and are displeased when the lease is renewed."[‡]

Cardinal Alfonso Gesualdo, a Neapolitan nobleman and pious reformer of the Church, was scorned because of his strange habit of bathing every day. Such eccentricity made his colleagues wonder if he was all right in the head. Cardinals Gabriele Paleotto and Giovanni Antonio Fachinetti were from Bologna, which weighed heavily against them. The Bolognese Pope Gregory had stuffed all the good Church positions with his countrymen. The ambassador of Urbino noted, "At court they are all Bolognese, and they pass the ball from one to the other."[§] Now, after thirteen years, the non-Bolognese cardinals wanted balls for themselves.

On April 22, there was still no clear favorite. The sound of cannon fire, the traditional sign that a pope had been chosen, suggested that a pope had been elected but, the cannon, it turned out, had been fired to quell a riot. Voting continued on April 23.

Cardinal Montalto did not get swept up in factional disputes. He spent much of his time alone in his cell, praying. When a cardinal

---

† Pastor, *Popes*, Vol. 21, p. 17.
‡ Hubner, Vol. 1, p. 142.
§ Adamson, p. 160.

attached to the interests of Cardinal San Sisto, Gregory's nephew, asked Montalto about his choice, he replied that the college must elect a man agreeable to San Sisto out of respect for Pope Gregory's years of service. He told Cardinal Farnese's supporters that he could not understand why their man had not yet been elected. He told the *conclavistas* of Cardinal de Medici that their master had the greatest merit in the entire Sacred College. According to Gregorio Leti, "He said much good about the others and showed great self-deprecation… He was angry that he didn't have as many votes as there were cardinals."[†]

The powerful factions of Cardinals Farnese and de Medici were blocking each other, and several compromise candidates had failed. Thoughts now turned to Cardinal Montalto, who was somewhere between sixty-three and seventy. Even if the younger age were true, it didn't seem as if he would last too long with all his wheezing and limping. It helped that he generally had a reputation as a good person, "completely quiet and grateful, not mistrustful of anyone, without family, zealous of serving God, by nature benign and loving."[‡]

Montalto's gentle, submissive air had won him numerous supporters. Unlike many cardinals, Montalto never pushed his opinions on others but was prepared to renounce his own sentiments and agree with other prelates as being more learned than he. He had earned many points by forgiving the slights of the Franciscan monks who had tormented him. "He was civil and courteous with everyone," Gregorio Leti reported, "even his servants, and particularly with those monks who had persecuted him the most and who had most openly declared themselves his enemies. He embraced them when he saw them, as tenderly as if they had always been friends."[§]

But the event that helped him most in obtaining support for the papacy was his startling forgiveness of his nephew's murderers. He had openly declared his acceptance of the murder as God's will, had publicly pardoned the malefactors, and had received Paolo Giordano

† Leti, *Sixte V*, Vol. 1, pp. 316-317.
‡ Gnoli, p. 242.
§ Leti, *Sixte V*, Vol. 1, p. 355.

and Vittoria with demonstrations of great affection. Such a man would clearly not be one to hold a grudge against cardinals or make their lives miserable.

At this point, Cardinal de Medici had two good reasons for voting in Montalto's favor. It is likely that he had received news of Paolo Giordano's marriage banns. If so, he must have been livid that after four years of embarrassing edicts against him, the duke continued to drag the family name into the mud with his irrational passion for an unsuitable woman. And once elected, Cardinal Montalto, always a supporter of Cardinal de Medici, could easily be persuaded to renew Gregory's decree against the marriage.

Naturally, Cardinal de Medici also had political reasons for electing Montalto. He desperately wanted to block the election of certain unfriendly cardinals and thought he could effectively use his friend to accomplish this. His enemy Cardinal Savelli was starting to gain support. And Cardinal Farnese, realizing he was too controversial to be elected, now pushed his friend, Cardinal de Torres, who was racing to Rome from Spain. Farnese and his party were planning on adoring him as pope the moment he walked into the conclave.

Like a scrutiny, an adoration was an accepted way of electing a pontiff. If it seemed that two-thirds or more of the cardinals pointed at a colleague and started crying, "*A pope! A pope!*" a scrutiny would be held to confirm the number of votes. Sometimes embarrassingly few cardinals joined in, and the adoration was an abject failure. Other times, however, cardinals feared to be the last ones to cry out. In that case, surely the new pope would notice their lack of enthusiasm and punish them. As a means of ensuring their survival in the next pontificate, many cardinals ended up vociferously supporting their deadliest enemies.

Cardinal de Medici knew that Cardinal de Torres was nearing Rome and would arrive any day. He began meeting secretly with the main supporters of Spain and France, who reported that their monarchs had nothing against the kind-hearted, harmless Cardinal Montalto, who seemed to have good will toward all.

When other cardinals learned that de Medici was hell-bent on electing Montalto, they "found strange his resolution ... to create as pope an enemy of Prince Don Paolo Giordano Orsini," wrote the chronicler, "because Cardinal Montalto had received not small disgusts from Orsini, the in-law of Cardinal de Medici, and among these they attributed the murder of the cardinal's nephew in Rome. At any rate, it seemed more important to him [de Medici] to exclude Farnese and de Torres than to keep the goodwill and respect of his in-law."[†]

On the night of April 23, Cardinals Bonelli, de Medici, and d'Este swept into Montalto's cell. Speaking in a very low voice so others couldn't hear him, Bonelli said, "Courage, Monsignor, for we have come to tell you some good news, that we have resolved to make you pope."[‡]

No sooner did Montalto hear this declaration than "he began to cough so hard it seemed he was rendering up his soul, which obliged him to say that his reign would be of few days, that besides the continual difficulty he had in breathing, he did not think he had sufficient strength to carry such a heavy burden."[§]

In addition to his poor health, Montalto pointed out that he had never worked in international affairs, or even in Roman government. How would he know what to do? He said he would accept the papacy only on the condition that "those signors would be obligated to assist him night and day to govern the state and the Church." Montalto seemed heartened by their promises and said they must accept powerful positions to steer the ship of state, since he would have no idea what he was doing. "These were the words that made these big fish swim into the net," according to his chronicler.[¶]

Having left Montalto's cell, the three conspirators spoke among themselves. They were pleased at the thought of running the Church and government for a sweet, sick old man. They would have the power and wealth. Nor was it likely that Montalto's family would

[†] Anon., pp. 145-146.
[‡] Leti, *Sixte V*, Vol. 1, p. 335.
[§] Ibid., p. 337.
[¶] Anon., p. 142.

push themselves forward, according to the chronicler, as they were young, unsophisticated, and fonder of gardening than politics. The cardinals agreed that "if we make him pope then we will surely have a great part in the papacy."[†]

The trio did not have enough votes to elect Montalto and had to win over Cardinals San Sisto and Farnese and their parties. Cardinal San Sisto, who knew his uncle Pope Gregory and Montalto had heartily disliked each other, was quickly brought around because, as Cardinal de Medici wrote, "He would have elected the devil himself to get out of the conclave and return to the arms of his mistress."[‡]

Perhaps it is no surprise that Cardinal Farnese held out longer than the others. He couldn't easily swallow the fact that a pig feeder was going to be placed on the pontifical throne, and not his own magnificent self. But even Cardinal Farnese came around. According to one report, he had good reasons for not blocking Montalto's election: Montalto's poor health, his pleasant and forgiving temperament, and the likelihood that he, Farnese, would have an important role in papal government.

Hearing that Montalto's election was likely, many other cardinals agreed to go along with it so that the new pope would never hear of any hesitation on their part. As one cardinal told another, "The party of Montalto is so much advanced that surely today he will be pope, and seeking to prevent it would be a waste of time and procure ruin for oneself, and shame, because they will do it without you."[§]

And so, the Sacred College was mostly in agreement. They would elect friendly old Cardinal Montalto, an outstanding Christian who had forgiven his nephew's murderers; a gentle soul who would never hurt a fly.

*   *   *

On the morning of Wednesday, April 24, the smell of succulent roasted meats wafted through the Orsini palace in the heart of Rome. The

---

[†] Ibid., p. 143.
[‡] Pirie, p. 113.
[§] Anon., pp. 147-148.

rooms had been festively decorated with colored silks hanging from walls and draped around doors, windows, and columns. The silver and gold serving dishes gleamed from their recent polishing. Crystal decanters were filled with fragrant wine from the duke's vineyards. In the enormous vaulted kitchen on the ground floor, cooks baked huge pies and decorated the crusts with gold leaf. Musicians gathered in the balcony overlooking the great hall, tuning their instruments.

In her bedroom, Vittoria was laced into her best gown, perhaps the one made of solid gold thread. She put on her jewelry of gold, rubies, and pearls. She donned a gauzy headdress and dabbed her neck with the finest perfume. Now, today, she would finally, indisputably become the Duchess of Bracciano. It would be the greatest day of her life.

Somewhere downstairs a fight broke out. A shot was fired. Those hearing the noise ran toward it and found the body of Paolo Giordano's twenty-four-year-old servant, killed by an unknown assailant. They could hardly have a dead body in the palace with the wedding guests coming. Some of the men carried the body to the church next door so the priest, who had been preparing for the wedding, could say the prayers for the dead. Then they carted the corpse out the back door just as Vittoria, Paolo Giordano, and the wedding guests walked in the front. Many believed this was a frightening omen, a sign from God that this would be a blood wedding, bringing death and destruction to those who partook in it.

It is likely that Paolo Giordano had been told of his servant's murder but didn't care. He had trailed corpses in his wake for years, and it never seemed to bother him. Now, for the third time, he married his beloved Vittoria. And this time, having read the banns, and Gregory's decree having died with him, they would be married for real.

After the ceremony, the wedding party returned to the palace and took their places in the banqueting hall. Among the guests was Lodovico Orsini, who had evaded the Vitelli family assassins lying in ambush for him outside Rome. He must have been beside himself that Paolo Giordano was marrying the greedy, unsuitable woman a third time. The music started. Wine as dark and red as blood was poured into crystal goblets. Food was brought in on gigantic platters, perhaps a peacock with his feathers sewn back on and flames shooting out of his mouth, or a giant pie with live rabbits inside. Vittoria sat in her chair next to the duke and smiled.

Ironically, Vittoria and Cardinal Montalto, who had each been hot in the pursuit of splendor for so many years, achieved their goals in the same hour. For no sooner had the banquet started in full swing than cannon fire thundered forth from Castel Sant'Angelo. Immediately afterward, all the church bells of Rome pealed out their joy, the sign that the cardinals had elected a new pontiff. The priest who had married the couple recorded in his parish registry, right under the names of the Duke and Duchess of Bracciano, that within an hour of the wedding ceremony, he heard the cannon and bells and knew that the pope had been elected.

The diners wondered aloud who the new pope could be, some believing it was this cardinal, others sure it was that. Paolo Giordano and Vittoria may have had a feeling of dread in the pits of their stomachs as they forced themselves to smile.

And then, a rider raced into the courtyard of the Orsini palace and reined in his horse violently. He jumped off, ran into the palace and cried, "*The pope has been elected! Signora Vittoria, it is your uncle, Cardinal Montalto!*"

She was now the duchess. But he was now the pope.

PART II

REVENGE SERVED COLD

Chapter 13

POPE SIXTUS V

He then began to speak to them in parables: "A man planted a vineyard. He put a wall around it, dug a pit for the winepress and built a watchtower. Then he rented the vineyard to some farmers and went away on a journey. At harvest time he sent a servant to the tenants to collect from them some of the fruit of the vineyard.

But they seized him, beat him and sent him away empty-handed. Then he sent another servant to them; they struck this man on the head and treated him shamefully. He sent still another, and that one they killed. He sent many others; some of them they beat, others they killed.

"He had one left to send, a son, whom he loved. He sent him last of all, saying, 'They will respect my son.'

"But the tenants said to one another, 'This is the heir. Come, let's kill him, and the inheritance will be ours.' So they took him and killed him, and threw him out of the vineyard.

What then will the owner of the vineyard do? He will come and kill those tenants and give the vineyard to others.

– The Gospel of Mark. 12:1-9

C ardinal Montalto's adoration occurred just as his supporters had planned. As the electors were assembling in the chapel, the master of ceremonies was reading the conclave bulls, lengthy documents that had to be read at the opening of the conclave and reread whenever another cardinal arrived. Cardinal d'Este interrupted, crying, "There is no longer time to read bulls! The Pope is made! Let us proceed at once to the adoration."†

Numerous cardinals began to shout, "A pope! A pope! Montalto!" They surrounded him and threw themselves at his feet.

† Pastor, *Popes*, Vol. 21, p. 22.

Most newly elected pontiffs cried from joy and humility. The cardinals certainly would have expected such behavior from a good-natured old soul like Montalto. But his expression remained unchanged. He didn't cry; he didn't even smile.

Now a scrutiny was held for the official vote count, and even Cardinal Montalto sat at his desk and wrote a name on the slip of paper. It was a unanimous vote for him, except his own vote, which he had cast for Cardinal Farnese, as he had promised.

According to his chronicler, "Cardinal Montalto now began to raise the fog of deceit that he had kept secret for fourteen years, along with the great ambition that reigned in him. Impatient to see himself on the pontifical throne, and hearing most of the votes favorable to him, he straightened his neck and rose to his feet, and without waiting for the end of the scrutiny, left the chapel, and threw towards the door his cane that he had carried to lean on. He stood up straight and seemed several inches taller, and what was more astonishing was that he spat at the ceiling with such great force, that a young man of thirty could not have spat with more vigor than he."[†] Then he knelt in front of the crucifix at the altar.

While the other cardinals were rubbing their eyes, wondering if perhaps God had suddenly healed the illnesses of their new pope, the shrewd Cardinal Farnese realized in an instant what had happened: they had all been hoodwinked. He turned to Cardinals San Sisto and de Medici and said, "Your plan seems to have been a mistake."

Cardinal Montalto turned a frightening face back to the cardinals and cried loudly, "Mistake? What mistake?"

As cardinal deacon, Farnese had been in charge of the voting. "The scrutiny wasn't right," he said, shuffling the vote slips.

But Montalto said, "It was right," knelt again, and started to sing a Te Deum so loudly that it echoed throughout the hall. When Cardinal de Medici saw this, he looked at the cardinal deacon and began to laugh, because only moments earlier Montalto had done nothing but cough.

---

† Anon., pp. 149-150.

According to custom, the conclave master of ceremonies asked the new pope if it pleased him to accept the papacy. Most new pontiffs nodded through tears or humbly said they were not worthy of it but would accept it as God's will. But Montalto scornfully turned his back towards the master of ceremonies and, looking sternly at the cardinals, started speaking in the royal *we*. "We cannot accept that which we have already accepted," he replied, "but if we could accept it another time, we would, because we know well that we have sufficient strength, vigor, and talent, through the aid of God, to reign over two worlds, not just one papacy."[†]

The master of ceremonies then asked him what name he would like to take, and Montalto, who had had the name picked out for decades, replied, "Sixtus V." He had chosen this name to honor Sixtus IV (reigned 1471-1484) who had also been a Franciscan monk.

Behind the altar were several papal robes of different sizes, ready for a cardinal of any height or width. While the master of ceremonies dressed Sixtus in pontifical garb, those cardinals instrumental in his election came up to congratulate him. Cardinal de Medici, delighted he had raised his dear old friend to the papacy, used "great familiarity" with him, perhaps clapping him on the back. Sixtus cast him a scornful look and said, "Not so much familiarity with the supreme Vicar of Christ."[‡]

Cardinal de Medici smoothly covered his surprise by saying that it was a very happy day. The pope replied ominously, "It will not be happy for everyone."[§]

Farnese then had the task of announcing to the world the results of the election and trying to look pleased about it. He and the pope went to a window fronting onto Saint Peter's Square, and Farnese cried out, *"Nuntio vobis gaudium magnum Italicus papam Dominime Felicem Montalti, Sacrae Romanae Ecclesiae Cardinalem, qui sibi imposuit nomen Sixtus Quintus."*[¶]

[†] Ibid., p. 151.
[‡] Ibid., pp. 152-153.
[§] Gnoli, p. 254.
[¶] Pittoni, p. 7.

We announce to you with great joy an Italian pope, Felice Montalto, Cardinal of the Holy Roman Church, who will take the name Sixtus V. Thousands of people had been camping out in the square for three days. When they heard the news, some were horrified that the new pontiff was a bent old man staggering around Rome leaning on a stick. But then a vigorous figure in papal robes presented itself at the window and extended a benediction. Many who had seen him before didn't recognize him as Cardinal Montalto. "Who is the pope?" they asked. Many said, "This can't be Cardinal Montalto, whom we saw falling down from weakness in the streets. Could that be the same man who couldn't hold himself on his legs, who had his head always leaning on a shoulder? This person that we see today is so straight and so majestic."[†]

Cardinal Montalto had been best known for his charity during the famine. Many poor Romans were pleased that they finally had a pope who would think about them, and not just the rich and noble.

The foreign ambassadors were surprised by the election. "I must add that the election of Sixtus V is looked upon as the work of the Holy Ghost," the Venetian Priuli wrote his Senate, "all the cardinals having so promptly cooperated in his exaltation, notwithstanding that the nephews of Gregory and their numerous adherents must have preferred any other candidate, knowing as they did how ill-disposed he was to Gregory, against whom, and those who governed for him or were near his person, he spoke ill, even in Gregory's lifetime. Neither the enmity of Paolo Giordano Orsini, nor his endeavors with each cardinal of the Sacred College to plead with them on his knees that they not elect Montalto, nor the aversion of the whole Court, which, remembering the severities of Pius V, was against a pope who had been a monk, could prevail. Such attempts, and even greater considerations, are of no avail against the will of our Lord God."[‡]

Sixtus was conducted to the papal apartments where he sat down and ate a dozen sugared biscuits and drank two glasses of red wine. All the cardinals left except for Bonelli and Rusticucci. "Illustrious

---

[†] Leti, *Sixte V*, Vol. 1, p. 380.
[‡] Hubner, Vol. 1, pp. 203-204.

father," said Rusticucci, "it is no longer time to inconvenience yourself but to take a bit of repose."

Sixtus replied, "Our best repose will be the efforts that we undertake with our pleasure." In other words, *Don't tell me what to do*.

Rusticucci, who was already regretting the election, added, "Your Holiness speaks in a very different manner than the way he spoke yesterday in conclave and the day before yesterday with this cardinal here." To which Sixtus snapped, "Because yesterday and the day before we were not pope, but now we are."[†]

Looking around the papal apartments, the two cardinals nervously began to give the pope's servants orders for his comfort. Sixtus, wrapped in a thick mantle of sudden pontifical authority, said, "Save yourself, if you please, the trouble. I myself know well how to see to the things of which I have need."

Sixtus's butler, who had served him for several years, asked him what he wanted to eat for supper, a request he always made at about that time of day. But this time, his employer stared at him haughtily and thundered, "Do you ask sovereign princes what should be served to them? You should cover our table as you would cover those of kings, and we will see what pleases our taste most." The poor butler retired "in great confusion."[‡]

Outside the papal apartments, red knots of cardinals stood around discussing the shocking transformation they had just witnessed. Farnese accused his supporters of betraying him. De Medici and Rusticucci felt like fools. Later that afternoon, the new Pope Sixtus V sat on his throne in the papal audience chamber and accepted the congratulations of all and sundry who could squeeze themselves into the room. The pope graciously thanked his visitors for their good wishes. But when Paolo Giordano Orsini knelt before him, the pope said nothing. The duke kept sputtering congratulations, and the pope just glared at him, as if looking for splatters of Francesco's blood on his ruff and doublet. Finally, in humiliation, the duke stumbled to his feet and left. He stopped by the palaces of Cardinal de Medici and

† Anon., pp. 158-159.
‡ Leti, *Sixte V*, Vol. 1, p. 384.

Count Olivares, ambassador of Spain, to ask them to obtain for him another audience with the pope the following day.

When Paolo Giordano returned to the Vatican, the room was still packed with well-wishers, many of them asking the pope for favors. The new Vicar of Christ was supposed to be generous to others as a sign of gratitude to God for his good fortune. The most common request was the release of a friend or relative from prison and, indeed, most prisons were thrown wide open on a papal coronation day in memory of Pontius Pilate liberating Barabbas on the day of Jesus's crucifixion. The individual who obtained clemency for the most murderers and robbers before coronation day was seen as being highest in the pontiff's favor.

Pretending that the pope's embarrassing silence of the day before had never happened, Paolo Giordano knelt before him again and cheerfully congratulated him. Then he asked him to release from jail a servant of his, the murderer Marco Bracciardini.

The pope silently eyed the duke, closely examining this bad seed, this rotten weed, which choked the life out of young and promising plants. At first, it seemed as if the pope would say nothing this time as well. Now Paolo Giordano, who had made popes tremble, began to tremble himself, and Sixtus was clearly reveling in his discomfort. Finally, the pope said, "No one desires more than I that in the future Paolo Giordano Orsini will lead a life worthy of Orsini blood and of a Christian nobleman. Whether or not he has done that up until now with respect to the Holy See, his family, and himself, he must ask his conscience. One thing is certain, however: the offenses done to Francesco, and to Felice, Cardinal Montalto, are pardoned."[†]

Then he rose to his feet and roared, "But if you offend Sixtus, if you offend Sixtus, he will not pardon you. I will be a good pope to a good Orsini, a terrible pope to a bad Orsini. Go now and immediately remove from Bracciano and your palace each and every bandit."[‡]

One chronicler reported that, "Sixtus always had a marvelous efficacy in his speaking, but when he flew into a rage and threatened,

---

[†] Cicogna, *Maritaggio*, 41a.
[‡] Gnoli, p. 254.

accompanied by his natural pride, it seemed as if he were throwing thunderbolts."[†]

The duke, pierced by those thunderbolts, stumbled awkwardly to his feet. Instead of walking slowly backwards and bowing three times on his way out the door as protocol required, he raced from the audience chamber as fast as he could, committing the huge faux-pas of turning his back on the Vicar of Christ. Reaching his carriage, he ordered his coachman to drive post-haste to the palace of Cardinal de Medici. There he told him of his terrifying audience with the pope.

Though Sixtus had been pope for less than twenty-four hours, Cardinal de Medici well understood the mistake he had made in pushing for his election. The cardinal informed Paolo Giordano that despite Montalto's earlier protestations of forgiveness, he had a vengeful spirit and had used deceit to be elected so that he could punish his enemies. The duke's life, and Vittoria's life, and the lives of all who served them, were in grave danger. If the new pope wanted to have them all executed, as absolute monarch he could do so immediately. "There is no time to lose," the cardinal advised. "Obey him and save yourself because neither I nor anyone else can do anything for you."[‡]

While Paolo Giordano had been calling on the pope, numerous grandees, ambassadors, and noblewomen had lined up to congratulate Camilla. That morning, the Venetian ambassador and Cardinal Santorio viewed with pity Camilla's scantily furnished rooms and noticed that the pope's sister and her four young grandchildren wore ragged clothing. But an extreme makeover was on the way. Santorio wrote that suddenly "the militia surrounded the house, furnished the rooms, and made everything ornate and worthy of dignity. Alessandro was dressed in dark purple, the sisters splendid with necklaces of gemstones."[§] Within moments, the entire house and its inhabitants were transformed almost as quickly as the pope himself had been.

One of the visitors shocked at the sudden change was none other than Vittoria Accoramboni, the newly minted Duchess of

† Cicogna, *Maritaggio*, 41b.
‡ Gnoli, p. 254.
§ Ibid., pp. 251-252.

Bracciano. She had ridden from her husband's palace accompanied by three coaches stuffed with noble matrons. It must have been a strange feeling for Vittoria as she entered the old house she had so detested. The chickens and pigs in the courtyard were gone now, and the servants wore gorgeous livery. Looking around at the well-born visitors congratulating the new pope's sister, she must have sighed that this had taken place too late. Too late for Vittoria, too late for Francesco.

Too late for Camilla, too. Bewildered by the throngs of powerful well-wishers, uneasy in her heavy bejeweled gown, Camilla spotted Vittoria. Perhaps she had a fleeting image of her as the fresh-faced sixteen-year-old bride she had welcomed with open arms into the Peretti family for the love Francesco bore her. And perhaps Vittoria, standing there in the wedding finery of a duchess, remembered the cheerful, loving young husband and their hopes for the future, back in the days when everything had seemed possible. If Vittoria had only waited, on this day she would have been not a mere duchess, but probably on her way to becoming a princess. It is likely that both women, staring at each other across the room as the crowd gaped in wonder at the sight, would have done anything to turn back the clock.

It was a bittersweet moment for Camilla. Her brother would ennoble her, she knew, giving her a territory of her own (she would soon become the marchesa of Venafro, near Naples.) There would be no more emptying chamber pots or plucking chickens for her. Her grandchildren would be cardinals and duchesses. But Francesco, that dearly beloved, happy-go-lucky son, was absent. Standing in front of her, however, was the woman who had caused his death.

The space between them was ripe enough to burst as Vittoria, graceful and charming as ever, swished up to Camilla and took her hand. According to Cardinal Santorio, who witnessed the scene, Vittoria said that "she wished great happiness from heaven for Camilla and the Peretti family, and that she wanted this for the love she had borne Francesco, for her prayers and her tears, and for the name of mother-in-law that Camilla had been to her and hoped she would not forget her."

This last was not likely. Camilla became red as a beet while listening and then wordlessly accompanied Vittoria to the top of the steps, as etiquette required, to show her out. Returning to the crowded room, she howled, "Oh, pompous wickedness! This iniquitous woman has dared to show her impure and cruel face to me within these walls!"[†] Then she dissolved into wretched sobs, crying, "Oh, my poor son!"[‡]

Though Vittoria had not heard these remarks, she certainly must have noticed the chilly reception, and it is likely one of her women friends raced after her to repeat what Camilla had said. It certainly didn't bode well for her happiness under the new papacy. She returned to the Orsini palace dismayed, only to find her husband terrified by his audience with the pope.

They both agreed with Cardinal de Medici's advice that they should leave Rome immediately. Paolo Giordano ordered his servants to pack for a trip to Bracciano, taking along the most valuable silverware and furnishings. As their caravan rumbled out of town, they saw the head of the duke's servant Bracciardini prominently placed on a pike so that anyone leaving Rome by the main gate would see it. This was, quite clearly, the pope's response to the duke's request for pardon.

Ambassadors and princes continued to line up to kiss the pope's feet, as was customary, throughout that afternoon. But when they began to congratulate him, he cut them short. He had been waiting for the papacy for decades now and didn't want to waste another moment in useless compliments. He had work to do. One of the few visitors the pope cheerfully chatted with was Francesco Filelfo, Lodovico Orsini's private secretary. The pope mentioned three times Filelfo's devoted service to him in the past and told him to let him know if he ever needed a favor. Before the year was up, Filelfo would need a very great favor indeed.

But the pope gave short shrift to other visitors and suddenly announced to the cardinals present that he didn't want to plan an

---

[†] Ibid., p. 252.
[‡] Ibid., p. 253.

official coronation several days in the future. Prodded by the feeling that he would have a short pontificate, he wanted someone to crown him immediately so that he could start his reign. The cardinals explained that he could start ruling right away, even before the coronation.

The custodians of the capital, those responsible for the law and order of Rome, presented themselves to the pope for the traditional request of bread and justice. The pope snickered that he would certainly provide bread better than his predecessor had, a remark that many thought was in bad form. He added that regarding justice, they could depend on his support if they did their duty but would suffer the direst consequences if they did not, including beheading. The custodians were stunned. They had come to render a traditional courtesy and been threatened with the loss of their heads.

The pope then issued a bull prohibiting the carrying of any kinds of weapons within the walls of Rome. Francesco had been shot first and then finished off with knives, and now his uncle, as if trying to undo a thing already done, forbade firearms, swords, and knives under pain of immediate execution. Many honest citizens carried guns to protect themselves from criminals and didn't want to give them up. Moreover, men and women alike carried knives, along with forks and spoons, in little wooden boxes called *cadenas* if they were going to a restaurant or a friend's house to eat. (They were unwilling to put other people's utensils in their mouths; heaven only knew where they had been, or how carefully they had been washed.) But the pope wouldn't listen to the protests of his ministers and insisted the bull be issued immediately.

On April 28, four young men of the same family, two brothers and two cousins, were arrested at the gate of Saint John for coming into Rome with firearms. Because they had not been in town when the decree was issued, most people believed they would receive an immediate pardon. Plus, the pope's coronation was coming up on May 1, and it was unseemly for any pontiff to start off his reign with executions.

When the governor of Rome, Monsignor Sangiorgio, asked the pope what to do with the young men, Sixtus dryly replied that the law must be observed. Many cardinals begged him for mercy. The men's family prompted Camilla to throw herself on her knees before her brother and intercede, but the pope waved her away. A group of cardinals raised 4,000 scudi they planned to donate to the papal treasury if the punishment was mitigated to life in the galleys.

But Sixtus decreed that all lawbreakers must hang. Contemporary documents differ on the characters of the condemned men; some said they were pure as the driven snow; others said they were four well-known thugs who deserved hanging for a variety of crimes unpunished under Gregory. Given Sixtus's subsequent efforts to determine guilt or innocence, we can assume that the latter was true.

What disturbed the pope's ministers most was the enjoyment Sixtus seemed to be deriving from planning their execution. It was as if in hanging these lawless young men, bristling with weapons and bravado, he was hanging the murderers of Francesco. The fact that they were different individuals didn't seem to matter. The morning of April 29, the four youths were executed on the Castel Sant'Angelo Bridge. The pontiff rode by to see the bodies swinging stiffly from the gallows and seemed greatly pleased. A chill of terror ran through the city. Sixtus V was not a forgiving old fellow after all.

The pope informed the cardinals instrumental in his election – de Medici, Rusticucci, Farnese, d'Este, and Bonelli – that he would give them no power. Jesus had given the Church to Peter, he pointed out, and not to the other disciples. "Oh, how deep are the divine judgments," Sixtus told them, "that to one boss and to one only he gave the authority of governing his sheep. *You are Peter, you alone are the pope, I will give you power to reign over heaven. To you I give the power to reign over and support the Church, to you, to you who are my vicar, and not to others who are simply ministers.*"[†] It was clear that Sixtus gripped the keys of Saint Peter in a tightly clenched fist and was not going to allow his cardinals to get anywhere near them.

† Ibid., p. 161.

In the days leading up to the coronation, according to the chronicler, the pope "spent the greater part of the hours and above all the night writing memorials in a little book that he always took with him for this purpose, without ever leaving it, fearing that someone might read what he had written, and he kept it in a little black velvet purse. In this book he noted all that he wanted to do, not only for the present day but for the rest of his life, and with such care that sometimes even while saying the holy office with his chaplain, remembering something he wanted to write down, or notes he had forgotten, he would take out his little purse and write in his little book." The pope's scribblings were to "put a brake on the insolent ways of the Romans, and their insufferable licentiousness and freedom of life."[†]

During a Vacant See, it was customary for criminals to turn themselves in to prisons and confess their crimes. There they waited until a new pope was elected, and during the general pardon that preceded the coronation they were released. Having received a papal pardon, they could never be charged again for the same crimes. Soon after Gregory's death, some five hundred malefactors turned themselves in. When other criminals heard that the new pope was the merciful old Cardinal Montalto, who had even forgiven his own nephew's murderer, long lines formed at the jails as dozens of murderers waited to confess their crimes.

According to a contemporary account, on April 30, the day before the coronation, Governor Sangiorgio and the vice castellan of Castel Sant'Angelo presented themselves to the pope with bundles of petitions for the release of prisoners. Bowing deeply, Sangiorgio said, "Most illustrious father, at the feet of your Holiness we have come seeking permission to give liberty to the prisoners, having brought the petitions so that your Holiness might deign to conform to the custom of pardoning the supplicants."

Sixtus cast the two of them a fierce look and thundered, "What pardons, and prisoners, and supplications are you talking about? We have often seen to our unspeakable pain the wickedness happening in

† Ibid., pp. 165-166.

Rome to universal scandal, in our own presence, with danger to our life, with the death of our nephew, and with the wounding of one of our servants, and of many other scandals and most grave evils. These guilty ones are not worthy of pardon. God forbid that such a thought enters into our mind.... The city of Rome needs justice, and during our pontificate we are a judge with a sword in our hand."

He continued, "We do not want the prisons to be opened, regardless of the nobility of the criminals. But more than this – listen carefully – we want them to be most strictly held and rigorously questioned until the end of their trials. We want to punish the guilty quickly to empty the prisons to make room for the new ones who must enter there. And they deserve to be punished so that all the world knows that God has placed us and elevated us to the See of Saint Peter to reward the good and punish the guilty. We want four of the guiltiest to be tried and executed tomorrow as a public spectacle for the eyes of the Roman people."[†] He ordered the executions to take place at the very moment he was being crowned in Saint Peter's.

Shocked, the governor and vice castellan bowed and shuffled backward out of the room, still clutching the petitions. According to a *relatione*, "The poor governor, distraught in his very soul, gave the order to hold the trial of the four most guilty, but it displeased him because he had convinced many dependents of great cavaliers and cardinals, his friends and patrons, to turn themselves in to the prisons voluntarily for hope of pardon. Now, seeing so many poor souls deceived, he didn't know what to do."[‡]

When he told the cardinals what the pope had said, they were equally horrified because there was not a single cardinal, prelate, or nobleman who did not have some relative, servant, or dependent guilty of some grave crime. Meanwhile, Cardinals Farnese, de Medici, Gonzaga, and Colonna raced to the pope, telling him that clemency should come naturally to the Vicar of Christ. It would be astonishing, they said, if the new pope closed his heart to pity, and above all on a day when Christendom rejoiced. The heretics would be scandalized,

---

† Ibid., pp. 170–172.
‡ Cicogna, *Conclave di Sisto*, Folio 92b.

seeing that the pope loved bloodshed better than forgiveness. They begged him to continue the custom of granting clemency to prisoners on his coronation day, pointing out to him that the honor of the Holy See depended on it because Christ was the father of compassion.

The pope had grown visibly irritated during the cardinals' lengthy diatribes. Now he cried, "Your remonstrances surprise me as much as they should mortify you and do you shame. When Jesus Christ confided the keys of his Church to Saint Peter, as we see in the gospels, he submitted him neither to the advice nor the lessons of the other apostles, and you are greatly mistaken if you believe you can have authority over us. Providence has raised me to the throne of his Church to reestablish all things in a better state… It is not the punishment of crimes but their impunity that scandalizes the heretics and God."

He continued, "You come, however, to ask my pardon for many criminals, under the pretext of establishing my reputation by pardoning crimes with which the Papal States have been infected for many years. God give me the grace to purge this filth."

He stormed out of the audience chamber into a private room as his servant scurried behind him and closed the double doors. The cardinals stood looking at the doors with mouths agape. But almost immediately the trembling servant threw open the doors, revealing a white-robed, red-faced Sixtus, who said, "I forgot to warn you that in the trials of the guilty, I also want to act against those who protect them." Then he slammed the doors shut.

When the Roman public learned that pardons would not be given and all confessed murderers would be immediately executed, their family members raced to the papal audience chamber to try to change his mind. A certain Sebastiano Ciacci had turned himself in to obtain pardon for murder and now learned that he would lose his head. His young wife, mother of his five children, threw herself at the pope's feet and begged for his life.

The pope looked on her with pity. "I am greatly touched, my poor woman," he said, "by the state to which I see you and your children reduced… But I am engaged in calling Justice back to Rome, from which she has been chased away, and I am dedicated to doing so."[†] And Ciacci was beheaded the next day.

In the days that followed, whenever anyone asked him for a pardon, Sixtus sneered, "The city has enough rogues without adding those from the prisons to them."

Sixtus sent for the governor of Rome, the jailers, and the judges of the criminal courts. He informed the jailers that if any prisoner escaped, the jailer would have to give up his own life as compensation. Then he ordered all of them to see that justice was done. "As long as I live," he thundered, "every criminal will die."[‡]

Before he dismissed them, he stood and cried out the words of Jesus in Matthew 10:34, "I am come not to bring peace, but a sword."[§]

---

† Leti, *Sixte V*, Vol. 1, p. 411.
‡ Sarazani, p.16.
§ Leti, *Sixte V*, Vol. 1, p. 389.

Chapter 14

THE SWORD OF GOD

Every morning I will put to silence all the wicked in the land; I will cut off every evildoer from the city of the Lord.

– Psalm 101:8

Most popes came from noble or at least well-to-do families, and their relatives were well versed in proper social behavior. But Sixtus's family, though they had lived in Rome for fifteen years, could potentially humiliate themselves and the pope if he wasn't careful. Because a pope didn't have a wife or daughter (at least, he wasn't supposed to), it was his sister or sister-in-law who became the first lady of Rome, playing hostess to noblewomen, the sisters and nieces of cardinals, and the wives and daughters of ambassadors and visiting royalty.

Although Sixtus delighted in Camilla's simplicity, earthy good sense, and piety, he also knew she wasn't exactly princess material. How could she engage with Europe's most refined men and women without making a fool of herself? It was his job to make a silk purse from a sow's ear, and fast.

Sixtus called Camilla to the papal palace and told her he was giving her the Villa Montalto, which he would have beautifully furnished and decorated. He realized it would be impractical for his sister to throw lavish banquets and balls, and admonished her to host only small gatherings, and those few and far between. "Close yourself in with modesty," he advised, "and live a life that is modest, retired, and private. To this end you will be provided with a decent court, but without grandeur, comfortable but without pride, and which will serve rather for edification than as a subject for gossip of the people."[†] And she should never, ever, forget her humble origins.

Camilla received a monthly allowance of 1,000 scudi for her maintenance, and four coaches, along with mules and horses. The pope carefully selected men of good character for her staff, and hired a lady-in-waiting, a major domo, a chaplain, secretary, butlers, valets, grooms, and cooks. Her servants wore livery of pear green (from the name Peretti, which meant *little pears*) and leaf green. One man's job was to instruct Camilla in courtly ceremonies. Sixtus debated whether he should hire a matron of honor to tutor Camilla in the etiquette required in dealing with Roman noblewomen. But Camilla "learned so quickly to compliment the ladies and succeeded in the necessary politeness and graciousness," that he didn't have to.[‡]

Pasquino, as usual, had his say. One day, he was seen wearing a filthy shirt, with a sign around his neck that he couldn't get clean shirts any more since "my laundress has become a princess and sister of the pope."[§]

They could laugh all they wanted to. Overnight, the laundress became one of the richest ladies in Rome. But true to her frugal upbringing, Camilla didn't squander her money on vanities. She bought land in Rome, built shops on it, and rented them out at high prices.

The coronation was held on Wednesday, May 1. As the first wave of criminals was being executed, Cardinal de Medici was crowning Sixtus V in Saint Peter's Basilica. Then, according to tradition, the papal master of ceremonies stood before him with a twist of flax burning on the head of a cane. "Holy father," he intoned, "so passes the glory of the world." It was a warning to each new pope that he, too, was mortal, and one day his power would disappear.

For six hundred years, other popes had smiled benignly and let the ceremonies continue. But Sixtus replied in a loud voice, "Our glory will never pass away because we have no other glory than

---

† Anon., p. 215.
‡ Ibid., p. 217.
§ Ibid., p. 355.

providing justice for all." Then, turning to the ambassadors, he said, "Tell your princes, our sons, the content of this notable ceremony."[†]

Sixtus had already planned the future of Camilla's two grandsons. Usually in a family with two boys, the elder would marry, and the younger go into the Church. Although it was not unusual at the time to give the red hat to very young relatives, Sixtus knew that an eight-year-old cardinal would be far more ridiculous than a fourteen-year-old cardinal. On May 2, the older boy, Alessandro, was made cardinal and appointed the pope's cardinal nephew. During his great-uncle's audiences with ambassadors, cardinals, and government officials, the youth sat quietly and observed. Later, he would discuss what had happened at the meeting with his teachers and the pope. In the course of time, Cardinal Montalto, as young Alessandro was known, would become one of the most distinguished cardinals of the Sacred College.

His brother, eight-year-old Michele, would be groomed to marry and sire a dynasty. While many pontiffs cleaned out the papal treasury to buy duchies for their relatives, Sixtus used his own salary to purchase small principalities for Prince Michele to allow him to live honorably after the pope's death. Sixtus did, however, immediately name him captain general of the pontifical guard and governor of the Borgo section of Rome, both positions with large salaries. Naturally, though Michele held the title and received the income, others did the work.

On May 5, the pope had his *possesso*, a ceremony in which he took possession of his titular church, Saint John Lateran. Many Romans who had not crammed into Saint Peter's Square for the election and coronation now had an opportunity to see their new pontiff as the procession wound its way through the main streets of Rome. They were shocked to see a man, who for years had been reputed near death's door, "all spunky on a horse," as one *avvisi* put it.[‡]

The pope had forbidden the traditional flinging of coins to the crowd, saying that the neediest people – the weak, crippled,

† Ibid., p. 204.
‡ Gnoli, p. 256.

and hungry – rarely got a penny. It was the strong and healthy who scrambled for it, knocking over the disadvantaged in the process. He asked parish priests to find the poorest families in Rome and give them alms directly.

Tradition decreed that after a pope took possession of the Lateran, the solemn ceremony was concluded with a lavish banquet. But Sixtus, knowing Gregory had left the Church finances in dire straits, canceled the banquet. He returned to Villa Montalto and partook of a simple meal with his servants. The rest of the day he spent in walking about the gardens examining his plants.

On May 10, Sixtus held his first consistory in which he declared to the entire Sacred College that he would devote his attention as sovereign to two things: the rigorous enforcement of justice and the plentiful provision of food for his subjects. Regarding justice, he issued an edict that took away immunity from cardinals, noblemen, and even ambassadors; no one had the right to deny law enforcement officers entrance to their palaces, and anyone harboring criminals would be punished as harshly as the criminals themselves.

Though Paolo Giordano had fled Rome two weeks earlier, many servants still lived in his palace. The pope had five men with bad reputations arrested in the Orsini palazzo, which so frightened the other retainers that they closed up the place and left Rome.

The pope further decreed that barons in their country estates must turn over all bandits to the pope's guards immediately. If any known bandits approached palaces or towns, those who recognized them were to ring church bells as a sign to request armed assistance. All those who heard the bells were required to stop what they were doing and try to capture the bandits. Anyone who did not ring the bells when they saw bandits, or who heard them but did not respond, would be executed.

Any law-abiding citizen who captured a bandit alive would receive a 400-scudi reward, and he would receive 300 scudi for each head he sent to Rome. In addition, all those who turned in bandits or their heads would receive a full pardon for the bandit of their choice. If they had any relatives sitting on death row, their sentences would be commuted to two years. If they were in the galleys, they would be immediately freed.

Sixtus issued an edict that saved his soldiers a lot of work: any bandit who turned in another bandit for execution and vowed to reform his life would receive a full pardon, a 500-scudi reward, and an honest job. The last was a clever move. Since many men joined bandit gangs because they didn't know how else to support themselves, the pope offered them good wages on his various building projects in and around Rome, with a chance to advance. Hard labor and a moral life would be well rewarded. Since there is little honor among thieves, the roads to Rome were jammed with reformed bandits holding their colleagues in chains.

Sixtus commissioned five hundred soldiers under three strict generals to ride throughout the Papal States to round up criminals and those protecting them – even dukes, cardinals, and princes. There would be absolutely no privilege for those of noble status. If found guilty, they would be executed, just like the poor. In August, the governor of Rome, Sangiorgio, resigned after only four months in office, disgusted by the pope's brutality. Sixtus appointed Mariano Pierbenedetti to the post, an old friend with a strict sense of justice, admonishing him "to attend to justice without respect of persons, and to particularly aid the causes of the poor."[†]

Gallows and scaffolds were erected in the main squares of Rome, and every day there were executions. The Romans suddenly acted like the most devout, law-abiding Christians in the world, but the pope wasn't fooled. In fact, he was in a hurry. "I know that under the next pontificate, the Romans will corrupt themselves again," he said, "which is why I want to hang all the bad ones during my pontificate."[‡]

To more efficiently conduct the hangings, Sixtus had a specially designed fifteen-man gallows built, where one day he executed thirty men in two quick shifts. After the bodies were taken down, the heads were cut off, affixed to pikes, and placed on city gates, public

† Pastor, Popes, Vol. 21, p. 79, n.
‡ Ibid., p. 489.

buildings, and bridges. The Castel Sant'Angelo Bridge displayed a veritable forest of heads on pikes.

During the summer of 1585, the *avvisi* were chock full of reports of heads. "Each day new heads of bandits appear." "Today four more bandits' heads appeared on the bridge."[†] As an insult to the families who had produced such evil-doers, the pope often had the name of the executed man on a placard hanging from the pike. "Head of Ercole Castrucci," read one sign flapping beneath a skull with patches of leathery skin and tufts of hair, the eyes picked out by crows, though perhaps the "head of" was unnecessary.[‡]

One day, eight bandit heads in sacks arrived in Rome, and the pope decreed that these, too, should be stuck on pikes on the Castel Sant'Angelo Bridge. According to an *avvisi*, "While these eight heads were on the bridge, two hours before sunset the pope came on horse, and wanted to see them, and stopping to look, you could tell the pleasure that the pope had of it, so that he went to the Church of Saint Mary Major to thank God for the blessing."[§]

Shortly thereafter, the pope told the governor that he wanted two criminal cavaliers to be beheaded in front of Castel Sant'Angelo. When he rode by to pick up the governor to take him to church, Sixtus wanted to see the executioner holding a head in each hand. The executioner, having whacked off the heads, was waiting for the pope's arrival, and as he passed, raised both heads by the hair, "whereupon the pope, very happy, went to the Church of the Most Holy Madonna of the Rotunda."[¶]

Whenever a particularly violent bandit was captured and executed, Sixtus cried with outstretched arms, "God be praised that he has given us so much favor to have assisted us with justice."[**]

Every two weeks, the pope called for his governor and expressed his astonishment at how few punishments had been meted out, saying that if he had been in his position he would have rounded up many

---

† Gnoli, pp. 267-268.
‡ Anon., p. 255.
§ Ibid., p. 281.
¶ Ibid., p. 441.
** Ibid., p. 385.

more criminals, and that the governor was getting quite lax. Whenever the governor was foolish enough to advise leniency in a particular case, Sixtus threatened to fire him and make him a defense attorney. The chronicler wrote, "So the governor was obliged to content the pope by watching night and day for the persecution and punishment of evil-doers, not pardoning even the lightest guilt."†

While the governor of Rome was responsible for law enforcement, traditionally cardinals had no such role. Yet Sixtus expected his cardinals to actively pursue criminals. Cardinal Marcantonio Colonna, like Sixtus, had been frustrated over Pope Gregory's leniency with murderers. He built twelve gallows between the towns of Anagni and Frosolone and decorated them with the chopped-off body parts of criminals he had executed. But Cardinal Alfonso Gesualdo had foolishly joined the Church without realizing he would be expected to kill people, and he lagged in meeting the pope's expectations. When the pope reprimanded him harshly, he hastily rounded up and hanged twenty-five bandits and sent the heads to Rome. The pope was "satisfied enough."‡

Realizing that the best way to win the pope's favor was to send him heads, and hoping to cash in on the rich rewards, some people started digging up dead bodies in graveyards, cutting off the heads, and sending them back to Rome in sacks as the heads of bandits.

Cardinal Farnese wanted nothing to do with heads and was as disgusted by the pope's behavior as he was with himself for having approved his election. Summering at his country estate, he didn't lift a finger to send a single head. When the papal complaints started to arrive about the lack of heads, he replied that he was not "the bailiff of the countryside, and he did not know how to dig up men at church and send their heads to Rome as if they were exiles, who were then found to be alive."§ But he did manage to find a few criminals and send their heads to Rome just to quieten the pope.

---

† Anon., p. 265.
‡ Gnoli, p. 268.
§ Ibid., pp. 268-269.

Though the pope was pleased with his heads, and "often went expressly to look at them," not everyone felt the same way. Usually, heads were taken off their pikes after a few days and either buried or thrown down an old well. But Sixtus didn't remove the heads. He liked to see them pile up, week after week, month after month, and kept an exact count of them. The problem of the unsightly heads became worse in the stultifying heat of a Roman summer. Black swarms of flies buzzed from head to head, and according to one report, the stench emanating from so many rotting heads revolted many.

Some of the cardinals – who were literally nauseated – asked the councilmen of Rome, who were called conservators, to remove the heads and bury them. The councilmen asked the pope if they could do so but, "The pope, greatly enraged, replied, 'Oh, what a delicate sense of smell you have, my lords conservators, that the heads of dead people stink to you, heads which don't harm anyone, while we find that living people who offend the liberty of others are the ones who really stink. We want them to stay put. Those who get nauseated and disgusted can leave Rome. We do not lack conservators and cavaliers who are less sensitive and more attentive to our service and to that of the city.' He then had the door closed in their faces, and left, and they were terribly scandalized by the pope's manners."[†] The request had been a grievous mistake. The pope was quite fond of his heads.

"The following day he issued a notice posted in all public places that anyone under pain of death should not dare to remove the heads from the places where they had been placed, and these were his words, 'There will be no regard for nobility of whatever grade, nor will any person be excepted, who will remove those heads, because the pope wants it this way.'"[‡]

But soon after, the pope arrived in his audience chamber to find gut-wrenching fumes rising from a "rotten stinking head" next to the papal throne.[§] Sixtus had his heads counted, and sure enough one was found to be missing. The Romans laughed at this wonderful joke, but

† Anon., p. 287.
‡ Ibid.
§ Ibid.

the pope didn't think it was very funny. He believed that one of the conservators who had complained about the heads had done it, but he didn't know which one. So he fired all four of them.

A report of September 18, 1585, stated that in the first four months of Sixtus's reign more bandits' heads had been exposed on Castel Sant'Angelo Bridge than melons had been brought to the Roman markets. Indeed, the heads were like so many over-ripe, maggot-infested melons harvested from the pope's garden. With such numerous executions, the pope needed more executioners than the two employed in Rome, who under Gregory had rarely had any work to do. Moreover, foreigners were traditionally executed by their fellow countrymen. So Sixtus hired numerous executioners from various parts of Italy, France, Spain, and Germany, and ordered them "to march once a week, two by two through Rome, nooses over their shoulders, or sometimes holding an axe, to strike fear into the hearts of citizens."[†]

One of the assassins of Pope Gregory's advisor, Vincenzo Vitelli, a certain Manlio da Sturi, was captured and admitted to having murdered eighty-two people. He was paraded through Rome strapped down on a cart as the executioner tore off chunks of his flesh with red hot pincers. His right hand was cut off before he was hanged. Safe in his palace in Florence, the bandit king Piccolomini said of Sixtus, "You can't joke with this pope."[‡]

Bandits, who for years had lived comfortably in castles and towns, were now forced to flee to woods and caves. Peasants hunted them like animals for the reward, riding out with nets and dogs hot on their scent. The Duke of Urbino knew of a gang of bandits who had entrenched themselves in an unassailable position in the hills. Knowing they were low on provisions, he sent a convoy of mules carrying food over the nearest mountain pass. As expected, the robbers plundered the satchels and ate heartily. But the food was poisoned. The next day the duke sent his guards to pick up the bodies, sever the heads, and send them to the pope, who was delighted.

[†]   Ibid., p. 218.
[‡]   Gnoli, p. 274.

Those bandits with money and connections fled to Venice, Tuscany, or the Kingdom of Naples. But Sixtus knew that they could still conduct raids on his territory and then return over the border to safety. Worse, after his death, they would return for good to the Papal States and once more plague his people. Within days of his coronation, Sixtus wrote to King Philip of Spain, asking him to order the rulers of his Italian principalities to refuse sanctuary to criminals from the Papal States. Philip agreed, as did the dukes of Urbino and Ferrara. The Grand Duke of Tuscany, however, was more reluctant. The pope had to threaten him with the public disgrace of excommunication before he complied.

Venice, too, was a problem. For centuries it had welcomed exiles, even murderers, who could offer their services or talents to the republic, and never questioned them about their crimes. The Venetians jealously guarded the right of sanctuary and rarely extradited anyone. Undeterred, the pope negotiated with the Venetian ambassador. "We want people to live in peace in the States of the Church," he explained, "and the best means of obtaining this end will be to deprive the evil-doers of any chance of escape. Every prince in Italy and His Catholic Majesty [the King of Spain] have assured us that they will refuse them an entrance into their territories; we trust the Doge will do as much, otherwise we will question his good will towards us."

The pope added that he did not mind if Venice sent these swashbucklers on military missions to fight the Turks, as long as they were far from Italy. "When it is a question of the respect due the Holy See, which must have more weight in the eyes of the Republic than a mere individual, I cannot believe, nor does it appear to me right, that the republic should favor rebels."[†] The republic was painfully aware of how badly it had treated Felice Montalto as inquisitor twenty-five years earlier. Would he hold a grudge against them, harming their trade? As a peace offering, Venice agreed to extradite to Rome any bandits the pope requested.

But not all bandits escaping to nearby nations were easily spotted upon entry. There were no passports with photographs, no drivers'

† Hubner, Vol.1, p. 287.

licenses to help the guards at the gate identify them. They were allowed in as law-abiding travelers, and once inside, started murdering and robbing again. Some ambassadors complained to the pope that he had driven his own bandits into their territories where they committed heinous crimes. Smiling, Sixtus replied, "If your masters abandoned to me their states, I would clean them as well as I have done the Papal States. If they followed my example, all Italy would be entirely safe. Monarchs make miracles happen when they want to."[†]

*   *   *

After leaving Rome on April 26, Paolo Giordano and Vittoria received frequent reports of the pope's executions. They were horrified to learn that immediately after the election, criminals across the Papal States, as well as those harboring them, were rounded up and executed, even those of the noblest blood, like Paolo Giordano.

The duke realized that the fortified castle of Bracciano itself was not safe if the pope intended to send an army to storm it. He and Vittoria had to leave the Papal States and find sanctuary in a place outside of Sixtus's jurisdiction. Once again, he returned to the idea of Venice, a nation that did not jump when a pontiff snapped his fingers. Venice would recognize the duke's marriage to Vittoria and would drag its feet for years at a request to turn him over to papal guards brandishing a warrant.

On May 21, Vittoria and her entourage jolted down the road that led from Bracciano to the northeast. It was remarked that she looked exhausted physically and emotionally. So much had happened in the past four years, and now it seemed as if the murder, the guilt, the imprisonment, and now the irony of Cardinal Montalto's belated election, had all been for nothing. If she had just waited, she would have been the pope's niece, a great noblewoman, with unlimited funds at her disposal for dresses, jewels, and banquets. Now she was in exile.

On May 26, the group reached the popular pilgrimage destination of Loreto, a small town of tidy houses huddled together on a windswept hill overlooking the Adriatic in the distance. Its only claim to fame, and indeed the only reason for the town's existence, was that at its epicenter stood the holy house of the Virgin Mary, the one-room stone building in which she was thought to have conceived Jesus, and where she had raised him. It was believed that angels, seeing the Muslims chase out the last Crusaders in the Holy Land in 1291, lifted the Virgin's house and carried it westward to safety, placing it first in Slavonia (present-day Croatia) and three years later plucking it up again and setting it gently down on the hilltop of Loreto.

Recent scholarship has shown that the story is not as ridiculous as it first appears. A family named de Angelis, which ruled the Greek Kingdom of Epirus, brought the stones back from Nazareth with the aid of the Knights Templars. The stones were first unloaded in Slavonia, and three years later they became part of the dowry of Margherita de Angelis when she married an Italian prince. Uprooted once again, they found their permanent home in Loreto. Given the legendary flight, more recently the Virgin of Loreto was made the special patroness of aviators.

At the altar, Vittoria Accoramboni and Duke Paolo Giordano Orsini, sinners sorely in need of forgiveness and redemption, got down on their knees and prayed to the wooden statue of the Virgin on the altar. Paolo Giordano promised the Virgin a beautiful new bejeweled crown if she would only help them. In Loreto, Vittoria met with the archbishop of Bologna, Cardinal Gabriel Paleotto, who was staying there, and asked him for communion. He noted "her deep piety and religion."[†] Or perhaps it was guilt.

From Loreto, the Orsinis went to Fossombrone to visit Vittoria's brother, Bishop Ottavio. Then they trundled on to Urbino, a tiny independent nation. Though he was an ardent supporter of the pope's campaign against bandits, Duke Francesco Maria II della Rovere had always been friendly to Paolo Giordano and now took Vittoria under his wing as well. It is likely that the couple wanted to know whether they could count on the duke to protect her after Paolo Giordano died.

And indeed, the duke's health had become alarmingly bad. He had gained so much weight recently that when he stood up it seemed as if rolls of meat were falling from him which stopped halfway to the floor. Perhaps goaded by his increasing obesity, the old arrow wound in his left leg opened up again. When the Orsinis reached the port city of Pesaro, the duke had to undergo treatment before he could continue. Doctors called such an infection a *wolf*, because the wound was flesh-eating. To prevent the wound from devouring the flesh around it, doctors put slabs of fresh meat on it and the infection devoured the meat instead. The disease spread to his face, causing a fire-red rash of oozing blisters.

The healing waters of the Abano baths outside Venice were generally believed to be the best remedy for such an affliction. Unable to rattle further over bumpy roads, Paolo Giordano asked the Republic of Venice to send two galleys to Pesaro to take him, his possessions, and his servants there. Because of the grandeur and merit of his family, which years earlier had been inscribed among the Venetian nobility, his request was granted.

The ships duly arrived. Groaning under the weight of their illustrious burden, four porters carried the great Duke of Bracciano on a stretcher onto the ship as Vittoria trudged wearily behind.

Chapter 15

JUSTICE FOR ALL

I know that the Lord secures justice for the poor and upholds the cause of the needy.

– Psalm 140:12

Once the pope had initiated the firestorm of activity to round up the bandits, he turned his attention to the courts. Sixtus personally examined the records of criminal cases going back several years and stayed up late at night reading the reports of trials, confessions, and interrogations. Seeing so many injustices in the reports he read, he ordered all governors of the Papal States to examine criminal cases going back at least ten years for miscarriages of justice, despite sentences having been completed by the defendants.

Those judges who had been too lenient were fired, especially if they had given a lighter sentence to a nobleman than they had to a poor man for the same crime. The defendant who had gotten off too easily was rounded up and hauled back to jail and, if he had murdered or raped someone, executed. One man who had obtained a slap on the wrist for a murder he had committed as a youth thirty-six years earlier was dragged from his home and beheaded.

Sixtus threatened all judges with immediate execution if they accepted bribes. He threatened citizens with execution if they knew something about a corrupt judge and refused to come forward with the information. Many judges fled the Papal States. Lawyers, who knew very well their clients were guilty but protested their innocence just the same, were thrown into prison. Unethical judges and lawyers were whipped naked through the streets of Rome to the laughter of the people.

Sixtus held regular open houses where every citizen of the Papal States, no matter how poor, could personally tell him of injustices, or at least present a petition to him that he would read later. He looked into every request. One day the pope received a petition from a poor widow who had been in litigation for three years over a little house she owned. The lawyers had bankrupted her. She asked the pope to render a decision since she could no longer afford to pay for legal counsel. Enraged, Sixtus hauled in the dilatory judge, made him pay her back all her legal fees, and fired him. He then decreed that judges and lawyers must move through their trials in a speedy manner so that the process cost the litigants as little as possible.

The pope had created an atmosphere in which every citizen was supposed to report crimes, injustice, and blasphemy or else be punished himself. Naturally, some people told false tales to avenge themselves on enemies. But Sixtus and his team of investigators looked carefully into every accusation, and those who had lied were punished more severely than people guilty of crimes. One man falsely accused a tailor whom he disliked. The tailor was thrown into prison. When examination of witnesses proved the tailor innocent, he was released. The false accuser was brutally whipped and sent to the galleys for life.

Sixtus was an equal opportunity employer on the lookout for men of a stern nature like himself who could work in the jails or the courts, depending on their education. He even searched for new employees on the streets as he rode by. According to the chronicler, "When he went throughout the city, looking at the people, and seeing some person with a bitter and severe face, he called him to his presence and asked about his quality, and if he found in this examination the person capable of rendering some service to the principality or the Holy Church conforming to his mind, he would immediately confer on him some office."[†]

Sixtus wanted to break forever the unbridled power of Roman princes like the Orsinis. He knew that the next pope could return to the old ways in a heartbeat, undoing all of Sixtus's laws. One means of ensuring that the nobles' power was broken for many years to come

† Anon., p. 225.

was to dilute it. He would create powerful new noblemen loyal to him, men who, after his death, could not be made to disappear with a signature, as a law could. The pope invited to Rome the distant relatives of noble families, men who wanted land and a good living and who were willing to devote themselves to serving the pope and the Church. These men would obtain their desires by serving Sixtus and not their baronial relatives who would enlist them in personal armies opposed to the pope. Any crimes they had committed would be pardoned, and they would be given prestigious titles.

Destitute, they trickled in and threw themselves at the feet of the pope, who gave them the titles of count, marquis, and even duke, and turned over to them the lands he had confiscated from bandit-harboring barons. This action offset the power of the old noble families such as the Orsinis, who were horrified that their poor cousins suddenly had equal titles.

The Romans were delighted that their new pontiff was tough on crime and did not spare the powerful their just punishments. No one could now saunter away from a murder or rape because of noble birth, high office, or important connections. Many nobles like Paolo Giordano Orsini, knowing the pope was out to get them, fled Rome.

Nor did Sixtus spare diplomatic staff. When the Holy Roman Emperor Rudolph II sent a delegation to recognize the authority of Sixtus, one of the delegates was arrested and flogged for causing a brawl. Although the ambassador protested vigorously, the pope replied that even if the emperor himself came to Rome, he would have to obey the laws or suffer the punishment. "This prince has no respect even for cardinals or the ambassadors of the crowned heads," reported a shocked *avvisi* writer on June 26, 1585.[†]

Sixtus even executed a cardinal's son. The Marchese of Gallese, the son of Cardinal Altemps, had raped the beautiful lady-in-waiting of a Roman noblewoman and thrown her out of a window. Sixtus had the man locked up in the Castel Sant'Angelo. Upon further investigation, it was learned that the marchese had in his past butchered a priest, taken out the eye of a Jew, raped a boy and thrown

† Ibid.

him out of a window, and had sexual relations with a nun. Considering his illustrious parentage, any other pope would have exiled the man. But Sixtus, who had, right before the conclave, made a very open declaration of his enormous goodwill and eternal obligations for Cardinal Altemps and his son, ordered the marchese's execution.[†] He also hanged Cardinal Decio Azzolini's nephew for murder.

There was a hierarchy of humiliation at an execution. Noblemen were routinely spared a public death, which was carried out to the jeers, hoots, and vegetable throwing of the mob, and were decorously executed inside their prisons. And the swift stroke of a beheading was considered far nobler than the slow choking of a hanging. Being strangled sitting stoically in a chair inside a cell was also considered a dignified death. But Marchese Altemps and the young Azzolini were hanged publicly, in front of Castel Sant'Angelo, as if they were the lowest-born criminals. Scarlet-faced, eyes bulging grotesquely from their sockets, grisly sounds gurgling out of their throats, they died after several excruciating minutes.

Under Gregory's reign, Sixtus had been perturbed at how women were frequently mistreated in the streets: raped, molested, pinched, kissed, and insulted. Now Sixtus had rapists executed. Although many Italians considered ass-pinching funny, Sixtus didn't. The pinchers were whipped severely and imprisoned. Even those who verbally insulted women in public or flirted with them in a bawdy way received harsh punishments. An employee of Cardinal Giovanni Sorbelloni's was whipped for uttering filthy words in front of ladies, even though those particular ladies liked what he was saying. The cardinal's personal intercession was, of course, scornfully rejected.

"It is incredible how Sixtus guarded the honor of women," the chronicler wrote, "whether noble or not, and what an enemy he was to those who harmed or insulted them, particularly on the public streets... So that the streets of Rome were so secure that the girls would go about freely and without fear, as no one dared to outrage

---

[†] Cicogna, *Conclave nel fu creato*, no page given.

their honor, whether they were noblewomen or servant girls, as there was no distinction of persons."[†]

Within a few months of his election, the city of Rome and the Papal States were almost completely free of crime. Indeed, people were afraid to argue with each other in case the argument got out of hand and it was reported to the pope. Bandits had either fled, or reformed, or died. According to one papal historian, "It was a matter of great pride and rejoicing to the pope, when ambassadors now arriving at his court assured him that 'in every part of his states through which the road had led, they had traveled through a land blessed with peace and security.'"[‡]

*   *   *

In the first half of June, Paolo Giordano and Vittoria, their servants, horses, carriages, and mountains of fine furniture trundled off the Venetian ships docked near Abano. It was a short carriage ride to the sulfurous baths. According to Michel de Montaigne, who visited in 1581, Abano was "a little village near the foot of the mountains, above which, three or four hundred paces higher, there is a place somewhat elevated and stony. This height, which is very spacious, has a number of springs of hot and boiling water spouting from the rock; around the source it is too hot to bathe in, and still more so to drink… The whole of the district is in vapor, for the streams which flow here and there into the plain carry the heat and the smell a long way."

He described two or three little bath houses into which water had been channeled. Heat and steam rose from the water, and there were places for an invalid to lie down and rid himself of evil humors through copious perspiration. He would then drink some of the water, swishing it around in his mouth to cool it. Montaigne found it very salty. Despite the baths' claims to cure all manner of disease, from lung ailments to leprosy, they did nothing to alleviate Montaigne's

---

† Anon., pp. 401-403.
‡ Ranke, Vol. 1, p. 342.

appalling kidney stones, though he did complain about "flatulence without end."[†]

While Paolo Giordano was partaking of the waters of Abano, the pope was focused on the water of Rome, or rather the lack thereof. A good gardener cannot tend his garden properly without water. Sixtus, the gardener of God, wanted to bring water to God's garden, the holy city of Rome. As soon as he had bought his hilltop villa in 1576, he had become painfully aware of the lack of water. As cardinal he had often met with the architect of his palace, Domenico Fontana, to discuss how it would be possible to bring water not only to his garden, but to all of Rome. Fontana, examining the various ruined aqueducts, thought that one of them, the Acqua Alessandrina, would be the easiest to repair.

In the time of the Roman Empire, fourteen aqueducts had supplied Rome's one million inhabitants with sparkling water from mountains some twenty miles away. The city boasted 1,300 fountains, hundreds of swimming pools, and dozens of huge bathing complexes where Romans could splash happily in cold, tepid, and hot water. Even public toilets had fresh water running through them. It often irked Sixtus that a city that worshiped idols had been blessed with water, while the home of Christ's Church had been a thirsty shambles for eleven hundred years. Certainly, God didn't approve. Now, as God's Vicar, he would bring renewed life to parched earth. He would baptize the city with fresh water, cleansing its ancient sins.

On May 5, the day of Sixtus's *possesso* ceremony, he had announced his intention to restore the Acqua Alessandrina. "These hills," he said, gesturing to the weed-bedecked mounds dotted with munching goats, "adorned in early Christian times with basilicas, renowned for the salubrity of their air, the pleasantness of their situation, and the beauty of their prospects, might again become inhabited by man."[‡]

Deploring Rome's lack of water, he said, "This condition that has lasted for many centuries has attracted our attention, especially

† Ibid., p. 211.
‡ Ranke, Vol. 1, p. 361.

because the low quarters of the city, which are densely populated, are very humid, unhealthy, and exposed to the frequent floods of the Tiber. It is therefore necessary to conduct water sufficient to render habitable the hill regions, which are distinguished by their excellent air and attractive position. Neither the difficulty nor the serious expense of the enterprise will discourage us."[†]

And indeed, there was plenty of discouragement. It would take decades to fix the aqueduct, experts warned, and millions of scudi. But with characteristic stubbornness, the pope said, "Nothing is impossible."[‡]

Domenico Fontana agreed. Using a team of 4,336 men, at a cost of 300,000 scudi, the pope fixed Rome's water supply within fifteen months. He ordered that the new aqueduct be called the Acqua Felice, after himself, but it also meant *happy water*.

Once Sixtus had his waterworks underway, he turned his attention to another problem that had been bothering him for decades: Rome's narrow, twisting medieval roads. Sixtus knew that the ancient Romans had built wide streets punctuated by large piazzas. But over the centuries, people had enlarged their houses by building additions into the streets or blocking up the streets altogether.

In 1575, Pope Gregory's master of ceremonies had written, "If a solemn festival be anywhere held, or if there be a confluence of people on occasion of any public rejoicing or spectacle, or the funeral procession of some cardinal or dignitary, whatever the cause may be, the roads and open spaces are so packed with the crowd of vehicles that it becomes impossible for foot passengers to move along; nay, even public ceremonies and processions are interfered with, to the great inconvenience and scandal of all, sometimes even with danger to life."[§]

But building the new streets involved knocking down ancient churches, convents, palaces, and Roman ruins. A howl of protest went up when the public heard of the pope's plans. Cardinal Santorio

---

† Pastor, *Sixtus V*, pp. 8-9.
‡ Anon., p. 424.
§ Thurston, pp. 90-91.

wrote, "When it was perceived that the pope seemed resolving on the utter destruction of the Roman antiquities, there came to me one day a number of Roman nobles, who entreated me to dissuade his Holiness with all my power from so extravagant a design."[†]

The pope insisted that he would "clear away the ugly antiquities."[‡] And down they went, their columns and stones hauled off to be used in finishing Saint Peter's Basilica. Impatient with what he saw as unproductive space, Sixtus wanted to turn the revered Colosseum into a wool factory, where the poor could live and work. He planned to hang a huge sign on the side which read, "Pope Sixtus's Wool Factory." Fortunately, his architects deemed the building unsuited for such an enterprise and too expensive to remodel.

Fontana was also put in charge of building the new roads. In his autobiography, the architect wrote, "Our Lord [Sixtus], wanting to facilitate the streets to those who show devotion, and who often want to visit the most holy places in the city of Rome, and in particular the seven churches so celebrated for the great indulgences and relics, opened many very wide and straight streets to these places, so that anyone on foot, on horse and in coaches can leave from wherever they want in Rome and go almost in a straight line to the most famous devotions. And this is filling up the city because in those streets which people frequent, they are building houses and shops in great number. Earlier, groups got scattered with great inconvenience on the long route, and on certain really rough streets, so that they couldn't arrive at the desired locations."[§]

The new streets, wide enough to hold five carriages across, and straight as swords, radiated out like the points of a star from Sixtus's favorite church, Saint Mary Major, to all parts of Rome. In six months, the pope's 1,500 workmen paved 121 dirt roads with large stones and built some 10,000 meters of new roads at a cost of two million scudi. Today, these are still the main arteries of Rome, and a lasting testament to Pope Sixtus V.

[†] Ranke, Vol. 1, p. 363.
[‡] Ibid.
[§] De Feo, p. 176.

Chapter 16

NO RESPECTER OF PERSONS

You will be like an oak with fading leaves, like a garden without water.

– Isaiah 1:29-31

Rome had its share of smells that summer, and not just from the ripe-decay stench of the pope's beloved heads. Sixtus caused a huge stink by removing diplomatic immunity. He gave all embassies fair warning that their employees, including the ambassadors themselves, would no longer be permitted to rabble rouse or carry firearms. He would, however, allow the embassy guards to carry pikes and halberds as a matter of tradition and prestige.

Most ambassadors didn't listen to his orders and carried on as if the immunity were still in effect. Cardinal d'Este, who was a close friend of the French ambassador's, repeatedly warned him to clean up the behavior of his large staff of ruffians, but the ambassador merely shrugged. Riding by the ambassador's palace, Sixtus could see for himself that the doormen at the gate were armed to the teeth with guns. Back at the Vatican, he commanded the governor to break down the gate and arrest all those inside with firearms. Awed by the regal power of France, the governor merely told the guards to put away their guns by order of the pope. Then he returned to Sixtus and told him that it would no longer be a problem.

When Sixtus heard this, according to the chronicler, his "face was greatly disturbed, and he said, 'Arrest them immediately, even if you have to go into the ambassador's bedroom. It is our task to free ourselves from these intrigues because on Sunday we want to make a public spectacle.'"†

† Anon., p. 304.

The two guards at the gate, still holding their guns, were arrested despite the furious complaints of the ambassador, who stated that he had given them instructions to carry firearms, and they should not be punished for following his orders. The pope replied that the two men would be carefully interrogated to see whether they were troublemakers or not. If they were law-abiding men, merely guarding the gate with guns as they had been ordered, they would be pardoned. But if they were criminals, he could not, as chief judge and strict Vicar of Christ, let them live.

Alas, it was found that these men were thugs and bandits. They had caroused late at night in the streets of Rome and beaten up honest citizens. In the time of Gregory XIII, they had often chased away the pope's guards with shots and threats. The men were hanged as an example to other ambassadors to keep their servants in line with the law.

The ambassador immediately fired off a letter to King Henri III of France protesting the incident. The king replied quickly, instructing the ambassador to read his angry response personally to the pope. But before he could finish, Sixtus chased him out of the audience chamber and commanded him and his entire entourage to leave the Papal States within forty-eight hours. There were repercussions, however, and Sixtus soon suffered a diplomatic tit for tat. When he sent a new nuncio to Paris, the king refused to receive him. The pope, in return, threatened to excommunicate the King of France himself.

Sixtus had even worse relations with the Spanish ambassador, Count Olivares, a scion of one of the richest families in Spain. The Kingdom of Naples was technically owned by the pope but leased to Spain in return for the annual tribute of a gorgeous white horse on the Feast of Saints Peter and Paul, June 28. The beautifully embroidered myth of papal jurisdiction soothed the pain of having lost the valuable kingdom centuries earlier.

During the 1585 ceremony, the first of Sixtus's reign, when the ambassador swaggered forward with the noble steed, instead of accepting it graciously, the pope said sarcastically, "Oh, what a nice compliment you are making us today, obliging us to exchange a kingdom for a beast. This will not last much longer."[†] The ambassador wondered if this meant a papal invasion of Naples.

Sixtus was furious with Philip II for saying that religion was too important to be left in the hands of the pope. How on earth, he fumed, could a foolish inbred king presume to tell Christ's Vicar on Earth what to do in matters of religion? Relations between Spain and the Papal States further deteriorated when the pope refused to ship grain to Naples and stored it up in large silos for his own people to use in time of famine. The grain of the Papal States, he said, was for the benefit of the people of the Papal States, and not for the people of Naples, who could grow their own grain if they ever got off their rear ends and planted some.

Most insulting of all, instead of allowing the Spanish ambassador to walk directly behind him in public processions, a time-honored tradition, the pope gave precedence to the governor of Rome as his top official. When the Spaniard angrily sputtered protests about this insult, the pope declared that he, as Vicar of Christ, and his judicial representative, held a status far above that of all earthly monarchs. Olivares returned to read a letter from his king insisting he take his rightful place and push the governor's delegation out of the way. The pope whispered something to a servant, and within minutes one of his executioners stood in the corner of the papal audience chamber, grimly holding a noose.

Because Olivares could not tolerate the dishonor of taking a place further back in the parade line, he pretended to be ill for the processions. To catch the ambassador at his own game, Sixtus instructed the governor to tell everyone that he was too sick to participate in the next parade. And sure enough, the ambassador's health miraculously improved, and he lined up with his entourage to march. But at the last minute the health of the governor also improved, and he pushed in front of the Spaniards with ten of his weapon-wielding officers. Olivares suddenly pretended to have an attack of kidney stones and stumbled from the parade line clutching his side.

[†] Ibid., p. 313.

Olivares didn't help matters by getting into shouting matches with Sixtus. As the personal representative of the most powerful monarch on earth, the ambassador had an inflated sense of self-importance and argued when other ambassadors would have trembled. Their audiences often ended with the pope rising from his throne in fury, running down the dais steps, and shaking his fist as he chased the ambassador down the long chamber and out the door. Younger and nimbler than Sixtus, Olivares always ran faster and raced out to his carriage before the pope could catch him.

It seemed the Spanish ambassador was forever angry at the pope for including Spanish citizens in his justice campaign. Under previous pontiffs, an ambassador need only say the word and the pope would release one of his compatriots for even the most heinous crime, with the request that the ambassador make sure he return home, far from the Papal States. It was a kind of diplomatic courtesy that was, by now, fully expected.

The Spanish ambassador was furious when the pope arrested his court poet, Carlo Matera, whom he had hired to write an epic poem recounting the glories of Philip II. Unfortunately, Matera wrote poems of a less worthy nature, including one which he circulated widely calling a certain Isabella Gigli *una gran puttana*, "a great whore."[†] Isabella Gigli was no whore but the virtuous wife of a successful Roman lawyer, who was livid when he heard about Matera's insulting poem. The husband paid servants in the Spanish embassy to steal a copy of the poem and bring it to him. Once he had the incriminating evidence in his hands, he obtained an audience with the pope.

"Most holy father," he said, "I protest that I do not hate this poet who has lacerated the honor of my innocent and honorable wife, nor am I trying to have him punished. I am come to the feet of your Holiness for the debt of honor and the rigor of your Holiness's justice which everyone praises, and which induced me to take this step, and to avoid causing the indignation of your Holiness." He was right about the last. If he had not protested to the pope, and Sixtus had

† Ibid., p. 360.

found out about the poem, then the husband would have been given the same punishment as the poet.

The pope replied, "You have done your duty, and we will do ours… Your cause is in the hands of a good judge."[†]

Matera was arrested as he came out of the ambassador's palace. Sixtus had him brought into the papal audience chamber where several cardinals, a criminal judge, and other prelates were sitting with him. Matera, who had no idea why he had been arrested, was unafraid, thinking he could talk his way out of any situation.

Sixtus read the poet some of his verses and asked if he was the author, to which Matera replied frankly that he was. Then the pope got to the line that read, "In short this woman is a great whore."

He asked, "Why are you dishonoring an honorable woman, calling her a whore?"

Matera replied, "Holy father, I swear at the feet of your Holiness that it was never my intention to offend the honor of this lady, because that word was only used in poetic license. It has always been the common opinion of the world that poets and painters are permitted everything, and your Holiness can see that the rhyme in the previous line was *fontana* [fountain], so that I called this lady *puttana* only to accommodate the rhyme, as is usual."[‡]

The cardinals burst into guffaws at this clever and impudent reply, and even Sixtus couldn't help but chuckle. "Oh well," he said, "if this poetic license to accommodate the verses is conceded to you poets, it will also be allowed to us popes, and we want to see if we can make verses and accommodate the rhymes to our taste." The pope thought for a moment and said, "He greatly deserves, this Signor Matera, to have his own room in the *galera* [galleys.]"

The poet suddenly lost his cockiness and found himself speechless with terror. The pope asked him if he liked his rhyme, but Matera didn't reply. Sixtus repeated his question, asking whether these verses did not make a nice rhyme. The poet murmured they did, and Sixtus had him returned to prison.

† Ibid., p. 361.
‡ Ibid., pp. 362-363.

The criminal judge asked the pope if he really wanted to condemn the man to the galleys for such a silly poem. Red-faced, Sixtus cried, "Why do you have any scruples? If you allow this great crime, vice, and insolence to go unpunished under the stupid excuse of poetic license, in the future every poet will be writing such verses and will be able to call the *pontefici* [popes] *eretici* [heretics.] The *Vaticano* [Vatican] rhymes with *Luterano* [Lutheran.] And you make us marvel when you ask us if you should execute the sentence of sending him to the galleys when the crime deserves, upon further reflection, the gallows. And it seems that you doubt this?"[†]

As Matera was being dragged off to the galleys, Olivares complained to the pope's grand-nephew, young Cardinal Alessandro Montalto, that papal guards had invaded the immunity of his palace three times, had executed two of his servants, and sent another five to the galleys, where Sixtus was now dispatching his poet, whom he had hired to write an epic poem. When Alessandro asked Sixtus to reconsider the sentence, the pope replied, "The sentence of the galleys was made out of respect to the Spanish ambassador because Matera deserved the gallows, and there are not so few poets on earth that another one could not be found to write verses praising Philip II of Spain. The ambassador should be grateful for the favor he has received and not go nudging around for more."[‡]

The pope began to focus on arresting poets. He said he wanted them to write their verses while on the gallows, in the galleys, or sitting in chains in jail. Sometimes in the morning when the biting pasquinades of the night before were brought to him, he would say of a particular poet, "If he applied his genius to virtuous and relevant matters, he would find his fortune with us, instead of running in danger of his life."[§]

One day, a certain Spanish gentleman was waiting in the papal antechamber when a Swiss guard walked past and unwittingly knocked him on the head with his halberd as he tried to clear the

[†] Ibid., pp. 363-364.
[‡] Ibid., p. 365.
[§] Ibid., p. 368.

crowds for the pope to pass by. The Spaniard took it as a mortal offense. A few days later at early morning Mass, the Spaniard saw the Swiss kneeling at the other end of the altar and grabbed the pilgrim's staff of a man kneeling nearby. He marched up to the guard and said, "You have insulted me with your stick, and now I will revenge myself with mine," and gave him a whack on the head, a tremendous blow that cracked his skull. The guard fell to the floor without even being able to confess, and could only extend his hand while the celebrating priest raced up to him and gave him absolution before he expired. The Spaniard fled from the church, but the Swiss guards, seeing their compatriot dead on the floor, ran after his attacker and arrested him.

The pope was enraged when he heard this story. He cried, "In the time of Sixtus they commit such wickedness in Rome? Hasn't everyone heard about the rigor of our justice? Very well, we will make them hear it now." Then he called for the governor. "Is this how they kill the men in Rome, Signor Governor, in the presence of God with no respect for his Church, and for his sanctuary? It is now your job to repair this crime with the execution of justice given to our authority."

The governor replied that he had ordered testimony to be gathered with all possible speed for the trial. To which Sixtus replied with a voice even angrier than usual, "What trial? In such cases trials are superfluous."

But the governor replied that it was necessary to have a trial because the accused was protected by the ambassador of Spain. Investigations and interrogations must take place as usual. The pope replied, "Get as much information as you want as long as this Spaniard is hanged before I eat lunch, and I want to eat early today because this morning I have a good appetite."

As the governor was leaving, the pope said, "Build the gallows in a place where I can see it from this window."

The chronicler continued, "The governor knew that the pope wanted him to be hanged immediately. So while he was leaving the Vatican Palace he gave orders to build the gallows right in front of the windows where the pope lived, and while it was being built he examined the criminal with a brief trial. There were only four and a half hours from the murder to the execution, and Sixtus did nothing else but talk about it to his servants and keep looking out of his window." Then the ambassador of Spain showed up with some cardinals, not to ask for pardon (they knew that to be impossible), but to request that Sixtus not dishonor the Spanish nation with a hanging but honor it with a beheading.

Sixtus replied angrily, "Such delinquents don't deserve favors, and his excesses merit the gallows and not the block. But we will give you more than what you ask; we will make his death noble by watching it ourselves."[†]

Sixtus remained glued to the window. As the hangman was placing the rope around the Spaniard's neck, the pope quoted a line from David's Psalms: "I will make die, in one morning, all the sinners of the earth, to purge the city of God of all those who commit iniquity."[‡]

According to the chronicler, "When the man was dead, the pope said to his servants, 'Bring us lunch, because we want to eat, serving this justice as a sauce to our appetite.' And they brought him the meats to his table and he began to talk to his servants, as he often did during his meals, about the justice, esteeming it a great thing that he had immediately punished this crime. Having finished his lunch he rose to his feet and cried, 'God be praised that this morning we have eaten with a good appetite.'"[§]

The next day, Pasquino was seen holding a bucket full of ropes, cleavers, and chains, with a sign around his neck stating that he was taking sauce to Pope Sixtus to give him a good appetite.

According to the chronicler, foreigners in Rome were frightened that a Spaniard protected by the ambassador could be arrested, tried, and executed in four hours. Ambassadors warned their servants to behave themselves in public and make sure they didn't fall into the pope's hands.

[†] Ibid., pp. 348-351.
[‡] Leti, *Sixte V,* Vol. 1, p. 192.
[§] Anon., pp. 351-352.

The pope liked to ride slowly through the streets of Rome with his little book in hand, noting down dilapidated buildings, dirty markets, and the bad habits of his subjects. But he found it hard to examine their daily behavior when everyone was apprised of his coming down the street well before he arrived. "Long live the pope!" they cried, as they had for centuries whenever a pontiff came their way. If those along his path had been gambling, carousing, or drinking, they would suddenly stop and become as grave as saints. He wanted to come upon them unannounced and catch them red-handed. Sixtus issued an edict that no one was to shout as he passed by. Now when he rode, Romans either ignored him and went about their daily business, or they sank silently to their knees and bowed their heads, probably praying he wouldn't notice them.

Mothers, concerned that young children would cry out and upset the pope, took to telling them to be quiet because Pope Sixtus was passing by. Over time, whenever children at home started to squawk, parents told them they had to settle down because Pope Sixtus was coming. Pretty soon, Pope Sixtus was going to get them if they didn't behave, an admonition that lasted for decades after his death. Sixtus became the boogeyman who hid under the beds of Italian children at night.

In his unannounced rides through Rome, Sixtus, to his great disgust, noticed the piazzas were teeming with idlers and vagabonds. According to the Venetian writer Tomaso Garzoni in 1585, "Amongst the other terrible and detestable occupations is that of the idle ... which consists in eating, drinking and enjoying oneself. They spend all their time passing through the piazza and moving from the tavern to the fishmongers and from the palazzo to the loggia, doing little all day except wandering from here to there, looking at glassware, mirrors, and rattles that are displayed in the piazzas. Now they move aimlessly through the market in the midst of the peasants, now they stop in some barber-shop to exchange songs and gossip, now they read the newspapers, and the bank news, which is simply for the ears of these lazy and negligent men."[†]

† Welch, p. 32.

Michel de Montaigne had noticed the same thing during his 1581 visit to Rome. "The most ordinary exercise of the Romans," he wrote, "is to promenade about the streets, and usually the effort of leaving the house is made solely to go from street to street without any fixed object."[†]

One day, while the pope was riding through the city, he spotted a group of men lounging about. He sent his minister to find out what they were doing. They replied they were from the countryside and were waiting for times to get better before they went back to work. The pope ordered them to work in building Saint Peter's Basilica, for which he paid them fairly. When they had fulfilled their obligations well, he then sent them to work on a farm outside of Rome.

Even those who lounged about the noble palaces were hauled off at the least infraction. "It was a marvel that all the wicked idlers who had hung around Rome in the time of Gregory were sent to the galleys," the chronicler wrote, "and any ruffian who let drop a bad word was immediately taken into custody, especially those who stayed in the Palazzo Orsini."[‡]

Romans had enjoyed playing ballgames in the piazzas and courtyards but now gave up such pastimes. Those who played early forms of soccer or rugby often got into loud arguments and fistfights; now they feared the pope would learn of it through his intricate web of spies in the city. Bowling in the piazzas had been popular, but even that gentle sport ceased as bowlers were afraid the pope, riding by, would accuse them of being idlers and send them to work on his building projects. "There had never been anything like it in any other pontificate," reported the chronicler, "so that it was universally observed that when people met friends in the street and asked where they were going, the reply was to a sermon, or to church, or to whip themselves."[§]

In addition to idlers and loungers, Rome had countless beggars spry enough to chase the wealthy for alms and intelligent enough to

---

† Montaigne, p. 155.
‡ Anon., p. 233.
§ Ibid., p. 269.

beg in several foreign languages. The pope had all beggars rounded up and examined to see if they were healthy. Those who were truly sick were given a begging permit, and the healthy received one hundred lashes and were sent to clean up the dirt in the streets or were sent to work in factories. Those who were good with arms were sent to war. Suddenly, Rome was cleared of its masses of beggars and vagabonds. Most now worked in the factories, in the docks, or in the trade of war.

Chapter 17

DANCE MACABRE

*A man tormented by the guilt of murder will be a fugitive till death;
let no one support him.*

– Proverbs 28:17

On June 28, Paolo Giordano, Vittoria, and their entourage
reached Venice, where the duke had rented the Dandolo Palace
on the Grand Canal. Strolling in Saint Mark's Square, Vittoria must
have been amazed by its size and elegance. One side of the square
had been torn down to make way for new government buildings,
the *procuratie nuove*, and construction was just getting started on a
long three-story building over an arcade. But Saint Mark's Church
glittered in the sun just as it does today, with its domes, mosaics, and
minarets. The church is a testament to Venice's centuries of contact
with the East, the spot where Roman Catholicism meets Ali Baba and
the Forty Thieves.

In the huge square itself, hundreds of people promenaded from
six to eleven in the morning and from five to eight in the evening,
local residents as well as visitors from across Europe, Asia, the Middle
East, and Africa. There was a babble of languages, a colorful palate
of skin tones, and a multi-ethnic panoply of costumes. Scattered
throughout the piazza, six or seven mountebanks performed on
stages, entertaining with buffoons and jugglers, and selling "oyles,
soveraigne waters, amorous songs printed, apothecary drugs, and a
commonweale of other trifles."[†]

Four year earlier, Montaigne had been amazed by Venice's
150 rich prostitutes "spending money like princesses on dress and

† Coryat, Vol. 1, p. 274.

furniture, and yet having no other livelihood but that traffic; and many of the nobles of the place even keeping courtesans at their own expense, in sight of and to the knowledge of all."[†] But prostitution was just one commodity that Venice traded in. Countless vessels from around the world bobbed in the harbor, loading and unloading luxury goods. Streets were lined with shops selling the merchandise: fine fabrics, rare jewels, porcelain, carpets, furniture, and Murano glass. Hundreds of inns and restaurants did a brisk business serving the nonstop onslaught of visitors. Venice was rich, bustling, ambitious, and yet despite this, law-abiding.

Perhaps the Dandolo palace didn't please Paolo Giordano, or maybe one palace wasn't good enough for a signore of his stature. Within a couple of days, he rented another palace in Murano, the nearby island that was known worldwide for its exquisite glassmaking factories.

Delighted that such a meritorious nobleman had moved to their territory, the Venetian Senate offered Paolo Giordano a military position. This was exactly what the duke had been hoping for only three months earlier, but now he replied that as a servant of the Most Catholic King of Spain, it would not be appropriate for him to accept a commission from Venice, a nation usually at odds with the arrogant Philip II. The Senate was stung by this reply, and we can only wonder why he changed his mind. It is possible that the duke was not feeling up to snuff, and now that Vittoria was indisputably his wife, he wanted to enjoy what little time remained to them as a married couple.

Lodovico Orsini had taken up his military commission in Venice a few months earlier, and now he welcomed Paolo Giordano to town. But almost immediately the old friction between the Orsini cousin and the Orsini bride started up again: the sarcastic comments, the sniping, and the bitter complaints of both to the duke. Lodovico was painfully aware of Paolo Giordano's precarious health and must have viewed Vittoria as a hovering vulture, ready to swoop in at the moment of death, and devour whatever she could sink her talons

† Montaigne, p. 93.

into. Lodovico equally detested Vittoria's brother, the swashbuckling Marcello, who accompanied the duke and duchess to the Venetian Republic. Marcello, it seems, had nudged Lodovico out of Paolo Giordano's favor.

It is possible that this antagonism was the cause of a bloody quarrel which erupted within days of the duke's arrival. Paolo Giordano's gang of bandits got into a sword fight with Lodovico's gang of bandits, and Paolo Giordano felt it best to separate Vittoria and Marcello from Lodovico. On July 5, the duke moved to yet another rented palace, this one in Padua, twenty-five miles west of Venice.

Padua had been an independent city-state until 1405, when Venice conquered it. The watery republic, shimmering incandescently on wooden stilts, was proud to own some solid terra firma, which especially came in handy when it came to growing crops and riding horses. It was a gentle seven-hour journey from Venice to Padua. Travelers were rowed in a boat for five miles to the mainland, where horses and carriages were kept. These were then strapped to barges which were pulled by three horses on one side of a canal for twenty miles up the River Brenta.

Unlike the scintillating city of Venice, Byzantine in its excessive ornamentation, Padua was decidedly earthbound, with a solid, tidy look. It had been a university town since 1222, where young gentlemen from across Europe came to study, primarily medicine and law. In addition to academics, Padua offered special schools for fencing, riding, and dancing. Both Montaigne and Coryat admired the arched arcades under the downtown buildings where citizens could walk comfortably for many blocks in the heat of the day, and in the wind and rain.

Paduan courts had an unusual way of dealing with debtors. Those who were willing to sit with bare buttocks on a pillar in their assembly hall on three occasions would be forgiven small debts, perhaps in return for the sheer entertainment value of such a performance. Coryat described "the impudent behavior of some abject-minded varlet, who to acquit himself of his debt will most willingly expose his bare buttockes in that opprobrious and ignominious manner to the laughter of every spectator. Surely it is the strangest custome that ever I heard or read of, though that which I have related of it be the very naked truth."[†] Coryat was glad that such a law did not exist in London, where hundreds of people would be running around with bare behinds to avoid paying creditors.

Though it would have been easy enough for Paolo Giordano to drop his pants to reduce his debts, the resulting horror of the sight might have been too much for Paduan authorities. Certainly, the dignity of his blue blood would not have permitted it. Indeed, instead of trying to reduce his debts, he racked up many more. In Padua, Paolo Giordano rented two palaces, in addition to the two he already had in Venice. Forever unsated, he was now treating palaces the same way he treated lamb chops and prostitutes.

The Zeni palace by the Brenta River had beautiful gardens for summer entertaining. But he and Vittoria spent most of their time in the Foscari Palace, a sumptuous U-shaped residence with a triumphal staircase and grand reception rooms, where "they held the most beautiful parties, balls, and dances, and he was always entertaining, going to all the castles in Paduan territory as it pleased him… being overall accepted with the greatest pleasure and favor," according to a Venetian *relatione*.[‡] It was a kind of dance macabre. With all the music, feasting, and dancing, no one noticed that one of the guests had not been invited and was carrying a sickle.

As if renting four palaces in his difficult financial situation was not enough, the duke went on a shopping expedition (on credit, of course) to stuff them with beautiful furnishings. Fearing the pope would confiscate his possessions, he had brought numerous wagonloads of furniture from Rome and Bracciano, but this was not enough to fill so many palaces. He stocked up on finely wrought items of ivory, gold, and silver.

One contemporary historian reported, "He had, among other things, two carriages, the roofs of which opened and closed, each

† Coryat, Vol. 1, pp. 280-281.
‡ Cicogna, 1439, *Strani Accidenti*, p. 2.

pulled by six of the most beautiful steeds. In one of these went the most illustrious duchess his wife."[†] Vittoria finally had her carriage.

Duchess Vittoria's beauty was lauded, as were her wit and grace. Local noblewomen and the wives of top government officials vied for her friendship. She reveled in these few weeks of glory, as the sun relentlessly dropped toward the unforgiving horizon. Soon, it would burst into blood-red fury before sinking into eternal night.

† Ibid.

Chapter 18

THE ROOT OF ALL POWER

Dishonest money dwindles away, but he who gathers money little by little makes it grow.

– *Proverbs 13:11*

While the Duke of Bracciano was digging a deep financial pit for himself and his heirs as quickly as he possibly could, Sixtus V was trying to climb out of such a pit made for him by his predecessor. Gregory XIII had left the papal finances in an awful state. When he had died in April 1585, every penny of Church income was pledged through October of that year. On May 22, Sixtus told the Venetian ambassador that he despised those pontiffs who did not know how to manage their income and left huge messes for their successors to clean up. He called Gregory and his ministers *scialaquatori*, squanderers. He almost spat when he said the word, and he said it frequently.

Sixtus further told the Venetian ambassador that he had had a nightmare in which Gregory XIII was screaming to him from the agonies of Purgatory, where God had placed him for wasting the Vatican treasury. Shaken by the dream, Sixtus had dozens of Masses said for Gregory in the hopes of winging him on his way to heaven.

Within a month of his election, Sixtus reduced his court expenses by 146,000 scudi annually. He dismissed nineteen grooms and a number of chamberlains, and the salary of those who remained was reduced. After a time, he stopped paying for his employees' holidays, saying that since he had no holidays himself he didn't see why they should have any.

The papal kitchen budget, which prepared meals for hundreds of Vatican employees daily, was greatly reduced. The court, including the pope himself, ate simply prepared dishes of chicken or fish, fruits, vegetables, and bread, though Sixtus did insist on drinking good wine. And there would be no more lavish Vatican banquets. No four-foot gilded pies stuffed with whole deer, no spun sugar sculptures or piles of quails' tongues. Visiting dignitaries would partake of the same basic but tasty foods the court ate regularly.

Each new pope had the opportunity to decorate his Vatican apartments from scratch as the servants of his predecessor usually pillaged all the furniture during his final illness. But Sixtus refused to order elaborate cabinets and expensive wall hangings and banished all signs of luxury from his apartments. His carpets, which were necessary in the brief but chilly Roman winter, were of common wool, and not the glorious colorful patterns from Turkey. His candlesticks were of wood, not gold and silver, his tables and chairs plain and functional. "With this parsimony the palace was almost reduced to misery," according to one contemporary.[†]

When Sixtus's shoes got holes in them, he didn't throw them away, but had them resoled at least once. Princess Camilla, still a laundress at heart, often reprimanded her brother for wearing patched, ratty shirts. The Vicar of Christ, she said, should at least be able to afford a new shirt. But Sixtus replied that he was no *scialaquatore*. "Our elevation, my sister, does not mean we should forget the place we came from. Patches and rags are the first coat of arms of our family."[‡] Sometimes, he took off his gorgeous papal robes and wore the simple habit of a Franciscan monk.

Despite the costs of repairing the aqueducts and building new roads, Sixtus vowed to squirrel money away for important purposes. Fighting the heretics, for instance, or the Turks, who still raided the Italian coasts plucking hapless Christians from the shore and enslaving them. Money was also put away for providing bread in time of famine, combating the plague next time it struck, or finishing the embarrassing half-built dome of Saint Peter's. When Christ's Church needed so many basics, buying clothes and furniture, employing

†   Strozzi, *Vita del Sommo*, Folio 48b.
‡   Leti, *Sixte V*, Vol. 2, p. 452.

hundreds of needless servants, and throwing lavish banquets seemed a sinful waste.

"Poor princes, and especially a poor pope," Sixtus said, "are a laughingstock even to children, especially in times when everything is accomplished by money; a wise prince ought to follow the example of the ants who during the summer store up provision for the winter."[†]

He announced to his cardinals his intention of socking away one million gold scudi a year in the treasury room of Castel Sant'Angelo to be used only in times of urgent need. But Cardinal Farnese was almost apoplectic when he heard this. "He sometimes opposed the plans of the pope with great agility," wrote one contemporary. "And he feared that the pope was a man greedy for money, wanting only to accumulate it, and not having it serve any purpose, but just because he was avaricious he would impose grave taxes. He said that his grandfather, Pope Paul III, had tried to save money, but it was impossible."[‡]

Sixtus was doubly offended – at being contradicted again by Cardinal Farnese, and that someone else had come up with his idea. He replied, "It is no great wonder, Monsignor, that your grandfather was not able to increase the treasury of the Church because there were many great squanderers who are not alive, thank God, in our time." According to the chronicler, "He went on to describe the multitude of sons and daughters the pope had, and nephews of all sorts, and the many and diverse squanderings of all sorts of ecclesiastical benefits to enrich them. When he heard this, Farnese was silent and said nothing more."[§]

In order to raise the money, the pope imposed a variety of taxes on goods and services and sold a number of Church and government offices. Each office sold was a kind of investment, paying a certain annual return until the office holder died. When that occurred, the Church could sell it again. For instance, under Gregory XIII the office of treasurer sold for 15,000 scudi. But Sixtus sold it for 50,000.

[†] Pastor, *Popes*, Vol. 21, p. 121.
[‡] Strozzi, *Vita del Sommo*, folio 45a.
[§] Ibid., folios 45b–46a.

Throughout the length of his reign, the sale of offices brought him 608,510 gold scudi and 401,806 silver scudi.

Gregory also saved money by reducing the number of papal troops. Every branch of government was instructed to reduce needless expenditure and operate only on strict necessities. The pope saved an additional 150,000 scudi a year by these measures.

Sixtus looked into the Vatican financial records and found that many nobles had borrowed large sums and never repaid them. He decreed that everyone who owed money to the papal treasury had two months to pay up or their property would be confiscated. Within those two months, the treasury received 600,000 scudi, some of which had been owed for twenty years.

The pope kept his promise of amassing the one million gold scudi a year, "dedicating them to Christ our Lord, to Mary, the blessed Virgin and Mother of God, and to the holy Apostles Peter and Paul."[†] It is likely that the above-mentioned individuals would have been bewildered by such worldly treasure, but the pope knew exactly what to do with it. Every three months, he went into the treasury room of the Castel Sant'Angelo and thrust a stick into the giant leather-bound treasure chests where the coins were deposited. He was overheard to say, "Now from a poor vegetable grower I have become a rich gardener."[‡] It was soon acknowledged that the pope was the richest prince in Europe, even if he did wear patched shoes.

Sixtus hired clever Jewish financiers to advise him in fiscal management. Over the centuries, Europe's Jewish communities had become well versed in the art of finance and trade. The New Testament prohibited usury (lending money at interest), which left the trade wide open to Jews. Christians frequently needed loans to build a house, finance a dowry, or wage a war, and Jews, prohibited from many other professions, were happy to oblige them.

But a pope employing Jews as his advisors shocked many good Catholics. Unlike his predecessors, Sixtus respected Jews because they, like he, understood how to save money and how to spend it without

[†] Pastor, *Popes*, Vol. 21, p. 123.
[‡] Sarazani, p. 97.

wasting it. A certain Jew named Lopez, of whom Camilla was very fond, became his chief financial advisor.

Sixtus also respected Jews for being his most law-abiding citizens. It was almost unheard of for a Jew to throw punches in taverns, pick pockets, set fire to houses, rape girls, or duel in the streets, crimes committed by good Christian Italians with alarming frequency. Those few misbehaving Jews were dealt with by Jewish community leaders.

For centuries, Jewish doctors had been known as the best healers in Europe. Their medical tradition was rooted in Islamic practices and had been passed down from ancestors who studied in Persia and the Moorish empire in Spain. In 1555, Paul IV decreed that Jewish physicians could not treat Christian patients, resulting in the unfortunate deaths of many a good Catholic at the hands of well-meaning Christian butcher-doctors.

Pope Paul had also forced all Roman Jews to live inside a walled and flood-prone section of the city next to the Tiber River, where their movements could be watched and controlled. They were locked in at night, and Christian guards were stationed at the gate throughout the day to note their comings and goings, requiring a fee for each entry and exit. This area became known as the ghetto. The first ghetto was created in Venice in 1516, when Jews were relegated to the area of an old foundry, called a *getto*, from the word *gettare*, "to cast."

In 1566, Pius V decreed that Jews had to wear a yellow circle on one shoulder and limited them to living in Rome and the Adriatic port city of Ancona, and he permitted that only to keep trade alive. Although Sixtus often agreed with the decisions of his mentor, here he diverged. He opened up the entire Papal States to Jews. Formerly prohibited from selling foodstuffs lest they poison good Christians, Sixtus allowed them to work once more in the food industry. He also allowed Jewish businessmen to work hand in hand with Christians for the economic advantage of the Papal States. Perhaps most shocking, he said that Jews and Christians could be friends without any punishment at all. Jews, he decreed, can "enjoy in the places where they are that utility, commodity and privileges that the Christians enjoy." They were permitted to "open schools and synagogues, where they perform their offices and rites."[†]

Former popes had taken away Jewish holy books and burned them. But Sixtus decreed, "We will tolerate these Jews and their rites, constitutions, and laws, and similarly we permit them to possess all Jewish books … [that do not] blaspheme the Holy Church."[‡]

One rude staff member of a noble house, when passing a Jew, grabbed his hat and threw it into the Tiber. It was a common insult, and by no means one of the worst. Jews were used to it, and it is likely that the Jew didn't file an official complaint about such a minor infraction. But every example of bad behavior found its way back to Sixtus in the form of a daily report, and when the pope read about this one, he was furious. He had the malefactor whipped through the ghetto to the jubilant hoots and howls of the Jewish population. Never had they seen a pope give them such justice. As a result, Jews were some of the fiercest supporters of Sixtus. He taxed them heavily, of course, as he did the Christians, but most of them didn't mind paying extra, "for the good life that they enjoyed without being molested by anyone."[§]

While Sixtus, with the help of brilliant Jewish financiers, was putting the papal finances in order, he expected his subjects to put their personal finances in order as well. During the two decades he had lived in Rome, he had observed how few people ever paid their bills, the most glaring example being the Duke of Bracciano, who at that very moment was renting no less than four palaces in the Venetian Republic and cramming them with furniture bought on credit.

Poor merchants who begged rich nobles to pay just a portion of what was owed were often scornfully turned away, sometimes beaten. Some merchants went bankrupt because of unpaid accounts and became a financial burden to the Papal States. Sixtus, who was planning to deal with this vexing issue eventually, was spurred into action by a certain merchant who delivered goods to the papal palace.

† De Feo, p. 163.
‡ Ibid.
§ Anon., p. 588.

The merchant complained to the pope about a client of his who had owed him a large debt for years and hadn't paid a penny. With the thought of Paolo Giordano's debts still festering, the pope had the debtor arrested, thrown into Castel Sant'Angelo, and criminally tried for having usurped the goods of others. The man was forced to pay the merchant in full, and the papal treasury confiscated 1,500 scudi of his property as a fine.

Sixtus issued an order to all merchants to bring him records of their debtors because he would insist that every bill be paid. When debtors heard about this, many of them "went to search for the merchants with money in their hands, begging them for the love of God to take their names out of the book."[†]

Of course, some debtors were in no position to pay their debts back so quickly. The pope assigned prelates to conduct personal interviews with them and look closely into their finances. If they truly could not pay the entire debt, the amount was reduced by half, with the pope personally paying the merchant the remainder. Those individuals who later came into money, however, were expected to pay the pope back. And those who lied about their assets to have their debts reduced were hanged.

The Roman economy suddenly surged. Business was brisk as merchants raked in old debts, paid taxes to the papal treasury on them, and invested the rest in their shops, expanding store fronts, hiring additional employees, and buying new goods to sell. Many merchants were now in a position to buy luxury goods for themselves from other merchants. Overnight, the middle class of Rome was flush with money.

Everyone was now obliged to base spending on income (a novel idea), and no one was permitted to live on borrowed money. Some families overwhelmed by debt fled the Papal States, but Sixtus didn't care. "A well-ruled state has no need of subjects who live at the expense of their creditors," he said. "The city will be much more tranquil. The rogues who think they never have to pay their debts will change their conduct in ceasing to eat the goods of others. And I hope that by these means the apostolic chamber will be much richer than ever before."[†]

Those individuals who blithely ignored the pope's new rules were the employees of cardinals. It had become a tradition that those working for a prince of the Church could not be imprisoned for debts or have their possessions confiscated to pay them. Many people who had never worked for a cardinal in their lives purchased letters from cardinals stating that they were employees. Sixtus decreed that within eight days all the servants of cardinals must pay their debts, and if they did not, the cardinals would have to pay the debts for them. Some cardinals agreed with the pope that the time had come to reform this abuse. But a delegation of twelve cardinals who would be obliged to cover their servants' massive debts went to the pope and said they were outraged at the insult.

The pope replied, "It is certain, my lord cardinals, that you must praise this resolution to remove from your houses the subject of such a scandal that ruins your decorum and good character…. What would the heretics say when they hear that those cardinals, who are expected to edify the world with a good ecclesiastical life…defend those who do wrong to their neighbors?" Such behavior, he continued, "not only scandalizes heretics, but mortifies good Catholics."[‡] Then he sent the cardinals away.

The pope ordered the governor to obtain from all Roman merchants lists of debts owed not only by cardinals' employees, but also the servants of Roman barons, such as the Orsinis, and even foreign ambassadors. The ambassadors were horrified that the diplomatic immunity of their debt-ridden servants was being wrested away and made a flurry of protests. But the pope stated that there was no advantage to his realm when foreigners came to Rome and stole from honest merchants. Such servants should stay home. From now on, those embassy employees who refused to pay their debts would be arrested and their possessions seized.

† Leti, *Sixte V*, Vol. 2, p. 30.
‡ Anon., pp. 257-258.

While Sixtus's measures greatly helped honest merchants, he was also on the lookout for dishonest ones. He hired six secret shoppers who saw first-hand the kind of merchandise being offered and noted which merchants treated poor shoppers worse than rich ones. Wandering through the market with baskets, they noticed quickly if a vendor used the wrong weights and measures. The foodstuffs of these merchants were confiscated and given to the poor. When bad fruit was being sold as good, it was seized and either thrown in the Tiber or given to pigs "so that no shop owner dared to sell bad merchandise," wrote the chronicler.[†]

Periodically, the pope would have his cortege stop in front of a bakery where he would order his servants to bring him bread. If it was not of good quality, if the baker were mixing in beans and stalks with the grain to pocket money, Sixtus would seize all the bread and give it to the poor. In one particularly egregious case, the pope hanged a baker for mixing ashes in with the grain.

"In the piazzas they found the very best [bread]," wrote a *relatione* author, "and in great abundance, and the bakers didn't commit any fraud in making it, nor in selling it."[‡]

Having been raised in a family so poor that they often went hungry, Sixtus understood the importance of nutritious bread at a fair price for the poor. He donated 200,000 scudi annually to subsidize Rome's bread supply and make loans to poor peasants outside the city to grow grain.

In another effort to help the poor of Rome, Sixtus passed a law that all taverns must offer a half-glass of wine because some people simply couldn't afford a full glass. Mixing a half-glass with water was still a satisfying drink for a poor person. One night, donning shoddy patched robes, he slipped inside a tavern and sat down.

When the tavern keeper asked him what he wanted to drink, Sixtus said he would like a half-glass of wine. The host replied there was no such thing as a half-glass of wine. Sixtus said in a shaking

† Ibid., p. 262.
‡ Strozzi, *Vita del Sommo*, folio 25a.

voice, "I only have enough quattrini for half a glass. And Pope Sixtus has ordered tavern keepers to sell a half-glass."

The host replied that he didn't care and added, "Go to the pope and tell him that I don't want to go up so many stairs for a half-glass of wine."[†] Sixtus obediently shuffled off. Back in the papal palace he gave orders for the governor to arrest the tavern keeper and build a gallows in front of the building. The tavernkeeper was hanged before noon the next day.

† Anon., p. 404.

Chapter 19

DESPERATION

We are troubled on every side, yet not distressed; we are perplexed, but not in despair; persecuted, but not forsaken; cast down, but not destroyed.

– *2 Corinthians 4:8-9*

Safely ensconced in Padua, Paolo Giordano received news from Rome that the pope's edicts were getting worse and worse with each day that passed. He must have realized that many of the decrees seemed to be payback aimed at him and Vittoria, and those like them. What would happen to Vittoria after Paolo Giordano's death? She would probably not be able to return to her family in the Papal States.

The duke wanted to extend a network of support for Vittoria outside the pope's territory. Already the dukes of Urbino and Ferrara had recognized the validity of their marriage. Now the ducal couple wanted Tuscany – far more powerful, and bordering the Papal States – to do so. This was an extremely naïve desire, considering how protective Grand Duke Francesco was of the eventual inheritance of his nephew and Paolo Giordano's son, Virginio, an inheritance which was clearly threatened by the charming new bride.

Undeterred by common sense, as soon as the duke and duchess arrived in Venice they called on the father and brother of Bianca Cappello, the former mistress and now the wife of Grand Duke Francesco of Tuscany. Three weeks later, on July 19, Vittoria wrote to the Tuscan grand duchess from Padua:

To the Most Serene and Revered Signora:

If up until now I have not made my respects to your Serene Highness, it was only out of observance and humility. Now, being come to Venice, where I have had the fortune to meet and be of service to your Highness's most illustrious brother and his consort, from whom I have received many favors and graces, I didn't want to wait for another occasion to make myself known as your most humble servant, as I have been for many years because of your virtue.

Not many spoke of Bianca's virtue, and we can only wonder if the grand duchess was puzzled when she read this. Vittoria continued:

Since my most excellent lord has deigned to make me worthy of being his consort, I am now much more obliged and wish to serve you. His Excellency is a particularly devoted servant of your Highness, and I ask you to accept me as a true and ardent servant, not ceding to anyone else in terms of respect and fidelity. I ask you to command me and to maintain me in the favor of his most serene Highness your consort. Kissing with humility the clothing of the one and the other Highness [Bianca and Francesco], I pray God to give you every happiness.

You most serene Highness's most humble and devoted servant, Vittoria Accoramboni Orsini[†]

When Bianca wrote back with a short note addressing Vittoria as *Excellency*, the honorific of a duchess, Vittoria practically fell over herself with gratitude. Many royal wives would not have lowered themselves to send polite letters to a dubious woman like Vittoria, but Bianca was not exactly to the purple born herself. For years, she had been the infamous mistress of the grand duke, who finally married her despite universal protest after his unloved Habsburg wife breathed her last. But recognition by the wife of the Grand Duke of Tuscany, as sweet as it was, was not the official recognition Vittoria wanted from the grand duke himself.

Determined to gain some hint of recognition of his wife's status, Paolo Giordano wrote to Francesco, giving him news of the safe arrival of himself and Vittoria in Padua, evidently hoping the grand duke would respond with some mention of her. But Francesco replied, "Your Excellency can imagine my contentment when I learned of

† Gnoli, pp. 446-447.

your safe arrival in Padua. Here the weather is varied and tends to coolness and to humidity… and it makes me happy that you can expect a season perfectly appropriate for taking the baths. I wish you good health with a good cure."[†]

The reply was shockingly rude in that it made no mention of Paolo Giordano's wife. Every letter of the time was supposed to send greetings to, and wish good health for, the close relatives of the recipient. Yet Francesco wrote as if Vittoria did not exist. Clearly, the grand duke did not acknowledge her as Paolo Giordano's wife. On August 10, Vittoria set to work once more on Bianca:

> To the most Serene and Revered Signora,
>
> I kiss the hands of your most serene Highness for the favor you have done for me with the very short letter, for which I remain to you in perpetual obligation… I beg you to favor me with your commands, and to favor me with your most serene consort, as a creature and servant of your Highness worthy of his favor and of his commands, kissing with all humility and reverence the hands of both of you, I ask God for your complete contentment.

The duke, too, worked on Bianca. The same day he wrote:

> It has pleased your Highness to show favor to my wife, even though your Highness is a princess so great…. A tranquil future for me and for my family depends on this as well as on many other favors that flow from the bounty of your Highness in this particular. Since it has pleased your Highness to favor me with so much signal favor, I ask you to work for me so that the grand duke my signor favors me with a similar favor, because all my fortune and my life will be spent for his Highness with all the honor and reputation I have.

Swaggering a little, he added, "I am not unuseful regarding friends, or things, or relatives."[‡]

Bianca wrote back that she had gotten absolutely nowhere with her husband, who steadfastly refused to recognize Vittoria. On September 7, Paolo Giordano wrote her again:

† Gnoli, p. 447.
‡ Ibid., pp. 448-449.

To the most Serene and Revered Signora,

> I kiss the hands of your Highness for the favor that you have done
> for me with the Highness of the grand duke, and I want again to
> ask your Highness to help me receive this signal favor from the
> grand duke, which I desire above anything else, she being already
> my wife… Since it is his duty as a just prince… to favor me with
> his protection and favor, he must not outrage my wife… And if
> there has been an error, his Highness with his authority should
> forgive my imperfections.†

But this letter, too, achieved nothing. The duke, who became easily
obsessed when he didn't get his way, wrote Bianca again on October
12, insisting she persuade her husband to recognize Vittoria. This
time there was no answer.

*   *   *

While most men of the time would have gladly lied about childhood
poverty, or at least not spoken about it, the pope brought up his
former indigence frequently. Looking around crowds of well-born
nobles, he realized they had had to accomplish very little to rise to
their positions, and frequently pricked them with this fact. He, on the
other hand, had accomplished a great deal. "Instead of blushing for
his poverty, he made it into an honor," wrote Gregorio Leti.‡

When foreign visitors delivered the usual flowery compliments
on the illustrious nobility of his family, he laughed, describing a house
with holes in the roof and walls. "With the sun coming in from all
sides," he said, "I can boast of having one of the most brilliant houses
in Europe."§ He then went on to describe his youth spent raising pigs,
cutting wood, planting vegetables and, as a monk, ringing the church
bells and sweeping the floors. Those listening were often too stunned
to respond; it was as if the pope had just confessed to horrible crimes.

Listeners were also shocked when the pope spoke of politics in
gardening terms: clipping, uprooting, fertilizing, pruning, watering,

---

† Ibid, p. 449.
‡ Leti, *Sixte V*, Vol. 1, p. 67.
§ Ibid., p. 68.

and harvesting. He liked to nip things in the bud and separate the wheat from the chaff. He spoke of the Biblical laborers in the vineyard, the barren fig tree, and the farmer sowing his seed on good soil and rocky ground.

Sixtus had no pastimes, unlike many of his predecessors on the papal throne who played cards for hours at a time. He took no vacations and was a "great enemy of recreation," according to a *relatione*, scorning the country pleasure villas of the popes and cardinals. "The treasure of the Church is for the Church," he said, "and must be saved only for the poor… The blood of Christ should not be spent for the recreation of popes and the pleasure of their relatives."[†]

He spent every waking moment working, and sometimes he didn't go to bed at all, reading and writing dispatches until dawn and starting a busy new day without a wink of sleep. At other times, when there were no emergencies, he slept long hours to catch up. Even in his sleep he talked out loud about government business. His servants were instructed to wake him at any time of night if a courier arrived with important news or letters. He said, "We want to be in control of sleep and not permit sleep to be in control of us."[‡]

Sixtus only left the papal palace to attend church services across town, to look into the needs of his subjects, or to check on his building projects. The pope felt that time was scarce. He always had the irksome feeling that his reign would be short.

Sixtus loved wine, and although he never became inebriated, he often had three or four different kinds served at each meal. He usually sat for two hours at meals, but most of this time was spent in discussing business with his guests or listening to his secretaries read dispatches and reports.

The Sacred College was shocked at his nonstop work, and several cardinals took a renewed interest in finding out exactly how old he was. As a wheezing, limping cardinal, he had added seven years to his age, giving the year of his birth as 1514. But once elected pope

[†] Strozzi, *Vita del Sommo*, 37b.
[‡] Anon., p. 499.

he deducted six, having been born, he declared, in 1527. Sixtus had gone from the age of seventy to fifty-seven in a matter of hours. The cardinals secretly sent to his birthplace for his baptismal records, which indicated that he had been born in December 1521.

Periodically, the pope would visit without notice his former monastery of the Saints Apostles. He would walk inside, knock on the door of a monk's cell chosen at random, go in and meet the monk. He wanted to see if the monk had a hangover, or a woman or boy in the room, or if he wasn't there at all, having perhaps spent the night at a tavern. Similarly, he wanted to see which monks were on their knees praying or studying Scripture.

Early one morning, he happened to knock on the door of a new monk who had just arrived from Naples and hadn't heard about the pope's unheralded visits. The monk was sound asleep when he heard the banging on his door. "Who is it?" he asked, groggy and irritated. "It's the pope," was the response. Thinking it was a fellow monk playing a joke on him, the monk cried, "You're full of shit."

The monastery's father guardian was horrified and wanted to barge in and punish the monk, but the pope, quoting from a Psalm, said, laughing, "The poor are lifted from the dunghill."[†] Clearly, he was referring to himself, and his having been born on top of a huge pile of the stuff. In a way, the foul-mouthed monk had been right.

All popes had to be aware of possible poisoning attempts and Sixtus, due to the hatred he had incurred among the cardinals, nobles, and ambassadors, had much more reason than most popes to be watchful. He had guards in his kitchen keeping their eye on his food the moment it was delivered, throughout its preparation, and all the way up to his table. Then food tasters nibbled from each plate, as everyone else in the room watched to see if they would grab their throats and collapse. Sixtus was even suspicious of the Holy Communion wafer. Instead of eating it whole, he broke it in half and gave one part to the sacristan standing nearby to eat, sometimes the right half, and sometimes the left. If the sacristan didn't fall over stone dead, the pope would consume his half.

† Ibid., p. 377.

VICES REBUKED

And the man that committeth adultery with another man's wife, even he that committeth adultery with his neighbor's wife, the adulterer and the adulteress shall surely be put to death.

– Leviticus 20:10

For years, Sixtus had looked on the moral failings of his fellow Romans with revulsion. Now, as pope, he was in a position to do something about it. Astrology, gambling, and taking the Lord's name in vain would be punished with fines, whipping, exposure in the stocks, and, for multiple offenses life in the galleys. But casting a horoscope, rolling dice, and saying *Goddamnit* were the least of Rome's moral problems.

It is likely that Sixtus, who had joined the monastery at ten, had never had sex in his life. He was known for his "egregious chastity," according to one contemporary report, and while he respected sex in marriage as the means of producing children, he despised illicit sex and was determined to punish it severely.† He issued a law prohibiting the hanging of obscene pictures in taverns, which served as goads to the private parts. Then he proclaimed that those guilty of incest, sodomy, and abortion would be executed. He was particularly horrified at parents who sold their children into prostitution. One woman was found guilty of peddling her young teenager to an older man; the girl was forced to sit in the front row and watch her mother's execution, wearing the jewels the man had given her.

But upon further reflection, Sixtus decided this didn't go far enough. He would make adultery a capital crime. The cardinals were horrified, fearing that half of Rome's population would be executed,

† Strozzi, *Vita del Sommo*, p. 34b.

and some were a bit worried about themselves. They ran to the pope, begging him not to issue the ordinance. But the pope replied that "an infected arm had to be amputated or the entire body would be vitiated."[†]

In fairness to the people, the pope gave them good warning. Old adulteries would be ignored, but with immediate effect new ones would be punished with the full rigor of the law. The pope was particularly disgusted by the custom of poor men selling their wives to lords and princes. "The husbands would support the family in this way, letting the lords have sex with their wives while they went to another place," the chronicler reported. "This greatly afflicted his Holiness, who thought there was nothing more monstrous in the world than men acting more like dogs than men, making a business off of their own wives."[‡] He offered rewards to people who reported the adulteries of friends, relatives, and neighbors.

Sixtus discovered that a certain Ludovico Piedemantello had kept a concubine for many years, despite the fact that the gentleman was married to "a lady of signal prudence" by whom he had sired five children.[§] The pope warned him in writing to cease and desist from visiting his concubine and then stationed spies outside her house.

It is odd that, initially at least, no one took the pope's warnings seriously. Sure enough, Ludovico was seen entering the house and arrested. Despite the pleas of his wife, who threw herself at the pope's feet, and the petitions of five noble families who were related to Piedemantello, the pope gave the order to behead him and his concubine. There were dozens of similar cases, and Roman men, who had looked on adultery as a prerogative of the male gender, suddenly found themselves obliged to be faithful to their wives.

The pope also wanted to eliminate prostitution in Rome. But when he floated this idea shortly after his coronation, the city council informed him that it would ruin Rome economically. Banks would fail as many had loaned great sums to prostitutes, who usually paid

---

[†]   De Feo, p. 114.
[‡]   Anon., p. 244.
[§]   Ibid., p. 319.

them back promptly. The customs duty officers, who had bought their positions, insisted they should be reimbursed 20,000 scudi a year for the taxes they would lose if the prostitutes – who imported luxury goods – were exiled. Landlords would lose good tenants who paid on time and in cash. Worse, when men didn't visit prostitutes, sometimes they visited the wives and daughters of virtuous citizens or, heaven forbid, satisfied their desires with other men.

An economic asset all around, the prostitutes were also good for tourism. As one Roman courtesan declared in a popular novel of the time, her clients were "the kind of men who come to see Rome, and having seen the antique rubbish, want also to see the modern kind – that is the ladies."[†]

Just such a visitor was Michel de Montaigne. After seeing the Vatican and the ancient monuments, he set out to gawk at the prostitutes and found them advertising their wares from their windows, seated on cushions and leaning out. The streets below were full of men shopping for women. "The more licentious," Montaigne wrote, "in order to have a better view upwards, have a sort of open skylight in the roof of their coach."[‡] Alas, the view from the street was largely an optical illusion. Montaigne reported upon meeting the women, they weren't nearly as attractive as they had seemed at a distance.

Pope Sixtus particularly hated prostitutes displaying their wares near the Vatican. He forced them into a kind of whore's ghetto, known as the Ortaccio, the only place they could work legally. Sixtus ordered the Ortaccio prostitutes to paint their doors green to make clear to all exactly what kind of house it was. Guards were stationed in the hallways behind the green doors to interrogate the men entering to see if they were monks, priests, or husbands. If so, they would be beheaded. Had the married Michel de Montaigne visited the prostitutes four years later, his status as a foreigner under the protection of the French king and ambassador would not have prevented an ignominious execution.

[†] Masson, p. 24.
[‡] Montaigne, p. 156.

Naturally, business declined steeply, as wealthy married men had been the mainstay of the prostitutes' earnings. Many women packed up their baggage wagons, jumped into their opulent coaches, and rumbled off to greater pickings in Naples and Venice.

The prostitute who dared to ply her trade outside the Ortaccio would be severely punished. A big, burly bailiff would hoist her over his shoulders, with her skirts pulled over her head, and expose her bare behind to a hooting crowd. The executioner would then whip her behind with fifty strokes. One visitor to Rome who witnessed such a performance reported that the executioner "in a short time reduced her white bottom to a bloody red." Having been set on her feet, the woman pulled down her skirts, shook herself like a dog, and staggered off "just as if she had come from a couple of weddings" to the loud cheers of spectators.[†]

Even virtuous noblewomen now had to behave more circumspectly. Each family's carriage bore a coat of arms on the doors (a kind of sixteenth-century license plate), and when the pope saw a carriage stuffed with luxurious bejeweled women, he made a note of the coat of arms and sent the governor to talk to them about their attire. On the streets of Rome, more modest clothing became popular.

Many of Sixtus's new regulations were inextricably connected to Francesco's murder. A group of lawless bandits had killed him, and the pope was exterminating every lawless bandit he could get his hands on. The weapons that had done his nephew in were knives and guns, and these he outlawed on the streets of Rome on penalty of death. An arrogant nobleman – Paolo Giordano Orsini – had arranged the murder, and Sixtus was putting all arrogant noblemen in their place, taking away their privileges and diluting their power. That particular nobleman had enormous debts, and the pope was forcing all his subjects to pay their debts immediately. Francesco's death had been caused by a flirtation (and many believed it had, in fact, been adultery) between his wife and a nobleman. Adultery was now punished with death. Remembering that Paolo Giordano had given Vittoria two gowns, one of gold thread and the other of silver, Sixtus

† Masson, p. 136.

decreed that women could only possess one such gown of precious metal threads.

*   *   *

The streets of Venice had become almost as dangerous as those of Rome had been under Pope Gregory. Now that Lodovico's gangsters could no longer brawl with Paolo Giordano's, who were tucked away in Padua, they picked on honest Venetian citizens, thereby disturbing the serenity of the most serene republic. The Senate decided that such men were wasted in civilization. Their swashbuckling violence would be put to better use in fighting Turks on the Greek island of Corfu, which was used as a Venetian trading post.

Lodovico was named governor of Corfu but found reasons to delay his departure. He needed to obtain the pope's permission for his wife, Giulia Savelli, to journey from Rome to Venice as he wanted to take her with him. He also required time to round up men, weapons, and provisions.

It seems likely that Lodovico kept postponing his trip because he was keeping a careful eye on the duke's health. Though he should have stayed full-time in his rented Venetian palace, collecting supplies for his voyage to Corfu, Lodovico moved into the Contarini Palace in Padua, a couple of blocks away from Paolo Giordano's Foscari palace. Vittoria could not have been pleased at the sinister shadow following her.

On October 30, the duke and duchess visited a Paduan notary, Francesco Rosati, to make a will, which Paolo Giordano wrote in his own hand. Feeling death approaching, Paolo Giordano was worried about Vittoria, who was "poor in reputation, as well as in possessions, little favored by the Orsinis, and without hopes of any support after his death," according to a *relatione*.[†]

He named his thirteen-year-old son Virginio his heir and stated that Vittoria should get back her 5,000 scudi dowry, as well as the super dowry of 20,000 scudi that he had promised her on their wedding day. In the two years following his death, she would receive

---

† Cicogna, *Maritaggio*, folio 43a.

an additional 60,000 scudi. Moreover, Virginio must give her 16,000 scudi cash to buy a palace and a vineyard or villa in Rome. Virginio was further required to let her reside in every palace he inherited from his father, providing her during her stay with bread, wine, and firewood for forty retainers, and straw and hay for fifteen horses.

Paolo Giordano left other legacies worth 16,800 scudi. Some 8,000 scudi were to be used to build a monastery in Bracciano as penance for his hefty sins, while another 1,000 was to buy the statue of the Virgin of Loreto a magnificent chalice, no doubt a bribe for her to convince Saint Peter to open the pearly gates. He wanted an ornate family tomb to be built in the Basilica of Loreto, with statues of himself and Vittoria and their coats or arms. He named as his executors the dukes of Ferrara and Urbino.

Later that day, the duke called in another notary, Tiberio Valento, to write a codicil, which Paolo Giordano signed. After all, it was possible that Virginio, guided by his cunning de Medici uncles, wouldn't give Vittoria a single scudo, let alone allow her and her forty-person entourage to reside at his palaces. Vittoria might not be able to return to the Papal States, not even to live with her parents, if the pope forbade her to do so, or if the Orsinis and de Medicis made threats. She might find herself penniless, friendless, and adrift.

But Paolo Giordano realized he could provide her with a legacy located in the Venetian Republic, where the pope and the de Medicis couldn't get their hands on it. This legacy consisted of the valuable items he had bought and stored in his various rented palaces. No matter that they weren't paid for; his creditors would have to look to his primary heir, Virginio, for payment.

Vittoria's indisputable inheritance would include the two convertible carriages the duke had bought; the twelve superb horses to pull them; the beds, wardrobes, tables, desks, and chairs of marquetry and ivory; the enormous expensive tapestries of mythological figures covering the walls; her sumptuous rainbow of gowns ornamented with pearls and rubies; her jewel box bursting with gold chains and gemstones; and the silver platters, gold cups, and porcelain dishes he had bought to entertain all those smiling noble couples who gladly recognized Vittoria as his wife. Such goods were called *mobili* – the word often used for furniture – but this literally meant *mobile items*, including animals, those things not cemented into or bolted onto a building.

Several contemporaries estimated the value of these goods at the eye-popping sum of 100,000 scudi. Armed with such valuable items, Vittoria could sell them, one by one, and live comfortably for many years even if her Roman legacies never materialized. The *mobili* were absolutely vital to her future.

But Paolo Giordano's grandiose wishes regarding his estate failed to take into consideration his mountain of debts. Creditors who waited patiently for years while their debtor was alive snarled for their payment like ravenous wolves the moment the debtor died. Virginio, as principal heir, would be required to satisfy hundreds of thousands of scudi in debts that his father had contracted before he even met Vittoria. He would have to pay Venetian vendors tens of thousands of scudi for her *mobili* and hand over more than 100,000 scudi cash as her widow's portion. But the estate had almost no cash. Virginio would be forced to sell much of his duchy to come up with it.

The duke's health deteriorated quickly. He had swelled to such alarming proportions that he could barely move and suffered constant pain. Worried about the harsh Paduan winter and Lodovico's menacing proximity, on November 1, the Orsinis moved to the beautiful town of Salò, on Lake Garda, some eighty miles west of Padua, where they rented a fifth palace. Unlike the other towns surrounding the lake, Salò relinquishes its grasp on summer unwillingly. It is a subtropical sliver, where thousands of lemon and orange trees thrive in its mild climate.

It would take time to pack up the numerous wagons with the expensive furnishings the duke had bought for his Paduan palaces. Servants were instructed to bring the items to Salò as soon as possible. Their new quarters had belonged to the recently deceased Sforza Pallavicino, Captain General of the Republic of Venice, and the property fronted the lake. The edifice was an architectural hybrid; a medieval fortress and turrets faced the narrow road that ran past it, but on the lakeside it was a Renaissance palace, with countless spacious windows. There were two main stories, with a servants' mezzanine under the roof.

The service quarters were located on the ground floor, including an enormous kitchen with a well reaching down into the lake water. A wide staircase led to the *piano nobile*; here, the central room was fifty feet wide and twenty-five feet high, with a ceiling of unpainted wooden coffers of hexagons and rectangles, interspersed with heavy beams. A gigantic hearth adorned one end, and seven doors radiated off the three interior walls to corridors and bedchambers beyond. This enormous room was designed for banquets and balls. But the Orsinis would be holding no festivities here.

The duke felt terribly unwell. It was fortunate for him that the lake was within a few yards of the palace itself, and the sound of the waves washing the shore must have gently lulled him to sleep, a place without constant nagging pain. As lovely as the palace was, Vittoria urged the duke to travel further from the threats of Rome and to shake off Lodovico, who was certainly taking his time going to Corfu. Switzerland, for instance, that bastion of heretics, would be safe from the long reach of Sixtus. In Switzerland, they would be physically safe, although the question of what they would live on was a difficult one to answer. It is likely the King of Spain would withhold all pensions from a couple who had chosen to live among Protestants, and the Grand Duke of Tuscany and Cardinal de Medici would make sure that all income from lands in the Papal States went to Virginio.

Another problem was the journey itself, which would require a jolting carriage ride over the Alps, along passes which by early November were already piled high with snow. How would they ever get their heavy wagons of valuable, unpaid-for furniture over the highest peaks in Europe? Moreover, a winter Alpine journey was a daunting proposition for the most robust individual. Clearly, the duke's health was not up to it, and he wanted to spend his last few days gazing at the shimmering lake, hearing the gentle slap of its waves against the shore below.

It was a beautiful, peaceful spot to die.

Chapter 21

THE LITTLE BOOK OF
DEBTS OWED

*I looked, and there before me was a pale horse! Its rider was named
Death, and Hades was following close behind him.*

– Revelation 6:8

In his first months in office, the pope had brought safety to the
Papal States. He had created a fair legal system and a good bread
supply. His engineers were creating reliable waterworks at record
speed and building wide new roads. Due to his stringent financial
measures, gold ducats were piling up in Castel Sant'Angelo to carry
the country through times of need. Now, Sixtus took the time to
look into the old leather-bound journals he had carried around for
decades, the little books of debts he must pay and debts he was owed.

As a monk, he had had a benefactor named Capponelli who
had provided him with money and advice. Sixtus sent out men to
search for Capponelli, who discovered that he had been dead for
some time, along with his wife, and they had had no children. But
there still remained a debt to be paid. Sixtus learned that Capponelli
had nephews. The eldest was in the army, and the pope made him a
captain of infantry. The younger boys he sent to the best schools, and
he bought houses for their parents.

Sixtus found one notation from the 1540s, when he had been
a young monk in the town of Macerata and needed to buy a pair of
shoes. The shoemaker wanted seven giulios for them, but Fra Felice
had had only six. He told the shoemaker that if he cut the price by one
giulio, he would pay it back when he became pope. "And I promise
to add interest to it," he said. Laughing, the shoemaker replied, "I am

happy to do it, seeing you so well disposed to accept the papacy." He sold him the shoes for six, and Fra Felice wrote the shoemaker's name in his little book for repayment once he became pope, which made the shoemaker laugh even harder.

Forty years had passed. According to the chronicler, "Having been made pope, he checked his little book to see what he had owed and sent word to Macerata to see if the shoemaker was still alive. He had the local governor send him to Rome without telling him why."

The shoemaker, now a venerable seventy-three, was mystified as to why Sixtus had summoned him. Word of the pope's severity had spread throughout the Papal States, and the shoemaker must have worried that he was going to be imprisoned or even executed. As soon as he arrived in Rome, the pope commanded him to come to the Vatican for an audience. After the man nervously kissed his feet, Sixtus asked, "Do you ever remember seeing me in Macerata?"

The astonished shoemaker didn't remember. He had seen the pope in Macerata? Afraid of contradicting the pope, he remained mute as a stone. The pope continued, "So, you don't remember having sold us a pair of shoes?" The shoemaker was more shocked than before. He had sold the pope a pair of shoes?

Summoning up all his courage, the trembling man replied, "Holy Sainted Father, I do not have such a memory."

"Well, we know ourselves to be your debtor, and we have sent for you to satisfy this debt."

The shoemaker didn't know what to do except stand stock still gaping at the pope.

Sixtus said, "You sold us a pair of shoes for a giulio less than you wanted for them because we agreed to pay you the giulio with all its interest when we became pope. Now that we are pope, we want to satisfy you and abide by our word."

The shoemaker suddenly remembered the funny monk who had haggled over a pair of shoes forty years earlier. "Good," the pope said. "Now we will satisfy the debt." Sixtus called his majordomo and asked him to figure the interest on one giulio for forty years. It came to three giulios, which the pope handed him as he bid him farewell.

In the waiting room, the shoemaker, having recovered his power of speech, complained bitterly to his friends that he had spent fifteen giulios to get to Rome, and would spend another fifteen to go home. But this was one of Sixtus's jokes. He had the man brought back and reunited him with his son, a monk, to whom he gave a wealthy bishopric in the Kingdom of Naples. "The pope asked the shoemaker if he had paid enough interest on the giulio, and the delighted shoemaker went back home blessing him."[†]

Leafing through his pages for 1564, the pope saw an entry for an Augustinian monk named Father Saluti. When he himself was a monk, Sixtus had been making a journey on foot to preach in a certain city and had stopped along the way at an Augustinian monastery, where he had been warmly received by Saluti. Felice borrowed four scudi from him and wrote an IOU. He had never paid it back, and now was the time for all paybacks. He commanded the general of the Augustinian order in Rome to find out if Saluti was still alive and, if so, to bring him into his presence.

At the time Father Saluti, now in his forties, was involved in a dispute with his bishop. Having heard of the pope's strictness, when four burly guards barged into his monk's cell and told him they had orders to bring him to Sixtus in Rome, he feared he was going to his execution. He was ushered into the pope's presence, where he began to sputter out his defense. Sixtus, who was unaware of the dispute, waved it away.

"That is not the reason we called you to Rome," the pope said, "but to accuse you of having wasted the money of your monastery, and we are resolved to make you render an account, but first we want to hear a confession from your own mouth."

Now, Father Saluti began to pluck up his courage, because he was extremely careful with the monastery's finances and had never pocketed a penny. He said he would gladly show the pope his account books and submit to any punishment if it could be proved that he had poorly administered the finances.

† Anon., pp. 327-333.

With a disdainful voice the pope said, "Think well on what you say because we have sufficient proof to convince us. Is it not true that in 1564 a monk passed by of our order, to whom you loaned four scudi, without getting it back? Isn't that throwing away the income of your monastery?"

Father Saluti remembered this occasion twenty-one years in the past. "It is true, holy father, that I gave that monk four scudi, and I would have given him more if he had asked for it because he seemed to be a father of esteem, virtue, and worthy of every service, but then I found out he was a rascal, because he had made me an IOU in a phony name, and no matter how hard I tried I couldn't find him."

"Oh, good, don't search for him any further," the pope said, laughing hard, "because you will certainly not find him. And we can tell you that he is no rogue who remembers his old debts, and you should be happy that we will pay you his old debt for him."

The pope asked him what the monk looked like. Saluti looked closely at Sixtus and seemed to recall that the monk had looked rather similar. He started shaking from head to toe because he had just called the pope a rascal. Father Saluti said, "Your Holiness, I have to say that he bore a certain resemblance to you."

The pope replied, "Since we bear a resemblance to that monk who benefited so from your generosity, it is high time that we begin to give you proof of our gratitude. You received that monk with so much courtesy that we want to receive you with the same courtesy."[†] Sixtus ordered Saluti to be lodged in the luxurious apartments of his grand-nephew, young Cardinal Alessandro Montalto. He stayed there a month while the pope tried to discover what position would please him most. He finally made him a bishop with considerable revenues in the Kingdom of Naples. Later that evening, Pasquino cried that bishoprics in Rome were being sold at a good price, four scudi apiece.

Sixtus had done his best to balance the books in terms of debts he owed and debts owed to him, except, of course, for the elephant in the living room no one dared mention. Yet when it came to punishing Francesco's murderers, he was in a bit of a bind. He had repeatedly

† Ibid., pp. 335-337.

and publicly declared his pardon and chalked the whole unfortunate episode up to God's will. But he firmly believed that a pontiff was required by God to render justice for old wrongs.

As eager as Sixtus was for vengeance, there was a part of him that unwillingly returned to that particular place of pain. He complained to Gregory's nephew, Cardinal San Sisto, that the murder had been committed during his uncle's reign and, despite his protests of pardon, the pope should have done something about it. "If your uncle had punished it, he would have saved me the pain and embarrassment of pursuing its authors, and I would not cry a second time over the death of a nephew whom I loved with such great tenderness."[†]

Camilla, who had been pushing her brother for vengeance for four years, was delighted when he finally agreed. Though the former laundress was now the marchesa of Venafro, living in a palace, with one grandson a cardinal and the other a nobleman, there was always someone missing at the dinner table. Paolo Giordano, Vittoria, Tarquinia, Marcello, and their gang of murderers must pay.

Brother Geremia of Udine, a spy of Grand Duke Francesco's in Rome, wrote his boss, "The pope's sister doesn't do anything except spur him on to vengeance for her son that was killed... This sister of the pope is an old woman with a vindictive character who never forgets anything."[‡]

The Venetian ambassador wrote, "The pope is in great thought about what he must do because on the one hand he pardoned them when he was cardinal. On the other hand, he is moved by justice, and by the offices of his sister, who often cries over the death of her son."[§]

Two of Paolo Giordano's servants had been abandoned in Rome when he and Vittoria thundered out in April. One of them, the wardrobe master, was arrested in June for committing a crime. Another, a bottler, was found hanging around the duke's Roman palace. Both were questioned about the murder of Francesco Peretti, and both spilled the beans about Paolo Giordano ordering the

† Leti, *Sixte V*, Vol. 2, p. 43.
‡ Gnoli, p. 294, n.
§ Ibid., p. 293, n.

murder. The Venetian ambassador to Rome informed his Senate that they must plan how to respond if the pope sent them a request for Paolo Giordano's extradition.

The pope wanted to read the interrogation records of the two servants; every word they uttered had been recorded by a court reporter. As soon as Sixtus started reading, he began to sob bitterly at his papal desk, tears running like rivers down his homely face. He read how Paolo Giordano Orsini had callously planned to ambush and murder Francesco. Relying on Francesco's affection for him, Vittoria's brother Marcello would summon him to the murder spot with a note asking for help. Had it never occurred to the revolting duke, to selfish Marcello, that this person to be so brutally butchered had a family who loved him, whose hearts would be broken forever?

Sixtus had not allowed himself to show grief immediately after the murder, perhaps not even in the privacy of his own bedroom, as he steeled himself for his convincing theatrical role of forgiving Christian. But now, reading the words before him, all the pain repressed for more than four years tumbled out. It was too much for him. His gnarled hands pushed the papers away, and he cried out that he didn't want to read any more, and he never wanted to hear another word about it. But Francesco's murder was like a virus thriving inside him; it would never really go away.

Courtiers hoping to win the pope's favor asked him why he gave justice to other families but not to his own. They pointed out that Paolo Giordano Orsini had been guilty of many other crimes, including murders. While the pope could issue a pardon in the name of the Perettis, he could not issue it in the name of other bereaved families. It was a clever stratagem: personal revenge served up without technically being revenge. The pope decided to charge the duke in absentia for having aided Lodovico in killing Pope Gregory's advisor, Vincenzo Vitelli. Witnesses were called, charges were filed, and the trial began.

In October, the pope's guards rode to Bracciano and arrested a group of the duke's friends and servants who had just arrived from Padua. According to an *avvisi* of October 30, these men were "very intimate favorites of Signor Paolo Giordano and served His Excellency as secretaries in all languages. It is the opinion that now a terrible edict is being created against that signor."[†] Three others were extradited from the Republic of Lucca at the pope's request, "among whom one person of account who knows all the secrets of Signor Paolo Giordano."[‡]

The gossip mill in Rome whispered that Cardinal de Medici and his brother the grand duke encouraged the pope to take the Duchy of Bracciano away from Paolo Giordano as punishment for his crimes, especially the crime of marrying beneath him, and give it to his son, Virginio.

In a cruel thrust aimed directly at Vittoria, the de Medicis further hoped to win the good graces of the pope by proposing a marriage between Virginio and Sixtus's grandniece, Flavia Peretti, the child of Camilla's deceased daughter Maria. The granddaughter of Camilla, whom Vittoria had scorned, would be the new Duchess of Bracciano. Vittoria, the former duchess, would be exiled and insolvent. Having fought so hard and endured so much for four years, Vittoria risked being butted off her privileged perch by a twelve-year-old. But Sixtus was revolted at the idea of having Paolo Giordano as an in-law. He waved away the suggestion. Flavia, he said, was too young.

Cardinal de Medici began to fear that once the pope took possession of Bracciano, he would give it not to Virginio, but to Camilla's other grandson, eight-year-old Michele. Though Sixtus had purchased small principalities for Michele, the large, wealthy Duchy of Bracciano was worth far more than all the boy's other lands put together and would instantly make him one of the most important barons in Italy. Cardinal de Medici was deeply concerned lest the duchy go out of the family. On November 10, 1585, the cardinal organized a large hunt around Bracciano, a ruse to introduce a hundred well-armed soldiers to defend the castle from papal forces if necessary.

[†] Ibid., p. 293, n.
[‡] Ibid., p. 293.

The contention over Bracciano was just one of many problems that would conveniently disappear if the duke were to die before the trial was over. Virginio would immediately inherit the duchy to the satisfaction of the de Medicis. And a dead man would not be convicted of murder, an eternal stain on family honor, which must have worried the prickly-proud Lodovico Orsini. Pope Sixtus, too, stood to reap great advantage by the duke's demise coming sooner rather than later; he would not have to wreak public vengeance on a man he had pardoned.

*   *   *

On Wednesday, November 13, the duke had difficulty breathing, the flesh on his massive chest weighing heavily on his sodden lungs. His doctors bled his arm and ordered him not to eat anything for several hours, as "the violence of his illness was caused by the great abundance of crude humors, which could only be subdued by abstinence."[†] Naturally, the recommendation of abstinence was not well received by the duke.

"As soon as the doctors left the room, he wanted to eat and drink as usual, there being no one who dared to contradict him. After eating he repented of it immediately and had such a serious flux of mucus in his throat that he lost consciousness, and two hours before sunset he also lost his life."[‡] Vittoria had been sitting in the room listening to his labored breathing. Suddenly, she realized it had stopped. She shrieked.

According to one contemporary, as Vittoria gazed on her husband's corpse, she realized the brief glory of her life as duchess was over forever, and the Peretti family, which she had always scorned as being far beneath her socially, "was now rising to greater and greater happiness."[§]

[†] Strozzi, *Vita del Sommo*, 12b.
[‡] Cicogna, *Maritaggio*, folio 43b.
[§] Ibid., folio 43b.

She grabbed a pistol in the duke's room and tried to load it to shoot herself in the head, but her servants prevented it. One of them ran out of the room to hide the gun, while others got thick ropes and tied her hands.

Chapter 22

THE WAR OF THE FURNITURE

*My inheritance has become to me like a lion in the forest. She roars at
me; therefore I hate her. Has not my inheritance become to me like a
speckled bird of prey that other birds of prey surround and attack? Go
and gather all the wild beasts; bring them to devour.*

– Jeremiah 12:8-9

M any whispered that the Grand Duke of Tuscany and the
pope had conspired to poison Paolo Giordano. Though the
duke had clearly been dying, they reasoned that perhaps his ox-like
constitution could have dragged on a few more months. Had his
gangrenous carcass finally, with a heaving groan, succumbed to the
deadly doses of steak and cake and given up of its own accord? Or
had his lumbering mass been gently pushed over the edge by a little
something added to his wine?

Having recovered from her burst of suicidal desperation, Vittoria
dried her tears, sat down at her desk, and wrote a begging missive to
Bianca Cappello, Grand Duchess of Tuscany.

To the most Serene Signora and my most respected lady:

Because I am obliged to inform your most serene Highness, as my
lady and signora, of every piece of news, even though I am certain
it will displease you infinitely, nonetheless because of my debt
to you I must inform you of the unexpected loss that I have had
today of my lord consort, and most illustrious and excellent lord
duke. I hope that your Excellency has compassion for my troubles,
and I supplicate you, with every affection of my heart, to deign to
protect my affairs… I pray God, who has been pleased to afflict me

with this incomparable loss, to give to your most serene Highness every sort of great happiness.

From Salò, November 13, 1585[†]

There would be no answer. Vittoria also wrote letters to the dukes of Ferrara and Urbino, to the Senate of the Venetian Republic, and to Cardinal Farnese (employer of her brother Flaminio and enemy of the de Medicis), informing them of her husband's death and asking for their protection.

Vittoria and the duke had been expecting the heavy furniture wagons to arrive in Salò after their plodding journey from Padua. Now that the duke was dead, Vittoria would be leaving Lake Garda and returning to Padua. But she did not want to send the furniture back to the city, where Lodovico was still lurking. Marcello sent a rider to inform the drivers to turn around and take the road for Chioggia, fifteen miles from Venice at the southern tip of the Venetian lagoon. There the items would be loaded onto a ship and taken south to Pesaro. From there they would be taken to a secret destination, where the Orsinis wouldn't be able to get their hands on it.

Vittoria hadn't written to Lodovico about Paolo Giordano's death, probably because she wanted to hide the furniture first. But one of Paolo Giordano's servants, a Sicilian named Patrizio, wrote to Lodovico with the news. Patrizio, who hated Vittoria as a social climber trying to siphon off Orsini patrimony, was appalled that she hadn't let Lodovico know immediately. Lodovico received the letter at four hours past sunset on Friday, November 15.

According to Francesco Filelfo, Lodovico's secretary, his master sent news of Paolo Giordano's death post-haste by courier to the duke's son, Virginio, in Florence. He also informed Cardinal de Medici and asked him for instructions on how to proceed, especially concerning the duke's furniture, which was on its way to Salò – evidently Patrizio had not heard of Marcello's machinations – and worth a great deal of money. Lodovico feared it would "meet a bad end," clearly a reference to Vittoria stealing it, and resolved to ride to Salò immediately.

[†] Ibid., p. 452.

Lodovico had missed the funeral, held earlier that day, to which he had not been invited. Paolo Giordano had been carted across the little road that passed by the Salò palace and buried in the Church of the Capuchins in a specially made, extra-wide coffin. Most people were buried the day after death, but Paolo Giordano was buried two days afterward, probably because they couldn't jam him into a regular casket and needed an entire day to fashion one to fit. Vittoria hoped to move him to the Basilica of Loreto at some point in the future, once the Orsini chapel had been built there.

At dawn on the morning of November 16, Lodovico left Padua for Salò, ostensibly to give his condolences to Vittoria, but really to start carting the furniture away as soon as it arrived. En route he ran into a messenger bearing him another letter from Patrizio, stating that Vittoria and Marcello had sent away the duke's valuable furniture to hide it from him, and it was on its way to Chioggia. Lodovico was livid. He sent Filelfo on a fast horse to Chioggia to explain to the authorities there that the duke's rightful heir was being robbed of his inheritance; the authorities should prevent the furniture from leaving the city. Filelfo did so, but the items had not yet arrived. The mayor set watches on the roads into the city.

Lodovico galloped toward Salò and met Vittoria's carriage on the road. She was leaving the sad, beautiful palace of death and returning to Padua. Lodovico accompanied her on the return trip, galloping beside her as a most unwelcome companion. He informed her that he would have the furniture sent from Chioggia to Padua, where it would be placed in escrow until the court could ascertain its rightful owner.

Vittoria agreed to the escrow and gave Lodovico a copy of the will. Looking it over, Lodovico saw just how much money Paolo Giordano had left her, but he remained unperturbed, believing she would never get it. According to one contemporary source, Lodovico "negated [the will] for his suspicions that such cases suggested feminine arts, when women find themselves the bosses of the will of aged lovers."[†] He was much more concerned with the *mobili* and saw to his relief that the

---

† Strozzi, *Vita di Sommo*, p. 14b.

will did not give her the duke's furniture, jewelry, and other items, though it mentioned a codicil which she had not attached.

When Vittoria emerged from her carriage at the Palazzo Foscari, it is likely that she carried her jewelry boxes inside with her as ladies kept such valuables close at hand when traveling. To her great annoyance, no sooner did she set them down than Lodovico began rifling through them, but "it didn't seem to him that he found the quality and quantity of jewels that he thought he would find at the death of Signor Paolo." Vittoria must have surmised that Lodovico would try to steal her jewels and had probably hidden the best pieces. Women in danger of losing their valuables often sewed them into the linings of their clothing, or in the hems of their skirts.

Lodovico couldn't exactly start ripping her dress off, though the thought must have occurred to him, but he did lecture her sternly, instructing her to return the jewels she had received from Paolo Giordano as they should go to his son, Virginio. Vittoria may have hidden the jewelry, but she would have had a harder time stuffing armoires, silver platters, and wall tapestries up her skirts. And whatever Vittoria had up her sleeve, it couldn't be the dead duke's horses and carriages. Lodovico assumed that he could easily take possession of the furniture, which would be guarded by the authorities until he had proved his legal case.

On November 21, the items finally arrived in Chioggia. The mayor turned the wagons around once again and sent them with an armed guard to Padua. Vittoria wrote a letter to the mayor of Padua agreeing to the sequestration of the furniture until she could send a notarized copy of the will and codicil.

But Lodovico had tasks to perform other than fighting over the will, tasks to honor the departed. He arranged for Vittoria's servants to dress in mourning, which meant buying black cloth and having outfits hastily sewn. Black cloth was draped over all mirrors, tables, and doors in her Paduan palace. Satisfied with himself, he wrote to Virginio and the cardinal, letting them know he had honorably provided for mourning. He also sent them copies of the will and boasted that as far as the furniture was concerned, they had nothing to fear.

While Paolo Giordano's will was Vittoria's most valuable possession, it could also spell her own sudden demise if the fury of the de Medicis and Orsinis reached a fever peak. Her brother Ottavio, the bishop of Fossombrone, feared the will was not a windfall so much as a possible tragedy for her. Vittoria, too, must have been worried. Again, she tried to line up the protection of the powerful. On November 22, she wrote once more to Bianca Cappello:

> I have returned to Padua to the same palace that the most excellent lord my husband had taken for his residence, from where it seemed I should make reverence to your most serene Highness, letting you know that at Salò I have left all my joy, having deposited that blessed corpse of my signor with as much honor as possible in the Church of the Capuchins. On this occasion I beg you to take me under your protection, which I have asked you other times. And reverently I kiss your hands.†

On the same day she wrote the Duke of Urbino:

> To the most Serene and Revered Lord,
>
> After having buried that blessed corpse of his Excellency, my lord, and having done it with the most honor possible, I went to Padua the next day where I find myself awaiting some order from your Highness, and it seemed I should give you this news out of my duty. I ask you again, with every affection of the heart, to protect me and my affairs, which your Excellency has always said that you would do for me. I humbly kiss your hands.
>
> From Padua, November 22, 1585.‡

Though Vittoria had hoped for protection from Bianca Cappello and the Duke of Urbino, she was counting on the goodwill of the Venetian Senate, renowned for protecting the downtrodden, the hunted, and the unfortunate. Ambassadors waving warrants from the most powerful princes in Europe were often received with a yawn and

---

† Ibid., p. 454.
‡ Ibid., pp. 454–455.

a shrug, as the lion of Saint Mark fearlessly shielded Europe's outcasts under his enormous wings. Vittoria wrote a heartbreaking letter to the Senate describing the dangers of her situation and her hope that Venice, renowned for its generosity to the abandoned, would help her. It was a letter designed to win their favor.

Strangely, she also wrote to the pope, apprising him of her intention to become a nun at a Roman convent. She had always been a devout Catholic, confessing and taking communion frequently, fasting and praying. The events of the past four years must have exhausted her, and perhaps she would find peace inside convent walls. Still, life in a nunnery must have been a last resort for a woman who loved beautiful things to such an extreme, and Mariano Pierbenedetti, Sixtus's governor of Rome, believed Vittoria was doing it out of fear of the de Medicis and Orsinis. Whatever the case, convents required an admission fee of a few hundred scudi, which Vittoria claimed she did not possess. She wrote to the pope asking him to give her 500 scudi. Surprisingly, "The pope was happy at this news and replied that he would give her as much help as she needed and sent off the required sum."

Why would Sixtus, the brutally just sword of God, give money to Vittoria to enter a convent? Perhaps he thought she had not known about the murder plans and had only flirted with the duke out of her love of finery. After Francesco's murder, it was likely her ambitious family had pushed her hard into the duke's open arms. Even if he did believe her guilty to some degree, Sixtus, who always had a sweet spot for her, may have hoped she could find redemption by devoting the rest of her life to God.

But when Camilla heard the news, she was horrified that Sixtus was going to aid the murderer of her son and complained loudly. Frowning at his sister's protests, the pope said, "If this poor girl, who has recognized her sins and repented of them, wants to return here to serve God, how can we, who are his Vicar, refuse to help her? We want at all costs to help her."[†] And so, Vittoria would be assured of at least one path to safety if she didn't end up getting the furniture.

† Ibid., folio 53a-b.

The de Medicis, frustrated about the furniture stuck in escrow, had a backup plan as well. Temporarily stymied in Venice, they could make sure that the Accorambonis had no access to valuables closer to home. Cardinal de Medici had heard that Paolo Giordano had given Vittoria jewels and other valuables when he first whisked her from Rome to his villa at Magnanapoli a few days after Francesco's murder. She had deposited these items with her sister Massimilla in Rome's Tor de Specchi convent; religious houses often served as safe deposit boxes because nuns rarely stole anything. At the cardinal's request, Sixtus put these items in escrow for the time being, saying that he didn't want so much as "a metal screw to leave the convent."[†] No Orsini and no Accoramboni would be able to lay their hands on them. A notary, Gian Domenico de Rossi, went to the convent on November 22 with the pope's order. There he found "three fir boxes to hold glasses," "two boxes of carved walnut," and a "convent armoire containing things of the Signora Vittoria, and finally a writing desk."[‡] The notary placed his seal on everything.

Lodovico had obtained from Vittoria a copy of the duke's will and forwarded it to Grand Duke Francesco de Medici. Studying the document, the grand duke was horrified. It was a will, he wrote his brother, the cardinal, on November 26, "in which will be seen so many extravagances that it is clear how much that woman knew to do. But you would do a great service to Virginio if you could find a means so that his Holiness would declare this obligation null and void by the prohibition that Gregory made against them marrying, and for the murder of her husband which, when it is proven that it was done by order of Signor Paolo, the law will declare that she cannot be his wife. Finally, this legacy is so damaging to Virginio that it must be well considered, and every effort must be made to annul it."[§]

The grand duke also wrote a letter to Sixtus, which Cardinal de Medici personally handed to him. "Your Holiness will have learned of the death of Paolo Giordano," Francesco de Medici began, "and his

† Gnoli, p. 308.
‡ Ibid., p. 308.
§ Ibid., pp. 306-307.

will that is so damaging to Virginio, his son and my nephew who, if he is not embraced by the great goodness of your Holiness, I do not see how he will overcome all the burdens left him by his indiscrete father."[†] The cardinal pointed out to Sixtus that poor Virginio was starting out his adult life crushed by his father's debts. His estate had almost no cash and was mired in dozens of lawsuits with powerful adversaries. Now he would need to give Vittoria 100,000 scudi cash. The boy needed the pope's help and protection.

Again, the pope did not wish to appear vengeful. Perhaps another reason for his reluctance to negate the will was his old fondness for Vittoria. Seeing the pope's hesitation, the cardinal once more pushed the idea of a marriage between Virginio and Flavia Peretti. If the pope agreed to the marriage, surely he would want Virginio and his grandniece to have the dead duke's entire estate, without giving the murderess Vittoria a huge chunk. There were also advantages for the Peretti family as such a match would ensure them powerful connections long after the pope's death. Sixtus, who had shuddered at the thought of being related to Paolo Giordano, was more inclined to the marriage now that the grotesque duke was out of the way.

But Camilla was still adamantly opposed to it. She wanted nothing to do with the family of the man who had murdered her beloved Francesco. Plus, she was hoping for a royal marriage for Flavia. Catherine de Medici, queen mother of France, had made her illustrious match to the French prince when she was a papal niece. Why should Flavia settle for anything less? Aware of Camilla's resistance, Cardinal de Medici requested that his brother, Grand Duke Francesco, send the boy to Rome to win the pope's favor.

While negotiations were being made for the future Duchess of Bracciano, in her sumptuous Paduan palace the former one received condolence visits from government officials and their wives, along with the local nobility. On November 22, her youngest brother, Flaminio, arrived in Padua from Rome to raise her spirits. Flaminio, who had served as a page in the court of Cardinal Farnese, was a sensitive young man who hated violence and loved to play the lute.

† Ibid., p. 307, n.

Cardinal Santorio wrote that Flaminio was the only member of the Accoramboni family who was a decent human being. Not so her other brother, Marcello, who, as if the family were not embroiled in enough intrigues, had murdered yet again.

A servant of his named Moricone wanted to leave Marcello's service and first asked him for some money that he had loaned him. Marcello refused to give it. As the Ave Maria bells rang out just after sunset on December 1, Marcello's servants fired guns at Moricone as he walked in the street outside Vittoria's palace. He lay on the ground wounded as Marcello swaggered up and dispatched him with a sword. Paduan authorities asked Lodovico, head of the Orsini family in Padua, for permission to punish the murderers. Lodovico gave his permission gladly, but by then, Marcello and his men had hidden themselves in a convent.

Lodovico was eager to see Marcello executed for murder. It was Marcello, when he first moved to Bracciano in 1580, who had pointed out his sister's charms to the duke. It was Marcello who had murdered her husband so she could marry Paolo Giordano. Marcello had elbowed Lodovico out of the way and become Paolo Giordano's right-hand man. Marcello, a minor nobleman in a family of too many sons, had edged out a noble Orsini. Now, greedy Marcello had tried to hide the valuable furniture in order to steal it.

Lodovico was a dangerous enemy with powerful friends. He evidently concocted a plot with the Grand Duke of Tuscany to kill Marcello. On December 10, he wrote to Liverotto Paolucci, the man he had hired to kill Vincenzo Vitelli two years earlier: "God aid you in what I will do. I don't want songs anymore. It is said that Marcello goes away by road. It will be good to do this service (or better, according to the other lesson, but I will see what needs to be done when I come, and I will do it. Wait for me.) Burn this letter."[†]

But there were other, more practical matters to attend to. Lodovico wrote to Cardinal de Medici asking for instructions on reducing the dead duke's *famiglia*, a word used not only for family for also for servants and retainers. It was expensive to pay so many

† Ibid., p. 315.

employees, he explained, and he wanted to know what he should do with them. He also needed guidance on what to do with the furniture once he obtained possession of it.

While waiting impatiently for a reply, Lodovico was furious to learn that Vittoria had in her possession the duke's most sacred object: the ring of Saint Bridget, which had a tiny piece of the Swedish saint's clothing under glass. Bridget had visited Rome in 1350, where she befriended the knight Latino Orsini and healed him and his son of illness. Lodovico insisted that the ring, a talisman of good fortune for the Orsini family for more than two centuries, should go immediately to Virginio. Vittoria didn't want the ring; it was an ugly old thing with a moldy piece of cloth inside, but she was certainly not going to give it to the interfering Lodovico. Virginio could have it, she said, if he wrote her personally asking for it. Virginio accordingly wrote, and Vittoria sent him the ring.

Lodovico visited Vittoria frequently to discuss the estate, and she always seemed pleasant to him. One day, wreathing her poison in smiles, she told him of the codicil giving her all the furniture, but she didn't show it to him. Lodovico told Filelfo, "She pretends also to have a document written in the hand of the signor which gives her all the furniture and things, as was cited in the will."[†]

On December 13, Lodovico received instructions from the grand duke to pay off Paolo Giordano's servants who wanted to leave. The others should go to Bracciano, where they would be employed by Virginio. The older ones, in particular, were to be looked after. "To Signora Vittoria Accoramboni, tell her for our part that she can believe that we are very unhappy for the loss she has suffered, but it being the will of God, it is right to accommodate herself as a Christian and with patience. Since her brothers are with her, she can take whatever resolution and path she wants. If she desires to go to Bracciano, which would perhaps be best, she will find Signor Virginio there, and she can negotiate with him and hope for everything fair and pleasant."[‡]

† Ibid., p. 314, n.
‡ Ibid., p. 316.

Clearly, Bracciano did not offer Vittoria everything fair and pleasant. She had never met her stepson, who had been groomed by his uncles to detest her. If she were foolish enough to visit the castle, it is likely that she, too, would have died suddenly after eating something.

"With regards to the possessions of the duke," Francesco continued, "sell the useless ones, or those that are too heavy to move, keeping and taking to Florence the precious items and the best horses and carriages."[†] He informed Lodovico that Paolo Giordano had kept money in a desk, which he should use to repay himself for his expenses.

On December 13, Vittoria wrote one last imploring letter to Bianca Cappello:

> I have many times written to your most serene Highness of my affairs, and I have not had a reply. I desire to always remain in your grace and protection. To demonstrate to you how much I am your most affectionate servant, I once more ask you to account me as such, as I offer you this great affection with all my heart. Kissing your hands without end, I pray God that he keep your Highness in all happiness.

Having signed the letter, she added a postscript. "I beg your Highness to console me in so much affliction and tribulation, and to hold me under your protection and favor me on all occasions as your most humble servant."[‡]

But Vittoria must have known that protection would probably not come from that quarter. She hired Italy's top lawyer, Marcantonio Pellegrino, to help her with her husband's estate. She showed him what she had not dared to show Lodovico, the codicil mentioned in Paolo Giordano's will that listed the furniture and other items she was to inherit.

Lodovico was beside himself to hear that Vittoria had hired a lawyer to fight him in court. He sent a letter to Filelfo, who had gone to Venice to work with the authorities there on Virginio's behalf. "He wrote me that Signora Vittoria had changed the cards in her hand,"

† Ibid.
‡ Ibid., pp. 457-458.

Filelfo reported, "not fulfilling her promises to him, but that he hoped with the means of the law to prevent himself from being cheated."[†]

On December 14, Pellegrino presented himself as Vittoria's lawyer to the mayor of Padua, Andrea Bernardo, and pointed to the sentence in the duke's will where he mentioned a document of donation. Then he presented the document signed by Paolo Giordano and written in the hand of the notary Tiberio Valento. Unfortunately, Valento had left the republic and could not attest to having written it at the duke's instigation or to having seen him sign it.

The codicil confirmed that all of the items in the Tor de Specchi convent belonged to Vittoria. Although she had already given it to Virginio, the ring of Saint Bridget could remain in her possession until her death. And finally, Vittoria should inherit "all gold, silver, jewels, and other furniture that I will buy during the time I am outside of Rome and my estates... Moreover, in the case that I die outside Rome or my duchy, I give all the gold, silver, and other furniture that I will have taken there with me."[‡]

In Vittoria's name, the lawyer demanded from the mayor all of the duke's *mobili* that were in the republic. To make sure that the signature on the codicil was not a forgery, the mayor visited the duke's remaining servants and showed them the document. They swore that the signature was genuine, then Bernardo ruled that Vittoria should get back all the furniture that she had tried to ship out at Chioggia. True to its reputation, the Republic of Venice was standing up for the underdog. Here was a beautiful, tragic, young widow, fighting the power of the de Medicis, the Orsinis, and possibly the pope for some furniture. The Venetian Republic was on her side.

Lodovico was flabbergasted to learn that Vittoria would be getting the *mobili*. He had already boasted to the grand duke, the cardinal, and Virginio of his cleverness in snatching it back from her and had assured them he would obtain it soon. Now he looked like an idiot.

[†] Cicogna, *Filelfo*, p. 48.
[‡] Gnoli, pp. 459–460.

On December 17, he fired off another missive to Filelfo. "Thursday morning," the secretary reported, "I received another letter in which he told me that Signora Vittoria had by means of the law won all of Signor Paolo Giordano's furniture by virtue of a note of donation made to her by Signor Paolo. Signor Lodovico claimed that this was forged due to many reasons, and that against this judicial act he could not do anything else except to force her to give security for these items. But he was not entirely satisfied, it seeming to him that he had been made a fool of by a woman, and he asked if I knew another path of justice to take these things from her."[†]

Now it was Lodovico's turn to hire a lawyer in Venice, a certain Falagnosta whom Filelfo visited with all pertinent documents. After examining them, Falagnosta told Filelfo that Vittoria had a strong case. Lodovico wrote back that Vittoria was not the duke's wife and therefore could not inherit. He also cast aspersions on the document of donation. The duke's signature, though genuine, meant nothing. Before Lodovico went to Venice, Paolo Giordano had given him several sheets of paper, which were blank except for his signature at the bottom. Lodovico could fill in the sheets with the text he deemed necessary in case of an emergency. Perhaps Vittoria had obtained such a signed sheet of blank paper and had a trusted friend or servant pretend to be the notary. Why else, Lodovico asked, was the body of the codicil not written in the duke's hand, as his entire will was, but written by Tiberio Valento, who had disappeared? Why had Vittoria not shown it to him earlier, when she had handed him a copy of the will? Why had she handed over Saint Bridget's ring for Virginio when the document stated she could keep it? The document must be a very recent forgery.

Lodovico didn't consider that Paolo Giordano, having composed the will, had probably been too tired and sick to write another lengthy document later that day and had asked Valento to do so. Valento then departed Venice on a trip he had planned for some time, without leaving a forwarding address. It is possible that Vittoria, when she first met with Lodovico to discuss the furniture, hadn't shown him

† Cicogna, *Filelfo*, pp. 48-49.

the codicil because she wasn't ready to reveal her full hand until she had consulted with lawyers. And lastly, she didn't really want Saint Bridget's ring and thought it correct that it should go immediately to her stepson.

All Filelfo could do was to obtain from Falagnosta "a letter from him directed to the mayor of Padua, requesting that [the *mobili*] be deposited in escrow."[†] But the mayor denied this request. On Friday, December 20, Filelfo returned to Padua from Venice after having spoken to a lawyer there. On the road, he ran into several of Lodovico's bandits, who had been banished from Venice for breaking into shops earlier that day. They asked if they could stay in Padua with Lodovico, and Filelfo agreed. Such gangsters would come in handy fighting the Turks in Corfu, and Lodovico was preparing to leave as soon as he had the furniture situation sorted out.

On Saturday morning, Filelfo and the group of thugs who had tagged along with him arrived at Lodovico's Contarini Palace in Padua. Beside himself about the furniture, Lodovico instructed his secretary to speak personally to Mayor Bernardo. But the mayor was unavailable. Filelfo went again on the morning of December 22 and was told to return later that afternoon.

Meanwhile, Lodovico, hand on his sword hilt, swashbuckled his way into Vittoria's palace for a showdown. According to one contemporary, "This signor, a youth of about twenty-five, was said to hate in secret the Signora Vittoria Corambona, and wanted to steal from her, as many said, the horses and the jewels left her by the most illustrious signor Orsini her husband. He went on Sunday, December 22, 1585, to find her where she lived. And she informed him with sweet words that she intended to keep for herself the furnishings that her lord husband had liberally given her in his will, and that she would sell some of them, and give a portion of the money to Signor Lodovico in lieu of what her husband would have given him."

Paolo Giordano had arranged to give Lodovico a quarterly stipend, and his widow was now offering to pay him part or all of it for the following year. But Lodovico was not pleased at being patronized

†   Ibid., p. 49.

by Vittoria. He didn't want the stipend; he wanted the furniture, which was far more valuable. Moreover, his honor was bound up in the tables and chairs, the horses, and jewelry, as he had promised the de Medicis that he would obtain them.

The chronicler continued, "Their conversation being cut off by certain gentlemen coming to visit, she retired to her chamber, but Signor Lodovico remained in the room, where it was heard that he angrily said many strange and injurious words about her, with many threats, and left her, and considered and discussed with his men what they could do."[†]

Filelfo bounced back to the mayor, who saw him only briefly. "Having explained my desires," he wrote, "he replied that justice would not be lacking for anyone, and I should return the following morning at the usual hour for audiences. I told this to Signor Lodovico, who replied, 'Now is a good hour,' and nothing more."[‡]

Lodovico had lost patience.

[†] Cicogna, *Strani Accidenti*, p. 3.
[‡] Cicogna, *Filelfo*, p. 49.

Chapter 23

THE DEATH OF BEAUTY

They will draw their swords against your beauty and wisdom and pierce your shining splendor.

– *Ezekiel 28:7*

After his brief and fruitless meeting with the mayor of Padua on the afternoon of December 22, Filelfo returned to Lodovico's palace and dilly-dallied the evening away with some of the other men. At least, that is what he wrote some time later while sitting in a jail cell. "I stayed with one or the other gentlemen in the various rooms until we ate supper as usual. The tables being removed, everyone retired to the rooms, some to the fire, and some to watch the gambling."[†]

Somehow, Filelfo failed to notice that around seven p.m. almost forty of the men disguised themselves "with fake beards and armed themselves with guns, pistols, and other weapons, and went to the palazzo of Signora Vittoria Corramboni, where she lived with her brother, without anyone suspecting anything."[‡] Two of Paolo Giordano's servants who hated Vittoria had agreed to open a back door to let in the assassins. Only eight of the men entered; the others kept watch in the surrounding streets, ready to prevent any visitors from entering the palace.

Upstairs, Vittoria was draped in widow's weeds from head to toe, preparing for the feast of Saint Vittoria, her patron saint, which started at sunset. Saint Vittoria had been a Christian martyr and virgin who refused to marry a pagan during the persecutions of Emperor Decian in AD 250. Her frustrated would-be husband turned her into the authorities as a Christian, and an executioner stabbed her through the

† Cicogna, *Filelfo*, p. 49.
‡ Cicogna, *Strani Accidenti*, p. 3.

heart. Six days later, it was said, the executioner suddenly died; God's punishment for murdering the beautiful girl. In past years, Vittoria had celebrated the day as a birthday with parties and gifts. But this year, there would be no celebrations. In front of her private altar, in a small chamber off her bedroom, she walked in circles carrying a crown for the saint, reciting prayers. Then she placed the crown on the altar, knelt, and prayed before a tall ivory crucifix.

The sun set early on that, the longest, darkest night of the year. Vittoria's altar was lit by candelabra, which flickered in the draft, casting strange shadows on the walls.

Flaminio was sitting on her bed, picking out a sad religious tune on his lute, according to a servant named Brancaccio who was sitting by the door. The bedroom, too, was partially lit by the warm soft glow of candles, as well as the crackling fire in the hearth. But those areas furthest from the candles and the fire were sunk in utter darkness.

One of the masked men silently slipped into the bedroom and held a dagger to Brancaccio's throat to keep him quiet. From the shadows, a ruffian named Splandiano Adami aimed a pistol at Flaminio and shot, but missed. The youth, hearing the noise, looked up, threw down his lute and began to run toward his sister in the chapel.

As he approached the door, another shot was fired, and this time the bullet ripped through his shoulder. He dropped to his knees, howling in pain, and dragged himself towards Vittoria, who looked over and saw three men stalking her wounded brother. The men seized her. According to the men's subsequent confessions, Tolomeo Visconti of Recanati held a knife above her and hissed, "Now you need to die. Behold the reward of your iniquity."[†]

Knowing she could not escape, Vittoria begged for time to confess her sins; in such moments, even confessing to one's murderer was considered good enough to lift the stain of sin from the departing soul. But in reply one man sliced her bodice down the middle. Vittoria cried that she pardoned them for the great sin they were about to

† Gnoli, p. 325.

commit. "I want to die dressed," she declared, wriggling her arms free from the assassins' grip and throwing them across her breasts.[†]

But the two men grabbed her arms and pinned them down again, while Tolomeo Visconti gazed for a moment at the breasts that had bewitched a duke. Then he positioned his dagger above what he judged to be her heart and stabbed her. "Jesus," she cried as the assassin plunged it in and withdrew it repeatedly. "Jesus."

"Does it stick you in the heart?" he asked, gloating. "Answer me, does it stick you in the heart?"[‡] He stopped stabbing her when she had stopped moving, and his companions let the body fall to the ground in front of the altar.

The three assassins ran to the wretched sobs of Flaminio. While his sister was being murdered, the wounded youth had dragged himself under her bed. The murderers pricked him with their daggers as sport, laughing at his shrieks of pain. Not as courageous as his sister, the boy cried and begged for mercy. They shot him through the mattress, then dragged him out and stabbed him repeatedly. Authorities would later count seventy-four separate wounds.

The murderers then searched for Marcello, looking under beds and in cabinets, calling for him, but without success. He was still hiding with his men in the convent, knowing the authorities wanted to arrest him for the murder of his servant earlier in the month. If he and his gang of bravados, always armed to the teeth, had been living with Vittoria, they might very well have saved her and Flaminio. Before leaving the palace, the murderers commanded Baldassare Muti, Vittoria's chief butler, to take care of the duke's furniture for which they were accountable to the grand duke. And then they slipped out the way they had come in.

A servant of Paolo Giordano's still serving Vittoria, Scipione Longo, had been in the palace when the murders took place. He hadn't recognized any of the masked men. When they left, he ran breathlessly to Lodovico's palace two blocks away with news of the

† Strozzi, *Vita del Sommo*, folio 15a.
‡ Gnoli, p. 325.

crime. Lodovico showed no surprise and instructed Scipione to take the news to the rectors, the city councilmen.

Lodovico summoned Filelfo. "I was called," the secretary wrote, "into the room of the signor, where there were many gentlemen of the house, and the signor said to me, 'Did you hear the news?' and I replied, 'What news?' And he said, 'Scipione Longo has just been here and says that some masked men entered the house of Signora Vittoria and killed her and Flaminio and searched for Marcello but didn't find him.' I was shocked and said that it would be good to go to the police. Lodovico replied that Scipione had already gone. The conversation was about this event until it was time to sleep, and I went to my lodging."[†]

The mayor and the rectors, many of whom had been roused as they were preparing for bed, were horrified to hear the tale and sent letters to the doge of Venice, informing him of the murders. They knew who was behind them. They also knew that Lodovico and his army of hardened ruffians would not peacefully turn themselves in. The rectors gave orders to the cannoneers and soldiers to present themselves at City Hall early the next morning and to keep the city gates closed so Lodovico could not escape.

Then the mayor and the rectors went to the Foscari Palace, pushing their way through the throngs in the street who had heard of the carnage. On the ground floor they called together the servants and interrogated them. Some were hauled off for further questioning as it became clear that somebody had opened a door for the assassins.

Holding their lanterns aloft, the officers tiptoed up the enormous staircase. Shining their lamps this way and that, they saw that the rooms had been rifled, the desks and wardrobes opened and emptied, with clothing and papers scattered all over the floor. The group quietly crossed the ballroom, then turned to enter Vittoria's bedroom. They saw a dark heap of something on the floor. It was Flaminio, riddled with gunshot and stab wounds. The laughing youth had been reduced in minutes to butcher's offal. Groaning and crossing themselves, the men went into the little chamber at the back of the bedroom. There

† Cicogna, *Filelfo*, pp. 49-50.

was the altar, the crown of Saint Vittoria on a red velvet pillow in front of the crucifix. Beside it were candlesticks coated with hard white droplets from the candles, which were guttering low in pools of wax.

Vittoria, face down, was stretched out like a sacrificial offering at the base of the altar. They rolled her over. She was white as a sheet, her bodice ripped asunder, the shreds of velvet and her breasts caked with dried blood. Beneath her a pond of blackened blood spread out across the floor.

They waited for sunrise to attend to the bodies. There was no money to pay for a funeral, indeed, no family member around whom they could even ask for money. As the cold, distant sun rose over a misty Padua, the officers obtained two wide planks to use as stretchers to carry the bodies. They hoisted Vittoria, her body sticking to the rubbery puddle of blood on the floor, onto one, and Flaminio, his guts and brains falling out of his monstrous wounds, onto the other, and carried them to the Church of the Eremetani across the street. Given the sensational manner of the deaths, and the fact that one victim was a duchess, crowds pushed to see the bloody bodies, particularly Vittoria's mangled breasts. The curious wept and groaned for compassion for the brother and sister cut down at such a young age.

Trying to save the city of Padua money, the officers bought the cheapest coffin possible from the monks and jammed both bodies into it. Then, as the distant midwinter sun started to slide towards the horizon, and as the gravedigger dug a hole just outside the church, the monks lit tapers at all four ends of the coffin and chanted psalms. "At sunset they put the coffin in the church in an earthly sepulcher, without any other funeral pomp," wrote a *relatione* author, "because those of their household having run off in great terror, they could find no one who dared to attend the service."[†]

Cardinal de Medici was the first person in Rome to hear news of Vittoria's murder. He raced breathlessly into the papal audience chamber and told Sixtus. The pope, who always firmly believed God would punish the guilty, seemed stunned. The news gave him

† Ibid., p. 5.

no joy. If anything, it seemed like another stone around his neck. If the pope's true feelings were unclear, Camilla's weren't. She was absolutely delighted.

The bloody murders of Vittoria and Flaminio were routinely called Lodovico's "excess," as if he had imbibed a bit too much wine or eaten a second piece of cake. The crime was also called an *accidente*, a word which can mean incident but also has nuances of the English *accident*, implying that he had slipped on a banana peel, or farted at a noble dinner party, or accidentally called together forty assassins, inadvertently handed them swords and pistols, and unthinkingly ordered them to murder an unarmed brother and sister. Some descriptions used both words. "This accident happened by the disposition of Divine Justice because of the excess committed against the house of the pope," according to a *relatione*.[†] They were polite words for bloody deeds, the usual Renaissance gilding over bones and guts.

"Such was the end of Vittoria Accoramboni," wrote another, "a woman who would have been lacking no happiness if she had been able to wait for things to come in their time. But wanting to run ahead, she tasted great bitterness in the end, so that few women have left behind such a bitter memory."[‡]

Another writer attributed her bloody end not merely to ambition but to complicity to commit murder, stating that Vittoria "paid with such a death for the sin committed in the consent she gave to kill Francesco Peretti, her first husband."[§]

One contemporary writer saw irony in the events. The duke, he wrote, had seen to it that she was well provided for after his death, "but such is the uncertainty of human plans that what he thought would secure her future was that which flung the poor girl off the precipice."[¶]

So ended the worldly ambitions of Vittoria Accoramboni. At the grand finale, she possessed half a coffin in an unmarked, unmourned

[†] Ibid.
[‡] Ibid., folio 46b.
[§] Anon., p. 621.
[¶] Strozzi, *Vita del Sommo*, folio 12b.

grave. But for eight months she had lived as Duchess of Bracciano. During that brief time, she had owned several large wall tapestries, numerous silver platters, and a marvelous carriage with a roof that opened up to let in the sun.

Clearly, it was a tragic accident, although many in Rome who heard of it uttered the same words that Cardinal Felice Montalto had said four years earlier in reference to another such accidental excess.

It is, they said, *God's will.*

Chapter 24

JUSTICE SERVED

They will come against you with weapons, chariots and wagons and with a throng of people; they will take up positions against you on every side with large and small shields and with helmets. I will turn you over to them for punishment, and they will punish you according to their standards.

– Ezekiel 23:24

The morning after the murders, Lodovico and his men swaggered over to City Hall to speak with the rectors. The gates around the building were closed and heavily guarded. Evidently, the rectors feared that he and his gangsters might try to harm or kidnap them.

Lodovico's prickly pride was irritated when the soldiers told him they had received orders from the rectors forbidding him to enter. "The signor suffered this with difficulty," Filelfo wrote, "and disdainfully and loudly spoke some words so that the order came for him to enter. We all entered, and the signor went alone into the chamber of the signor rectors and spoke a while with them."[†]

Lodovico haughtily complained that he had initially been prevented from entering the building. He, an Orsini, had never suffered such an insult from kings or popes. Then he gave the reason for his visit. Since an unfortunate accident had happened the previous evening to Vittoria Accoramboni, he wanted the dead duke's furniture. The rectors' jaws must have dropped at this request. Given the angry men bristling with weapons waiting just outside in the hall, the rectors nodded and smiled, agreeing that he should take possession of the furniture immediately. Lodovico then asked to send a courier to the Grand Duke of Tuscany and Cardinal de Medici with news of Vittoria's accident, and they agreed.

Smiling still, the rectors began to ask him where he had been the night before, and what he might know about Vittoria's death. Lodovico angrily replied that he knew nothing about it. When the rectors asked if they could question his men, he replied haughtily, "My peers do not undergo examination."[†] With that he stood up and marched out.

The rectors had soldiers follow Lodovico's courier and arrest him a few miles outside Padua. They hoped to learn from his letters whether Lodovico had instructed his thugs to kill Vittoria. It was always possible, they knew, that when a man ruled over a personal army of lawless murderers, they might kill without the instructions of their boss in a misguided effort to please him. "Will no one rid me of this troublesome priest?" Henry II of England had groaned in 1170 when he heard of new problems stirred up for him by the annoying archbishop of Canterbury. Within days, Thomas Becket had been stabbed to death by four of Henry's friends.

The rectors recognized that such could have been the case with Lodovico and Vittoria. It had not helped his position, of course, when Lodovico showed up to demand the furniture and refused to answer their questions or allow his men to be interrogated. Such behavior, however, was not necessarily a sign of guilt but could have been caused by his nettlesome Orsini pride.

Nonetheless they were very interested to see what he wrote in his letters to the de Medici brothers. The messenger was duly searched, and in addition to the letters in his leather pouch containing bland accounts of the killings and the furniture, another letter was found in his shoe. "With great contentment of spirit, I give you news of how the business occurred," Lodovico wrote, "which happened quietly enough."[‡] His guilt was confirmed by his own hand.

In Venice that morning of December 23, a letter of the Paduan authorities describing the crime was presented to the powerful

---

Council of Ten in Venice, which was now faced with the most heinous murders in recent memory. They decided to send to Padua one of the three Venetian *avogadori* (top criminal prosecutors), Luigi Bragadino, to investigate the crime. Later that day, the council received from the Paduan authorities copies of Paolo Giordano's will and codicil; witnesses' accounts of the arguments between Lodovico and Vittoria leading up to and including the day of the murder; a report of Lodovico's arrogant behavior toward the rectors of Padua that morning; and copies of the incriminating letters he had sent to the grand duke and Cardinal de Medici.

Clearly, the murders were not committed by Lodovico's men in a bumbling attempt to please their innocent boss. Lodovico himself had instigated it. The council immediately sent a courier to Padua with orders to keep the gates well-guarded so that neither Lodovico nor his men could flee. The following day, despite the fact that it was Christmas Eve, they convened the entire Venetian Senate. The council proposed that Lodovico be taken into custody immediately, dead or alive. There were one hundred and forty-nine votes for the proposal, and twenty-two against it.

The Senate sent the following letter:

To the rectors of Padua and to Chief Prosecutor Bragadino in that city:

The most atrocious case … of the death of Signora Vittoria Accoramboni and her brother has greatly disturbed us, not only for the interest of justice, but much more for the dignity and security of our republic if such nefarious things were tolerated in our state. We are certain that having received the order that we sent you this morning by express courier, you will have used every means to keep the gates well-guarded so that Lodovico Orsini, greatly implicated in the above-mentioned excess, and his men cannot leave…

We command you to procure with all industry and diligence this Lodovico with as many of his men as possible, dead or alive, in whatever way is easiest and most expedient, using such force and artillery as are required… So that the above-mentioned Orsini and his men come securely, dead or alive, into your hands, you have orders that if they try to escape, they should be followed and taken or maltreated and killed.†

Meanwhile, poor Filelfo, loyal to the bitter end, was fretting about his employer. "Many people all over Padua were already saying that this event had taken place by order of the signor," he wrote, "and I too, fell into this opinion but didn't tell him."‡

Seeing battalions of soldiers march into Padua throughout the day, Filelfo thought that Lodovico should leave the city, which was obviously gearing up for battle. But he didn't feel comfortable bringing up Vittoria's murder as the reason. "I, who knew his humor, also knew that when he didn't feel like talking about a subject, he felt it was an impertinence when someone brought it up." But there was a good excuse to pack up and leave; Signor Contarini had been angling to get his palace back, which he had only loaned to Lodovico for a short time.

"Since we were not sure of having the house in Padua with any certainty, and since he would not be able to do anything about Signor Paolo's property during the Christmas holidays, I suggested we go to pass the holiday with his wife at Venice. He replied that he didn't want to leave and asked me if I wanted to. I replied no, and then I was silent."

Filelfo then pretended to go for a walk, but his purpose was to see if the nearby city gate was guarded. To his surprise, he found that it wasn't. "I told this to the signor laughing and said that if whoever killed Signora Vittoria was in Padua, they could leave because the gates were open and all without guards. He didn't reply." Filelfo had heard that the criminal magistrate would be arriving soon and advised Lodovico to visit him and look as if he were cooperating in the investigation. Again, Lodovico refused.

"Now the morning of Christmas, I got up at my usual early hour and went walking in the street in front of the Church of San Agostino… During Mass I heard a certain monk and others say loudly, perhaps to be heard, that all the piazzas and streets were full

† Ibid., pp. 337-338.
‡ Cicogna, *Filelfo*, p. 50.

of armed people who came to the front of the signor's house to arrest those who had killed Signora Vittoria. Hearing this, I lifted my gaze and saw the bridge of San Giovanni and that of San Thomaso and the street full of people and the walls with muskets, and a piece of artillery on a gate directed at the house."[†]

Filelfo saw that even now the city gate next to the church was unguarded, and he could have escaped if he wanted to. "But I was guided by the love and loyalty that I had for the signor, and by my own innocence, to run into the house to give them this news, so that nothing happened unexpectedly. I found him being dressed by Master Honorio Adami and told them what I had heard and what he should do. He replied, 'Let them come,' and ordered the crossbar [to bar the door] and his moneybag. He told me to call the others if they were not yet awake, which I did."[‡]

Meanwhile, the rectors were raising the citizen militia. Soldiers beat drums and blew trumpets, while others cried out, "To arms! To arms, sons of Saint Mark! The most excellent Senate commands you to run to the house of Orsini for the most atrocious and nefarious murders he has committed. Those who do not go will be hanged! To arms! To arms!"[§]

Many Paduans were sitting in Christmas church services when they heard the call. They stood up, rushed out of the churches in droves, and scattered down side streets to retrieve their weapons from home. Once the citizens had assembled in front of Lodovico's palace, the chief of the militia, Captain Soardo, instructed them to drive carriages and carts into the surrounding streets, unhitch the horses, and leave them there as blockades. Now Lodovico could not ride out and escape.

Armed men clambered onto the roofs of surrounding houses. Others stood guard at the windows. More cannon were hoisted aloft the nearby city wall and aimed at Lodovico's palace. An official standing in front of the crowd announced that anyone who turned in

† Ibid.
‡ Ibid., p. 51.
§ Gnoli, p. 340.

one of Lodovico's men, dead or alive, would receive a reward of 500 ducats. Anyone bringing in Lodovico himself would receive 2,000 ducats, and the release from prison of two criminals of his choice.

Filelfo had followed his master's commands and roused the other men, who were dressing and arming themselves. "Then I went to the window and saw the street full of people, and I asked in a loud voice what they wanted. A man armed with a gun said that they wanted me."[†]

They had evidently mistaken the well-dressed secretary for Lodovico. Filelfo started to reply, but Lodovico pushed him away from the window. A gentleman appeared on behalf of the rectors and yelled up to Lodovico that they wanted him to turn himself in. Feigning ignorance of his crimes, Lodovico said that he did not know why all Padua was in arms around his palace, and he, an Orsini, was certainly not going to be forced out; he would only go of his own free will once the streets were cleared of men and artillery. The gentleman withdrew into the crowd to consult with officials and then returned, letting Lodovico know that the government of Venice negotiated with nations, not with private individuals. They would accept no conditions.

"The assault was begun," Filelfo reported, "with the greatest noise of muskets and of artillery that battered the house." Lodovico ran furiously back and forth with a gun in his hand, encouraging his men to fight, and guiding the old men and female servants to shelter, probably in the wine cellar.

Lodovico's men tried to fire out of the windows, but were met with a hail of bullets. Cannonballs ripped through the walls, and the men threw mattresses against the holes in an effort to stop the bullets flying in. The three men who had killed Vittoria – Tolomeo Visconti, Paganello Ubaldi, and Splandiano Adami – were the bravest fighters, knowing what was in store for them if taken alive. Lodovico ordered Filelfo to take dictation, as he paced back and forth, and the bullets whizzed by, and cannons fired, and somewhere a wall collapsed.

† Cicogna, *Filelfo*, p. 51.

"The signor told me to throw outside a note dictated by him and written by me," the secretary recounted, "in which I had tried to convince him to soften his rigor with gentle words, though it still seemed to me to be a bit haughty."[†]

The letter was as follows:

Signor Rectors:

I am astonished at the harsh measures being taken against me and my house for reasons I do not understand. And I am Lodovico Orsini, son of Giordano, nephew of Valerio and Bartolomeo de Alviano, and each one of them have promptly and on many occasions risked and in the last case given their lives in the service of this state. So this is the reward for the long, faithful and continuous service of my family… I will await the ending of this business with that intrepid spirit that is required by a member of the Orsini family.

Since your gentlemen do not want to proceed with me on the ordinary terms of justice, to which I will always be most obedient, I protest, and I call the world and God as witnesses, that before committing an unworthy act, I will sacrifice that life that you apparently want to take from me against all terms of piety and justice. I will be forced to reply to such treatment with bloodshed, leaving a clear and unhappy example with my death of my innocence and of the bad fortune of the Orsini house with this republic. With this I kiss your hands.[‡]

December 25, 1585

Clearly Lodovico, who had just murdered a woman and a defenseless youth, and who two years earlier had ambushed Vincenzo Vitelli in his carriage, and had killed countless others, did not believe these to be unworthy acts.

Filelfo was disturbed by the tone of the letter. "After the signor had signed," he recalled, "I added two lines remitting myself to the

---

† Ibid.
‡ Cicogna , 1439, pp. 15-16.

free will of the signor rectors, and I tried to throw this note into the streets, but a bullet grazed my hand, taking off some flesh."[†]

Lodovico grabbed the blood-splattered letter, opened it, and saw the submissive terms Filelfo had added. He added a sentence of his own. "Since you do not accept any conditions, everything will be done to save our lives."[‡] One of Lodovico's men, Colonel Lorenzo de Nobili, took the letter and for an unknown reason – perhaps because he was waiting for a lull in the firing to throw it out – stuffed it into his sock.

Instead of firing wildly at the palace, the cannoneers decided to end the assault quickly by bringing down the façade with strategic shots. A row of columns on the first-floor loggia held up the second floor of the house, and a cannon ball had already nearly severed one column. Now they aimed carefully at the columns, and just as Colonel de Nobili, Vitelli's assassin Liverotto Paolucci, and a man named Francesco Ranieri were placing mattresses against the front walls of the second floor, the cannon were fired, the columns shattered, and the front of the second floor collapsed.

The crowd cried out, and then there was a profound silence. As the dust settled, they saw two men whose fall had been softened by landing on top of mattresses. Shocked and bruised, Colonel de Nobili and Francesco Ranieri stood up. But the spectators, thinking of the 500-ducat reward, grabbed them and cut off their heads. The third man, Liverotto Paolucci, tried to save himself by clattering onto a neighbor's roof, but was shot and fell. His head, too, was cut off.

Those who had cut off the heads argued violently over which one would get the reward. But the rectors declared they would not give it to any of them because even an idiot could cut off the head of a corpse or a severely wounded person. The reward would go to the cannoneers who had bombed the façade.

Seeing the front of the building blown off, a pallid Filelfo asked his master what they should do. "Don't you see," Lodovico replied, "that they don't want to listen to anything?" Filelfo suggested he

† Cicogna, *Filelfo*, p. 51.
‡ Gnoli, p. 346.

send someone out to the rectors. "You go," was the response.[†] The trembling secretary tied his white handkerchief to a pole, raised it outside the door, and timidly stepped outside. Officers sprang on him, almost suffocating him, and led him to prison.

At this point, Lodovico turned himself in. He walked outside into the rubble and saw the mutilated corpses of his men. "Oh, my poor brothers, how you are beaten. Have mercy, Signor Soardo," he said, "and see that they are buried."[‡]

He was led on foot because all the streets had been barricaded. Part of the crowd followed or poked their heads out of windows to see the arrogant young man who had killed the Duchess of Bracciano and then dared to resist arrest. He marched with a sure step, his head held high, and got into a coach once they had passed the blockades. He asked his captors why there were so many people in arms throughout the city, and they replied, "Don't pretend to be so surprised because you, more than anyone else, know the reason for it."[§]

After Lodovico's arrest, thirty-three of his men turned themselves in. Lodovico, Filelfo and the three dead men made thirty-eight. Several more were thought to have escaped.

Lodovico was confined alone in a cell with walls of wood paneling rather than cold and clammy stone, the best one in the jail. But the haughty prisoner didn't feel that his accommodations were suitable to his dignity. Pacing back and forth, he declared, "Pope Sixtus would have treated me more honorably! But if God grants me life, that will be enough." He resumed pacing and then cried, "The Senate of Venice can boast of having Lodovico Orsini in prison. Not even Pope Gregory or other lords could do that."[¶]

Meanwhile, the rectors diligently searched Lodovico's house, carrying away his documents and other evidence, which removed any lingering doubt of his crimes. They found daggers covered in dried blood, false beards and masks, and a silver tankard that, according to the testimony of Vittoria's servants, had been in Flaminio's room when

[†] Cicogna, *Filelfo*, pp. 51-52.
[‡] Gnoli, p. 348.
[§] Ibid., p. 349.
[¶] Ibid., p. 350.

he was killed. It must have been an ill-starred tankard; it bore the coat of arms of the strangled Isabella de Medici. Paolo Giordano had taken it after he killed her and given it to Vittoria, whose murderers had stolen it. Outside the house, the investigators searched the clothing of the beheaded men and found Lodovico's letter stuffed into Captain de Nobili's sock.

Poor Filelfo and the other men were interrogated under torture. Filelfo steadfastly claimed to have had no foreknowledge of the murders, and the other men backed him up. But they also said that Lodovico had planned the crime from start to finish: getting two of the dead duke's servants to open the door, obtaining masks and disguises for the men, instructing eight to enter the house, and the rest to stand guard in the street. The murder was committed, they agreed, so that Lodovico, having exhausted all legal means, could finally obtain Paolo Giordano's furniture.

It was decided that Lodovico was too noble to torture, and besides, they had enough testimony against him. Later that Christmas Day, 4,000 Venetian troops entered the city to guard the gates, the piazzas, and the government buildings. It was feared that Lodovico's friends might bring an army of bandits to town in an effort to free him.

Chief Prosecutor Bragadino and the rectors sent a messenger to Venice to report the arrests to the Council of Ten and ask for further instructions. What on earth should they do with Lodovico? Would the Venetian Republic dare to execute an Orsini?

Chapter 25

AN ILLUSTRIOUS DEATH

The days of punishment are coming, the days of reckoning are at hand.

– Hosea 9:7

I n the city of lagoons, each year December 26 was a day of festivities. It was the Feast of Saint Stephen, the first Christian martyr. The doge held a banquet in the ducal palace on Saint Mark's Square for the Senate, the top magistrates, the ambassadors, and their wives. The Hall of the Great Council, 180 feet long and 82 feet wide, was the largest room in Europe and could seat some 1,800 people. The great fire of 1577 had nearly destroyed the hall, but it had been quickly repaired, except for the magnificent wall and ceiling paintings which had not yet been replaced.

The beginning of the banquet was open to the public, who came to gape at the finery. The sparkling silver plate and Murano glass had been crafted to represent the glories of Venetian history. The gentlemen gave the ladies in attendance gifts of fruit, flowers, and pastries. The doge himself walked about complimenting them. Once the spectators were cleared out, music was played, and the feast began.

After the banquet, the doge's grooms offered each guest a basket of delicious pastries decorated with his or her coat of arms. The gondoliers of male guests entered and took their masters' baskets out to their gondolas; each would row out to the home of a woman selected by his master and deliver the basket. Venetian courtesans waited eagerly on their balconies, hoping a gondola would stop at their house. The gentlemen's wives, sitting in the banquet room, must have wondered who was getting their husbands' baskets.

It was a time of frivolity and flirtation, of pastries and ribbons and compliments. But this year, just beneath the jovial veneer, there was a smear of blood and a whiff of gunpowder. The mood was tense. The banquet was a hurried affair, and the ladies left disgruntled. As soon as the festivities were over, the Senate convened to read the letters sent the day before by Chief Prosecutor Bragadino and the rectors.

As frightful as the murder of Vittoria and her brother had been, in the eyes of the Venetian Senate, Lodovico's outright resistance to authority was a much worse crime. Though Venice boasted a low crime rate, murders did occur periodically, but resisting arrest was unheard of. When the Senate considered his punishment, no one, not even those friendly with him, dared to ask for a mitigation of his penalty. One senator even suggested that he suffer the disgrace of dying publicly. But unlike Pope Sixtus, the nobles of Venice were not pleased at treating another noble as if he were a plebeian. In the vote which followed, one hundred and seventy-two were for a private execution, six against, and thirty-one undecided.

The Council of Ten sent the following instructions:

> To the Rectors of Padua and to the Criminal Prosecutor of the Commune in that city:
>
> To reply to your letters of yesterday and today, with which you have advised us of your success in arresting Lodovico Orsini and his men, we and the Senate praise your prudence and diligence in executing such an important task… After you give Lodovico Orsini three hours to confess himself and order his affairs, you will have him strangled in prison and order the public hanging of those of his men whom you know to be guilty of this torment, and you will do all this as soon as possible.

The Senate wanted to execute Lodovico as a clear example of Venetian justice for so heinous a crime. But it was urgent to do so before his powerful friends could intercede for him. They were fairly certain that Grand Duke Francesco of Tuscany and Cardinal de Medici were behind Vittoria's murder, and they were not so sure about the pope. If the Papal States and Tuscany demanded that Venice exile rather than execute Lodovico, the senators would find themselves squirming. Trade relations and military treaties could be threatened if they didn't comply. It would be far easier, the Senate realized, to apologize abjectly after the deed was done.

The letter continued:

> The others can wait a bit for the continuation of the trial, and you may summarily punish with the worst torture those who merit it. Those who seem to have minor guilt, or are not guilty at all, you will not release but send us their names and the summaries of their involvement to await our orders. We advise you to inquire with all diligence about that Filelfo, whom we know to be Lodovico's agent and very intimate with him, conscious of all his thoughts and orders, to find out the truth.[†]

At six a.m. on December 27, officials entered Lodovico's cell. One of them said, "Most illustrious signor, it has always been the firm intention of the most serene doge that the laws of his state be obeyed. And it being his wish that you must die within the next three hours, the most illustrious rectors have chosen me to inform you of your death."[‡]

Lodovico bowed his head and said to himself, "Patience!" More horrifying than death was the thought of being ignominiously hanged or executed publicly. He asked, "How will I die?" The chancellor replied, "A death worthy of your station, in prison."

"And will I be buried?" Sometimes the bodies of executed criminals adorned the city gates for several years, with crows picking at the flesh and sparrows nesting in the ribcages. Hearing that his body would be decently interred, he seemed satisfied and shook the chancellor's hand, saying, "I ask your lordship to kiss the hand of the most illustrious rectors for me. I ask them to do me a favor and allow me to see them, which I would consider to be a great favor."

The chancellor left to take Lodovico's request to the rectors and the mayor, who hurried to his cell and offered words of Christian consolation. Lodovico stated that he wanted to confess, and that death didn't bother him so much as not knowing why he must die.

---

† Gnoli, pp. 353-354.
‡ Ibid., p. 355.

The mayor replied, "You, signor, know the reason quite well." He shrugged and was silent.

Then he said, "I beg you to do me a favor and take off these handcuffs so that I can write a letter to console my poor wife and write to her of my wishes."[†]

The handcuffs were removed from his right hand, though his left one was cuffed to his chair. A monk and a priest entered the cell to hear his confession and give him Holy Communion. Then he began to write.

Most illustrious lady, my most beloved consort,

Because it has pleased Lord God that I pass to the other life, for which I thank His Divine Majesty, having made myself guilty of having greatly offended him, I wanted to write to your most illustrious self these few lines, with the only purpose being to ask you, exhort you, and conjure you to take all this with the necessary patience… In addition to this wish, I ask your Excellency to pay all the persons whom I owe money, so that this weight does not rest on my soul.

He then listed several debts owed from his student days in Perugia, Masses to be said for the repose of Paolo Giordano's soul, the distribution of funds to various loyal servants, and a donation of fifty scudi as dowry to allow a poor girl to marry. He continued:

And because the age of your most illustrious ladyship does not comport that you should remain a widow the rest of your life, I ask and command you to remarry because that would make me most happy, and I am leaving and giving you all the jewels that you have… In the event that you don't want to remarry but stay a widow, I make you my universal heir for as long as you live, intending that after your death everything goes to Monsignor my brother if he is alive, and if he's dead, to the nearest relative of Monterotondo [a branch of the Orsini family.]

And because they are allowing my body to be buried in a place that is pleasing to me, put me together with that of my father in Santa

Maria of Horto near that of Signor Valerio of happy memory, and
at your death you should be buried there with me.

From the Camozzana prison, December 27, 1585.
From your most illustrious consort and servant,
Lodovico Orsino

But he had forgotten some things and resumed writing, bequeathing
his wife a jasper necklace and instructing her to collect cash and silver
items in a chest he kept at the house of a friend. The parish priest of
Saint Clement started talking about Lodovico's upcoming journey,
but the condemned man couldn't stop thinking about loose ends and
wrote one last letter informing her that he had spent some of his own
money on travel in the fight for the furniture, evidently so that the de
Medici family would reimburse her.

The executioner and several Jesuit priests had entered the cell
as he wrote, and now they began to sing prayers. They intoned the
litany of the saints while he stood and called himself to blame for
his sins. He asked pardon from those present for the scandal he had
caused and asked God to forgive him for his offenses. He embraced
everyone in his cell, even the executioner, who was appalled at having
to strangle a nobleman. "I confess, most illustrious signor," the man
said, "that I am not worthy to put my hands on you, yet I must do so
to fulfill the task assigned to me by the minister of justice. However, I
ask you a thousand pardons."[†] Lodovico wholeheartedly forgave him.

Many of those present began to cry. With a firm step, Lodovico
approached the strangulation chair and sat down. He took off his
doublet and untied the red silk ribbon around his neck from which
hung a crucifix, then undid his shirt collar and made the sign of the
cross. Handcuffs and ankle cuffs were put on him and tied to his waist.
He asked that someone stand next to him repeating "Jesus, Jesus."

The executioner slipped around his neck a noose of crimson
silk, the privilege of condemned nobles, and inserted the stick into
a loop in the back and twisted it. As it was being twisted, the silk
noose broke, as it always did. As the executioner replaced it with a

---

† Cicogna, *Morte*, no page given.

thick knotted rope, Lodovico did not say a word, perhaps because he couldn't.

At one p.m., forty Jesuits carrying torches accompanied Lodovico's body out of the prison on an open bier. The corpse was carried around the piazza of the Senate to the cathedral and put in the middle of the church on a table covered with black cloth. Four torches burned brightly, one at each corner of the bier.

The people of Padua, roused to righteous indignation over the murders of Vittoria and Flaminio, and Lodovico's resistance to authority, now pressed around to study his corpse. True to the Italian spirit, they oozed compassion. This young man, of noble birth, quick intelligence, and good looks, lay there with a contorted face, his hands stiffly on his chest. His courage, which could have made him a hero, had turned him into an executed murderer.

Lodovico's death was the first of many. The following morning, December 28, the two traitors in Vittoria's household – Furio Savorgnano, a beloved servant of the duke's, and Paolo Giordano's secretary Domenico di Citta di Castello – were hanged. Meanwhile, the remaining men were being interrogated, often under torture. The rectors asked them whether Lodovico had come up with the idea to murder Vittoria himself, of if he had been commissioned by someone else to do the job. But the head of the Council of Ten instructed the rectors to stop this dangerous line of questioning. Testimony was emerging that the Grand Duke of Tuscany had given Lodovico the orders.

On December 29, one of Lodovico's men who had escaped his besieged palace on Christmas Day reached Florence and told the grand duke what had happened, ending with his master's incarceration. Since Lodovico had been acting on Francesco's orders, the grand duke wanted to save him without getting personally involved. He wrote his brother in Rome that he must take action "immediately so that you can help Lodovico, who has acted so badly, however it seems best to you."[†] They had no idea that Lodovico had been dead for two days but learned soon after.

† Ibid., p. 364.

When the pope heard of Lodovico's execution, he called in the Venetian ambassador and greatly praised the republic's administration of justice. But then he admonished them for thinking they could make use of such evil-doers by employing them in foreign wars. The republic, he said, should be "good with God and not hold account of these rogues, as God alone is the one to send legions of angels in favor of good princes."[†]

On the morning of December 30, thirteen men, one after the other, were hanged. Among them was Visconti, the man who had plunged the dagger into Vittoria's heart. He had already been sentenced merely to hanging before others revealed his vile deed, and the Senate was legally unable to increase his sentence. But his two companions, those who had held down Vittoria's arms, suffered the full penalty. Splandiano Adami and Paganello Ubaldi were each chained to a large table on a cart and rolled through town as crowds gawked. During this last, horrible journey, their flesh was torn out by red hot pincers. Then a knife was plunged into the flesh next to their hearts, in imitation of what they had done to Vittoria, but placed so that it did not cause immediate death. For half an hour they lingered in unspeakable agony. Their corpses were each divided into four parts, and the parts were hung on gallows at the four city gates.

Ten of Lodovico's men were found innocent of any foreknowledge of Vittoria's murder; they had either not gone to her palace that night or had merely followed their master's orders to watch for pedestrians in the street, unaware of what was happening inside. Nor had they taken up arms and fired at authorities. Several men received sentences of one or three years; they had thrown up mattresses to defend Lodovico's palace at his orders.

But Filelfo was given a fifteen-year prison sentence. Although the three murderers under torture had cleared him of any involvement in or knowledge of the plan to kill Vittoria, investigators found it suspicious that he had brought the murderers into Padua the night before the "accident." It seemed to them unlikely that it had been a chance meeting on the road. It was also believed that Filelfo might

† Gnoli, p. 381.

have prodded Lodovico to kill Vittoria to maintain family honor. This last was unlikely; Lodovico had hated her for years and required no goading.

Filelfo had a two-fold purpose in denying any involvement in pushing Lodovico to murder Vittoria. Clearly, he wanted to get himself off the hook and was angling for an early release from prison. Second, it was an insult to Lodovico's memory that some were pinning the blame on Filelfo, as if so great a cavalier could be persuaded to such an extraordinary act by a mere servant. Lodovico had been clearly motivated by a feeling of outraged honor.

In his 1586 pamphlet, *Defense of Filelfo*, written in prison, the secretary stated, "Those who want to calumniate me stain the good reputation of that unhappy cavalier as if he had committed this homicide without cause and at the instigation of others and not for the interests of honor and justice, the only two causes that save a gentleman from infamy… Though I was not informed of the causes that pushed the signor to do this, at least I was informed of his honorable thoughts on other occasions, and I am sure that he resolved to do this because he thought he was obligated for honor and justice to do it."[†]

Filelfo, who described himself as "buried" in prison, and "miserable and depressed," hoped that Pope Sixtus would remember his years of service and his promise to help him if he ever needed it. "The words of such a prince towards his servant lead me to believe I can hope for something notable," he wrote, "and the world will be the judge."[‡]

Did Filelfo serve his fifteen-year sentence and emerge blinking in the dawn of a new century? Did he die of illness in prison as so many convicts did? Or did Pope Sixtus live up to his promise and spring him from his cell? Venetian archives, which chatter loudly in many voices about Vittoria's murder and Lodovico's execution, are silent about Filelfo's fate.

---

† Cicogna, *Filelfo*, p. 54.
‡ Ibid., p. 60.

Chapter 26

VENGEANCE UNMASKED

Swing the sickle, for the harvest is ripe. Come, trample the grapes, for the winepress is full and the vats overflow – so great is their wickedness!

– Joel 3:13

Although Vittoria and Lodovico were dead and buried, there was still the small matter of Paolo Giordano's furniture to attend to. The Venetian Senate had decreed that it legally belonged to Vittoria. Marcello, as her brother, could claim it as her heir, cart it out of the Foscari Palace, and hide it from the Orsini family. On January 10, 1586, Vittoria's father, Claudio, instructed his lawyer to start legal proceedings to obtain his daughter's estate.

But Grand Duke Francesco was not about to let the furniture slip into the hands of the remaining Accorambonis. On January 11, 1586, the grand duke wrote to Cardinal de Medici that if the items from Padua "be molested by Marcello, as it is thought they will try to do, it will be necessary that you order the appropriate authority to defend them and get them back for Virginio."[†] Despite two months of death, murder, execution, and legal wrangling, the furniture situation hadn't changed a bit.

Whatever happened with the furniture, Vittoria was no longer in a position to siphon off Orsini patrimony, which must have delighted the de Medicis. Crammed, as she was, into half a coffin, there would be no dowry for her, no pensions or palaces, no room and board for forty of her attendants and their fifteen horses. Virginio wouldn't have to sell or mortgage his lands, bankrupting himself in an effort to fulfill the instructions of his father's will.

The de Medicis also heaved a huge sigh of relief when it became clear that Pope Sixtus was no longer thinking of taking the Duchy of Bracciano away from the Orsinis. Clearly, Paolo Giordano had deserved punishment for his many misdeeds, but little orphaned Virginio did not, and the justice-spouting pontiff would hardly penalize an innocent child. Instead of swiping the duchy and giving it to a Peretti family member, Sixtus would obtain the duchy for his family through a marriage, a much more elegant means. He finally agreed to betroth his grandniece, Flavia Peretti, to Virginio and hold the wedding when she became of suitable age. Flavia would be the new Duchess of Bracciano, effortlessly enjoying for decades what Vittoria, after so many years of struggle, had possessed for only a few nerve-wracking months.

Vittoria's death was the clarion call for Sixtus to seek revenge against the murderers of his nephew. The pope had been keeping tabs on them through his spy network. He knew exactly where they were, scattered over much of Italy, and asked all princes to arrest them and send them to Rome. It is surprising that in an age before photographs some criminals were easily apprehended. The pope sent detailed descriptions of the men: their height, weight, coloring, scars, accents, missing teeth, and aliases. They were duly arrested and shipped off to the pontiff's executioner.

Unfortunately for Sixtus, many of the key players had followed Paolo Giordano to the Venetian Republic, which usually denied requests for extradition. One Sunday, the Venetian ambassador to Rome, Lorenzo Priuli, saw Governor Pierbenedetti speaking with the pope at church. After the service, the governor asked Priuli, "Could they not take in hand those wicked ones who so cruelly killed the pope's nephew?"[†]

The ambassador said he could not give a certain reply; on the one hand, the republic was very independent-minded, and some of the criminals wanted by the pope had been promised sanctuary. On the other hand, he knew the senators desired the pontiff's good will and would be ready to agree to his wishes. This desire to comply was

† Ibid., p. 378.

heightened by the lucrative shipbuilding contract Sixtus was talking
about awarding Venice to build ten galleys to fight the Turks.

Later that evening, Governor Pierbenedetti presented himself at
Ambassador Priuli's residence. He had spoken once more to Sixtus,
and now the governor asked the ambassador "with great insistence,"
Priuli wrote to the doge, "to write to your Serenity, asking you to
hold the men listed below, who are deserving of the death penalty …
assuring me that this would be the greatest favor to the pope and his
sister."[†]

Curious to see if the pope was making an official request,
Ambassador Priuli asked the governor "if the order came from his
Holiness." But the pope and the governor were wary of such a trap.
"He replied to me that I could assume that without the consent of his
Holiness this petition would not be made," the ambassador explained.
"Whenever this case is spoken of, he [Sixtus] does nothing but cry and
sigh, saying that justice should be done without giving any particular
order. He [the governor] told the pope's sister that he would meet me
for this purpose, and she was glad to hear it. And he affirmed that
your Serenity can rest assured that this would be the most signal favor
for the pope and his sister."[‡] This last statement surely signified the
immediate signing of the shipbuilding contract.

The pope named four men involved in Francesco's death whom
he wanted executed: Marcello Accoramboni, Paolo Barca of Bracciano,
Marchio of Gubbio, and Lelio of Vicovaro. He gave the ambassador
written descriptions of the men. Some might already be in a Paduan
jail, the pope said, serving light sentences for Lodovico's last excess.

Public sentiment in Venice was on Marcello's side, the poor man
having just lost his brother and sister in such a brutal way. Nor would
the authorities wish to take a third child from the bereaved parents. In
the middle of January, he returned to Padua from Parma, where he had
been hiding from Lodovico, and gave himself up for the murder of his
servant Moricone. As expected, the authorities absolved him. When
Sixtus heard the news, he was furious. Marcello, killer of Francesco

† Ibid., p. 379.
‡ Ibid.

Peretti, Cardinal Pallavicino's brother, the pharmacist's assistant, his own servant Moricone, and probably several others, had once again gotten away with murder. Sixtus contacted Venetian authorities who, on February 1, imprisoned Marcello again, though he could not be charged with the same crime. The reason given for his detention was "the pleasure of his Holiness."[†]

The Accorambonis were terrified that they would lose another child. They sent Marcello 700 scudi, part of which was probably for his maintenance (prisoners had to buy their own food), but the bulk of it available to bribe his way out. Unfortunately for Marcello, it was not as easy to bribe one's way out of a Venetian jail as it had been out of a Roman one before Pope Sixtus. The pope's nuncio to Venice wrote, "Marcello has been conducted to the secure prisons of the Council of Ten, according to the instructions of your most illustrious Holiness, and at the moment nothing else is planned. As time goes by, the compassion for his losses is reduced with each passing day."[‡]

On February 15, the papal secretary, Monsignor Decio Azzolini, wrote the nuncio in Venice, "With regards to Marcello Accoramboni, he having committed a murder in the state of those lords ... we believe that those lords will not fail to do justice, and your lordship with the necessary prudence and deftness will procure it *without mentioning the name of his Holiness*."[§]

On February 22, the nuncio replied, "Regarding Marcello, I know that justice will not be served if he lives in liberty, and I believe the others agree. I will bring this up when it is appropriate, *without mentioning the [pope's] name*."[¶]

Sixtus was also out to get the Greek enchantress, thought to be responsible for poisoning his niece Maria in 1581. He ordered a bishop to launch a trial against "a woman in Padua believed to be a witch, who served Signora Accorambona for many years, and it is

[†] Ibid., p. 381.
[‡] Ibid., p. 384.
[§] Ibid., p. 382.
[¶] Ibid.

believed that she bewitched Signor Paolo Giordano, other bewitchings being imputed to her."[†]

It would have been easy enough to burn the witch, but Marcello's fate was more difficult. Venetian law, tradition, and the dignity of the republic prevented them from retrying a man who had been pardoned. By negating one law, the Senate would bring into question all laws and make an open declaration that the republic could no longer be trusted. Worse, they would look like the dancing puppet of Rome. They could, however, send Marcello to Rome, where the pope could try him for the murder of Francesco. But the pope found himself in a similar bind. He had publicly pardoned Marcello years earlier and couldn't try him for the same crime. He wanted Marcello to be executed in Venice.

The Venetian Senate, who so studiously avoided quagmires, now found themselves stuck in a deep one. They met several times to find a way out of the dilemma. They knew that Sixtus's friendship and, more importantly, the shipbuilding contract, depended on Marcello's execution. On March 1, the nuncio wrote to Monsignor Azzolini, Sixtus's secretary, "These lords have called the Senate many times without being able to come to the desired conclusion. The difficulty is this, that Marcello being absolved totally of that murder … the laws prevent the republic from retrying the case… It seems to me that the most successful way would be to send him to Rome, but I do not have orders to procure this." Then the nuncio came up with a clever solution. "The sea route up to Ancona would be easy, where justice could be carried out without sending him to Rome."[‡]

The Venetian Senate liked this idea that the place of execution would be neither in Rome nor Venice. They decided to deliver Marcello, along with other bandits wanted by the pope, to Ancona, the Adriatic seaport of the Papal States. Though Venice insisted the pope promise not to retry him for the murder of Moricone, he could charge him with other crimes and no one could point the finger at

† Ibid., pp. 381-382.
‡ Ibid., pp. 383-384.

the republic for not upholding its own laws. The pope, too, could dispatch him quietly outside of Rome. It was the perfect solution.

On May 19, Marcello boarded ship in Venice, along with the Greek witch and five bandits. The pope gave explicit orders that the food given to Marcello be carefully guarded from poison in case the Accorambonis, to save their honor, tried to prevent the shame of an execution. Just a few years earlier, the murderer Pietro Ramberti had avoided execution in Venice when his brother, giving him a farewell kiss in his jail cell, passed a poisoned pellet into his mouth which he had concealed in his own. Pietro bit down and immediately died, salvaging the family honor. Sixtus wanted Marcello to die at the hands of the law, the just punishment for Francesco's murderer.

Disembarking in Ancona, the others were conducted overland to Rome, but Marcello was put in the local prison and tried for the 1580 murder of Cardinal Pallavicino's brother. It was odd, some thought, that he had been interrogated in Venice for the murder of Moricone, and now in Ancona about the murder of Pallavicino, but he had never been asked about the real reason for his imprisonment: the death in a garden of Francesco Peretti, five years earlier.

Aware that he would, finally, pay for his crime, Marcello fell gravely ill. When the pope learned of this, he feared that a natural death would take away the satisfaction of his long-delayed revenge and ordered the governor of Ancona to have him beheaded immediately. Marcello received the news of his imminent execution courageously and said he wanted to die like a good Christian. He gave thanks to the pope for allowing him to die a Christian death. He asked those present to remember him and asked the executioner to do his job quickly. His head was cut off with the cleaver, and the beheaded corpse displayed to the curious public. And now the pope's revenge on Vittoria's conniving mother, Tarquinia, was made manifest.

The *avvisi* of June 18 said that Marcello was beheaded in secret, dying "intrepidly and as a good Catholic." Just before the execution, Marcello had asked the pope for absolution of the murders of Pallavicino and Moricone "but not for that other murder that was attributed to him," according to an *avvisi*.[†] Everyone agreed to pretend that Francesco's murder and Marcello's execution were not connected in any way, but no one was fooled.

Until his death, Sixtus continued the relentless hunt for the murderers of Francesco Peretti. In 1590, the last accomplices in Francesco's murder were ferreted out and executed. The harvest of justice was complete, and the pope lay down his pruning shears. His garden, God's garden, was now properly trimmed, all the life-choking weeds uprooted.

† Ibid., p. 388.

Chapter 27

FALL OF THE COLOSSUS

A good name is better than fine perfume, and the day of death better than the day of birth.

– Ecclesiastes 7:1

Long forgotten now are Sixtus's revenge on his nephew's murderers and his rigorous efforts to end violence in the Papal States. The most recognizable relic of his short reign is the red granite obelisk that stands in Saint Peter's Square. Carved for Pharaoh Ramses II, it had been abandoned at the Egyptian holy city of Heliopolis for 1,000 years before it was loaded onto a ship and brought to Rome. Emperor Caligula erected it in the center of the circus on Vatican Hill, which he built about AD 40 to hold chariot races. It had seen the crucifixion of Saint Peter.

Many popes before Sixtus had looked into moving the obelisk to the front of the basilica. But Rome's top architects – even Michelangelo – declared the task impossible. Sixtus was incensed to think that pagans had brought the thing from Egypt, but the Vicar of Christ couldn't cart it a mere two hundred and seventy-seven yards. He hired his favorite architect, Domenico Fontana, to move it using iron pulleys, hundreds of yards of rope as thick as a man's arm, forty winches, 1,907 men, and sixty-five horses. Fontana stood in a tower issuing orders by means of a trumpet. The obelisk was raised into its present position on September 10, 1586.

Sixtus finished another project that had plagued many of his predecessors – the dome of Saint Peter's. When Sixtus came to the throne, trees sprouted from the unfinished dome, which greatly embarrassed him. The pope began the work on December 22, 1588, with eight hundred construction workers laboring day and night.

It was completed in May 1590, except for the lead sheeting. Sheer willpower, aided by threats of physical violence to slack workers and financial rewards to energetic ones, had accomplished in a matter of months what other popes had been unable to achieve in several decades. Additionally, Sixtus built new, light-filled papal apartments, enjoyed by all pontiffs since then, and a new wing housing the Vatican Library. He sent out scholars across Europe to find rare manuscripts, and he set up the first Vatican printing press

For almost his entire pontificate, Sixtus had enjoyed good health except for a high fever in 1587, which caused him to fall into either a deep sleep or a coma. All the cardinals were supposed to make a big show of going to the local churches and, kneeling solemnly in front of a crucifix, pray for the pope's recovery. But many Romans believed the cardinals were, in fact, asking God to put Sixtus out of their misery.

At one point, the pope's doctor was alarmed that his patient had so little color in his face. Believing him to be unconscious, the doctor thwacked the pope's nose to see if any blood rushed to it. The pope opened his eyes immediately and said in an angry voice, "You have a lot of nerve to thwack the nose of a pope." According to the chronicler, "The poor doctor was horrified, believing the pope would never again want to see a man who had placed his hands on his nose. He ran home and took to his bed with a fever, which in a few days killed him."[†]

Unlike the doctor, Sixtus recovered quickly from the illness, which might have been malaria, a common complaint in Rome, and especially in the Vatican, which had been built on top of a swamp. Aside from bouts of insomnia, he remained healthy until April 1590, when he developed flu-like symptoms, headaches, and a slight fever. Though his appetite remained strong, he began to look haggard. In June, he suffered from cold sweats and high fevers.

The pope had good days and bad, and on every one of them he worked at least twelve hours, sometimes many more. On August 10, against the vehement protests of his doctors, Sixtus went to a church service celebrating the return to Catholicism of the German margrave

† Anon., p. 382.

of Baden. He returned from the service sicker than ever. When his grand-nephew, young Cardinal Alessandro Montalto, begged him to rest a little, Sixtus replied, "You must know, my nephew, that a prince only stops commanding when he dies. He is like the nightingale, who sings until death." To others he said, "A prince must die in action."[†]

On August 20, the pope had another violent shouting match with the Spanish ambassador. "Does the king want to become pope?" he thundered, referring to Philip II. "In that case we should make him a cardinal first."[‡] After Olivares protested, the pope cried, "We are not the servant of your king. We do not owe him obedience, nor an account of our actions. We are the father of all Catholics and do not expect that our children, without being asked, impose their advice on their parents... You, who carry a sword at your side, do you believe that you know theology better than we, who have studied it all our life? With what right, during the heat of August, do you come to molest us? You would have done better to have stayed home."[§]

After the audience, Sixtus developed a violent fever. The next day, he insisted on meeting with the cardinals' committee on French affairs, but when he spoke, he rambled unintelligibly. On August 23, he was back to being himself and dealt with affairs of state. By evening the fever had disappeared. The following day, he presided over a meeting of the Inquisition. He had no appetite but an insatiable thirst.

On Sunday, August 26, the pope agreed to his doctors' recommendation that he receive a suppository to draw out the feverish humors in his body. But instead of improving, he became markedly worse. The following day, it was clear that he was dying. When Cardinal Alessandro Montalto asked him how he felt, he said weakly, "I have a great heat in my head, which seems to be on fire."[¶] His last official act was to assign a large bread subsidy for the people of the Papal States, as harvests had been bad and the price of bread was rising rapidly.

---

†   Ibid., p. 571.
‡   De Feo, p. 132.
§   Ibid., p. 135.
¶   Anon., p. 574.

Some cardinals brought Sixtus the holy sacrament as his last communion, but his throat was so swollen he could not swallow it. A priest gave him extreme unction, anointing his body with holy oil, as the pope slowly breathed out the fire of his spirit. "In that instant when he gave up his soul," wrote one contemporary, "the most extraordinary thing happened. It began to thunder and lightning, the sky becoming black and wild, with clouds full of fire racing towards the Monte Cavallo Palace, where his Holiness was, shooting out thunderbolts, one of which they say struck the arms of the pope above the gate of the Jews."[†] Romans wondered if the Devil were coming to take Sixtus for executing so many people. Others thought it was God welcoming him home with a dazzling show as the heavens opened to receive him.

Vatican physicians set about performing an autopsy on Sixtus. Most doctors loved performing post-mortems, and it was especially amusing to pry open royal bodies, bring out the organs, and give them a good poke. Unfortunately, they usually didn't have a clue what they were looking at. Such was medical ignorance that if they found an abnormality in the stomach, they couldn't be sure if it was cancer, a ruptured gastric ulcer, poison, or a benign mark which had nothing at all to do with the individual's death. In the 1590s, physicians examining the corpse of King Henri IV's twenty-six-year-old mistress agreed that she had, in fact, been killed by a "corrupt lemon."[‡]

And now, as they prodded the cadaver of Sixtus, they found "very sincere" intestines[§] (probably meaning healthy) and a "rotten"[¶] brain with some water on it, which might have indicated poison. Physicians of the time believed all food and smells ended up in some form in the brain – clearly alcohol did, so everything else ingested must also find its way up there. According to this theory, it was not impossible that poison could have traveled north instead of south.

Some also wondered about the deleterious effects of the enema he had received the day before he died. Back in 1517, several cardinals

---

† Strozzi, *Conclave nel fu creato Urbano*, folio 109b.
‡ Lewis, p. 267.
§ Strozzi, Conclave di Urbano, foglio109b.
¶ Anon., p. 578.

had bribed the physician of Pope Leo X in a thwarted plot to give him a poisoned enema; given his reputation for homosexuality, they saw this as a fitting end. In the case of Sixtus, after some debate it was agreed that poison administered through the rear end couldn't rise up to rot the victim's brain while leaving his guts sincere.

There were ample reasons for Spain to kill the pope. Sixtus had stymied Spanish pretensions in France, publicly admired Spain's arch-enemy, Queen Elizabeth, insulted Spanish ambassadors, refused to pay for the armada and, more recently, he had seemed to be angling to take back the Kingdom of Naples. The Spanish protested loudly that they had not killed the pope (though they were certainly glad he was dead), and their enemies the French were spreading the slanderous rumors of Spanish poison. Indeed, it is highly unlikely that Sixtus was poisoned. He had felt unwell for months with intermittent fever and headaches, while poison was usually administered in one fatal dose. Moreover, heavy metal poisons, including arsenic, that darling murder weapon of the Renaissance, do not cause fever.

Due to the ghastly heat, the pope was buried temporarily under Saint Peter's Basilica. A year later when, it was hoped, he would be reduced to non-odiferous bones, he would be taken in a solemn procession to the tomb he had prepared for himself in his favorite Church of Saint Mary Major, just across from his gorgeous Villa Montalto, and his beloved gardens.

Sixtus had often said, "I am convinced that the Romans will slide back into their disorders under another pontificate."[†] And he was right. Succeeding popes would gleefully dig into the money he had so carefully put aside, spending it wildly. More merciful Vicars of Christ would return to the hallowed tradition of pardoning murderers, rapists, and robbers, setting them at liberty to begin committing crimes afresh. But many of Sixtus's achievements still exist as lasting testimony of his incredible reign: those tourist magnets, his obelisks; his wide, straight Roman roads; his life-giving aqueducts; his expanded Vatican Library and printing press; and his light-filled Vatican apartments.

† Leti, *Sixte V*, Vol. 2, p. 443.

Never before Sixtus had a pope achieved so much in so few years, and never after. The Venetian envoy, Paolo Paruta, wrote, "Anyone who sees the many and extraordinary works of Sixtus V, the long aqueducts and the public fountains, the streets and palaces and churches, could hardly believe that all this had been brought into being in so short a time."[†]

Shortly after the pope's death, the Benedictine abbot Angelo Grillo returned to Rome after a ten-year absence. He wrote a friend, "Here I am in Rome, and yet I cannot find the Rome I know; so great are the changes in the buildings, the streets, the piazzas, the fountains, the aqueducts, the obelisks, and the other marvels with which the glorious memory of Sixtus has beautified this old and ruinous city, that I cannot recognize nor find, so to speak, any trace of that old Rome which I left ten years ago, when I came away; and so it would seem to your lordship if you saw it in its new guise."[‡]

Sixtus's early chronicler wrote, "Only Christ, as God, who can do anything, could have done more than Pope Sixtus in five years."[§]

† Pastor, *Popes*, Vol. 22, p. 305.
‡ Ibid.
§ Anon., p. 376.

Chapter 28

AFTER VITTORIA

And I saw the dead, great and small, standing before the throne, and books were opened. Another book was opened, which is the book of life. The dead were judged according to what they had done as recorded in the books.

– Revelation 20:12

V ittoria's tragic death had all the elements to make poets swoon with ecstasy. She had been gorgeous, ambitious, and possibly adulterous and murderous. Her story was chock full of irony – if only she had waited for Pope Gregory to die, she would have been Princess Montalto with a handsome young husband at her side, beloved by her family. Due to her acquiescence in Francesco's death, she found herself a dubious duchess, shackled to a huge, rotting, spendthrift husband, whose family killed her for some furniture. Her end was dramatic in the extreme – a murder before a crucifix, complete with bodice-ripping, and followed by a shoddy burial in an unmarked grave.

Soon after her death, many poets wrote as if they were Vittoria, which led to the legend that Vittoria herself was a great poet. Though no contemporary records mention her poetry, it is tempting to picture the doomed beauty in the five weeks that remained to her after the duke's death, thick black tendrils of hair curling down a frilly white nightgown, as she penned sad verses by the light of a single candle. Numerous poems attributed to her are located in the Florentine State Archives, though none are signed by her.

One sonnet attributed to Vittoria was definitely not her creation, since we can assume she would not have referred to herself as dead:

I am the great Victoria who plucks the prize
of beauty from the Greeks and Latins.

> And dead, I, too, bring wars and ruin,
> And turn Rome upside down with my rank.
> In the proud and glorious city,
> Mother of heroes, high queen of the world,
> I was born endowed with divine beauty
> And lived among so many, who never found fame.[†]

Another depicts her plight shortly before her death in the Palazzo Foscari, waiting for doom to descend:

> Reckless thought
> Elevated to the sky, eager and light
> Not to rejoice on high,
> But to make me fall with a mortal leap.
> You in my audacious flight
> Promised me a tranquil peace.
> Then, throwing me to the ground,
> You fatefully gave me a perpetual war.
> Oh, that others died
> Because of my immoderate daring!
> When I so often think
> Of the good that's past, I increase the present pain.
> Thus if my thought
> Was the only cause of my proud haste,
> Cry much, my painful eyes
> Until life seeps away in tears.[‡]

In late Elizabethan and Jacobean England, poison, murder, revenge, and adultery were thought to thrive under the warm Italian sun just as bacteria does in heat. Shakespeare's *Merchant of Venice, Othello, Romeo and Juliet* and other plays reflected and encouraged this trend. In 1612, Daniel Webster wrote a popular play about Vittoria called *The White Devil*. Webster had evidently heard from a traveler of the astonishing events twenty-seven years earlier, though the details were a bit hazy, allowing the playwright to embellish. In order to marry the Venetian courtesan, Vittoria, the slender dashing Paolo Giordano kills his first wife Isabella by smearing poison on the lips of his portrait which she devotedly kisses every night. Vittoria's husband is killed the

[†] Gnoli, p. 19.
[‡] Ibid., pp. 310-311.

same night, his neck broken. The Duke of Bracciano dies by putting on a poisoned helmet.

At least Webster got the finale right – a pile of freshly killed bodies heaped up on the stage as the curtain swings shut. Regarding Vittoria's character, perhaps the only correct part was her courage in the moment before death:

> I shall wellcome death
> As princes doe some great embassadors.
> Ile meet thy weapon halfe way…
> I will not in my death shed one base tear
> Or if I looke pale, for want of blood, not feare.[†]

Public contempt for Lodovico's murder of a defenseless woman is expressed in her next line:

> 'Twas a manly blow!
> The next thou giv'st, murder some sucking infant
> and then thou wilt be famous.[‡]

Camilla, the mother-in-law Vittoria had scorned, lived to a great old age, beloved for her charity to the poor. Like the pope, Camilla never forgot where she came from. Refusing to waste her wealth on selfish extravagance, she gave to those who suffered hunger and poverty, as she had. She died in 1606 at about the age of eighty-seven.

Camilla's grandchildren all had illustrious careers. On March 20, 1589, seventeen-year-old Virginio Orsini, Duke of Bracciano, married sixteen-year-old Flavia Peretti. The murderer's son married the victim's niece. The same day, her fourteen-year-old sister Felice married fourteen-year-old Marcantonio Colonna and became the Duchess of Paliano. Out of his own money, Pope Sixtus gave each of the brides a dowry of 80,000 scudi cash, and 20,000 scudi in jewelry and furniture, "in order," he said, "that they may buy a pair of shoes without asking their husbands' permission."[§]

Out of Virginio and Flavia's eleven children, five of them became friars – penance, perhaps, for their families' sins. Flavia and

---

[†] Webster, pp. 178-179.
[‡] Ibid., p. 179.
[§] Hubner, Vol. 2, p. 141.

Felice's brother Michele became the prince of Venafro, and over time young Cardinal Alessandro Peretti would become a prelate of great distinction.

After the execution of Marcello, the Accorambonis lost the urge to get Paolo Giordano's furniture. If they pushed for it, perhaps new charges would be made against the rapidly diminishing family, or some of them would eat a meal and suddenly keel over dead. Cardinal de Medici took possession of the furnishings as if the duke's will had never existed, and gave them to Virginio, along with Vittoria's items in Rome's Tor de Specchi convent.

In 1691, Accoramboni descendants thought back on her estate and tried to take the ruling Duke of Bracciano, Flavio Orsini, to court. But they lost the case. The court ruled that a will could not be contested more than a century after the testator's death. The court also found grave doubts about the legitimacy of Vittoria's marriage to Paolo Giordano. Perhaps she had never been duchess at all.

The spendthrift Orsini gene was passed down until the family spent itself into near oblivion. In 1696, the last Orsini duke sold the Duchy of Bracciano to the family of Pope Innocent XI (reigned 1676-1689), the Odescalchis, who still own it today. The castle became a part of recent pop culture when in 2006 Tom Cruise married Katie Holmes in the main reception room.

In October 1587, Grand Duke Francesco of Tuscany and his courtesan-wife Bianca Cappello died within hours of each other from either malaria or poison. And, indeed, recent research has indicated they may have been given arsenic in medications they were taking for malaria. Many fingers pointed at Cardinal de Medici, who had been in charge of the sick rooms. He had hated his brother's second wife and wanted to prevent her from inheriting anything. Perhaps he was afraid of another protracted fight over furniture. Ferdinando gave his brother due funerary honors, but he tossed Bianca into an unmarked grave, just as Vittoria had been. Like Anne Boleyn before them (whose decapitated corpse was thrown into an arrow chest as no coffin had been provided), such was the fate of ambitious women who used beauty and sex to overstep their bounds.

Suddenly, the new Grand Duke of Tuscany was a cardinal. Like most royal younger brothers who joined the Church, Ferdinando had only taken minor orders and had never been ordained a priest, which was thought to tattoo the soul forever with a sign that the individual couldn't marry. Sixtus had been forced to allow the cardinal he disliked to doff his red robes and become the ruler of neighboring Tuscany, where he was in a better position to squabble with the pope. Ferdinando married Christine of Lorraine and had nine children.

Some of the places associated with Vittoria's story still exist, though, sadly, with the exception of the grandest of them all. In 1784, Villa Montalto was bought by a tasteless merchant who sold most of the statues and knocked down the splendid two-hundred-year-old trees that Sixtus had planted before he became pope. The palace itself was razed in the 1860s to build Rome's main train station, Termini. Those passengers arriving in Rome should remember as they alight that here a cardinal once tended his vines and plotted his vengeance.

The building where Vittoria was murdered miraculously survived both the Allied bombs of March 1944, which were dropped across the street, and the gentler but equally devastating hand of time itself. Known as the Cavalli Palace after the family who bought it in the seventeenth century, today it is part of the geology department of the University of Padua. The glorious rooms are used as offices, or filled with dark and dusty bookshelves, functions incongruous with its illustrious architecture.

It is not possible to say exactly where in the house Vittoria was murdered, though we have a good idea. According to contemporary reports, her altar was a small room off her bedroom, which was off the ballroom. There are two rooms off the ballroom, currently used as offices, which would have been the right size for a bedroom. At the back of one of them is a door to a small chamber, which today houses not an altar and crucifix, but a lavatory. Perhaps this is the spot of Vittoria's death, somewhere between the sink and the toilet.

The Salò palace where Paolo Giordano heaved his last breath is little changed since that day and remains in private hands. Mysterious and lovely, it slumbers at the very edge of Lake Garda, its ancient dreams undisturbed by the living. The current owner wonders if Vittoria hid her best jewels somewhere on the property – the ones Lodovico couldn't find in her jewel box – and Paolo Giordano's remaining gold. Perhaps she planned to retrieve them once Lodovico had finally sailed east. Maybe even now they lie forgotten in a palace wall, under a floor, or buried in the garden.

It is not known exactly where Vittoria and Flaminio lay. They had been placed, according to a contemporary report, "in the ground" at the Church of the Eremetani. There had been no marker, since nobody was around to pay for one. The bombs which spared the Foscari Palace blasted the German headquarters next to the church, which was largely destroyed, including numerous tombs and church records.

The exact location of Paolo Giordano's body likewise remains a mystery. Like most Renaissance corpses, his was dragged across the street to the nearest church. There is no tombstone in or around the church bearing his name, though his will requested that one be made. It is likely that as soon as Vittoria arrived in Padua, she was concerned with matters other than her dead husband's tombstone, fighting as she was with Lodovico over the furniture. But tombstone or no, where is his body?

According to the nobleman who currently owns the Salò palace, after Vittoria's death Sixtus sent word to the Capuchin monks that a serial killer could not be entombed on sanctified soil. The frightened monks, knowing of the pope's violent reputation when his edicts were not followed, immediately disinterred Paolo Giordano and laid his coffin on the ground outside the church. After a period of time, not knowing what to do with the coffin, the monks opened it up and tossed the duke into the lake which, it is said, never gives up its dead. Whatever was left of the duke's bloated magnificence became a feast for fish. Perhaps that ending is the most fitting of all.

Sixtus had always planned for the future, and as pope he was thinking ahead to Judgment Day. When the trumpet was sounded, he wanted to crawl out of his grave, brush the dust from his clothing, and greet loved ones with gladness. He certainly didn't want to be buried in Saint Peter's Basilica and wake up to find himself in the company of dozens of other popes, many of whom he despised, such as the weak Gregory XIII and the horrible, sex-crazed Borgia, Alexander VI.

The one pope he wanted to embrace on Judgment Day was his saintly friend and mentor, Pius V. In the summer of 1586, Sixtus built a tomb for Pius in a large side chapel in Saint Mary Major. He erected a beautiful statue of the pope, standing and giving a benediction. The figure wore the papal tiara with rays of the sun extending behind it. The plaque below it states that Sixtus constructed the tomb in gratitude. When the tomb was finished on January 8, 1588, the pope had Pius's body moved from Saint Peter's. In the same chapel, Sixtus had his own tomb built, but his statue is far more humble. He is kneeling, his hands in prayer, and his papal tiara is placed on the floor behind him.

That same year, Sixtus moved the bodies of Francesco and Maria to the chapel, too, in separate mournful ceremonies attended by numerous cardinals. Francesco's coffin, covered in a rich cloth, was placed on an open carriage and carried through the streets of Rome in a slow procession attended by eighteen cardinals wearing fuchsia mourning vestments. Monks carrying torches surrounded the funeral carriage.

In the crypt below Sixtus's chapel were deposited the remains of the young man who had never attracted public attention except by his tragic end. He now attracted it a second time by the splendor of his belated funeral, held seven years after his murder. But once the slab was dragged into place, Francesco was once again forgotten by all but his mother and uncle. The day of the re-internment, Pope Sixtus V shed many tears over Francesco's coffin and gave orders that when the time came his own should be placed beside it.

And there, until this very day, rest the young man who had enjoyed the amazing good fortune to marry the most beautiful girl in Rome, and the uncle who avenged him.

If you have enjoyed this book, the author would love a review on the channel through which you purchased this copy.

BIBLIOGRAPHY

Johnny Acton. *The Origin of Everyday Things*. London: Think Publishing Limited, 2007.

Adamson, John. *The Princely Courts of Europe: Ritual, Politics and Culture Under the Ancien Regime 1500–1750*. London: Weidenfeld & Nicolson, 1999.

Ajmar-Wollheim, Marta, and Flora Dennis. *At Home in Renaissance Italy*. London: V&A Publications, 2006.

Albala, Ken. *The Banquet, Dining in the Great Courts of Late Renaissance Europe*. Chicago: University of Illinois Press, 2006.

Alper, Nicole and Lynette Rohrer. *Wild Women in the Kitchen: 101 Rambunctious Recipes & 99 Tasty Tales*. Newburyport, MA: Conari Press, 1996.

Anonymous manuscript, *Relatione della Vita e Morte di Sisto V e tutto cio, che gl'occorse nel suo pontificato. Relatione della Morte di Francesco Peretti, Consorte della Signora Vittoria Accoramboni, poi passata alle seconde nozze coll Ecc.mo Signor Don Paolo Giordano, Orsini, con la morte dell medisimo*. Early 17th century.

Baumgartner, Frederic J. *Behind Locked Doors: A History of the Papal Elections*. New York: Palgrave MacMillan, 2003.

Brentano, Robert. *Rome Before Avignon: A Social History of Thirteenth-Century Rome*. Berkeley: University of California Press, 1990.

Burckhardt, Jacob. *The Civilization of the Renaissance in Italy*. New York: The Modern Library, 1954.

Canosa, Romano, and Isabella Colonello. *Storia della Prostituzione in Italia dal quattrocento alla fine del settecento*. Rome: Sapere 2000, 1989.

Coryat, Thomas, *Coryat's Crudities, hastily gobled up in five moneths travells in France, Savoy, Italy, Rhetia commonly called the Grisons country, Helvetia alias Switzerland, some parts of high Germany and the Netherlands : newly digested in the hungry aire of Odcombe in the county of Somerset, and now dispersed to the nourishment of the travelling members of this kingdome.* London: T. Thorp, 1611.

De Feo, Italo. *Sisto V, Un Grande Papa Tra Rinascimento e Barocco.* Milan: Mursia, 1987.

Della Casa, Giovanni. *Il Galatheo, de Costumi e Modi che si debbono tenere o schifare nella commune conversatione.* Florence, Italy: 1560.

Della Casa, Giovanni, *Il Galateo, A Renaissance Courtesy-Book of Manners and Behaviors.* Boston: Merrymount Press. 1914

Erlanger, Philippe. *The Age of Courts and Kings, Manners and Morals, 1558–1715.* New York: Harper and Row, 1967.

Firenzuola, Agnolo. *On the Beauty of Women.* Philadelphia: University of Pennsylvania Press, 1992.

Frick, Carole Collier. *Dressing Renaissance Florence.* Baltimore: The Johns Hopkins University Press, 2002.

Gnoli, Domenico. *Vittoria Accoramboni, Storia del Secolo XVI.* Florence: Successori Le Monier, 1870.

Gregorovius, Ferdinand. *History of the City of Rome in the Middle Ages.* London: George Bell, 1900.

Hübner, Joseph Alexander. *The Life and Times of Sixtus the Fifth.* Two volumes. London: Longmans, Green, 1872

Langdon, Gabrielle. *Medici Women, Portraits of Power, Love, and Betrayal.* Toronto: University of Toronto Press, 2007.

Leti, Gregorio. *La Vie du Pape Sixte Cinquieme.* Paris: Michel David, 1713.

Leti, Gregorio. *Il Nipotismo di Rome, or, The History of the Popes Nephews.* London: John Starkey, 1673.

Lewis, Paul, *Lady of France, A Biography of Gabrielle D'Estrees, Mistress of Henry the Great*. New York: Funk and Wagnalls, 1963.

Martinengo-Cesaresco, Evelyn. *Lombard Studies*. New York: Charles Scribner's Sons, 1902.

Masson, Georgina. *Courtesans of the Italian Renaissance*. New York: St. Martin's Press, 1975.

Montaigne, Michel, *The Diary of Montaigne's Journey to Italy in 1580 and 1581*. London: Hogarth Press, 1929.

Murphy, Caroline. *Murder of a Medici Princess*. Oxford: Oxford University Press, 2008.

Pastor, Dr. Ludwig. *The History of the Popes From the Close of the Middle Ages, Drawn from the Secret Archives of the Vatican and Other Original Sources*. London: Routledge & Kegan Paul, 1949.

Pastor, Ludovico von. *Sisto V, Il Creatore della Nuova Roma*. Rome: Poliglotta Vaticana, 1922.

Pirie, Valérie. *The Triple Crown, An Account of the Papal Conclaves from the Fifteenth Century to Modern Times*. London: Spring Books, 1935.

Pittoni, Leros, and Gabrielle Lautenberg. *Roma Felix, La Citta di Sisto V e Domenico Fontana*. Rome: Viviani Editore, 2002.

Prescott, Orville, *Princes of the Renaissance*. Random House, New York, 1969

Ranke, Leopold. *The History of the Popes, their Church and State, and Especially of Their Conflicts with Protestantism, in the Sixteenth and Seventeenth Centuries*. London: George Bell and Sons, 1881.

Ruggiero, Guido. *Binding Passions: Tales of Magic, Marriage, and Power at the End of the Renaissance*. Oxford: Oxford University Press, 1993.

Sarazani, Fabrizio. *La Roma di Sisto V*. Rome: Editrice I Dioscuri, 1979.

Santorio, Giulio Antonio. *Vita del card. Giulio Antonio Santori detto il card. di Santa Severina composta e scritta da lui medesimo*. Archivio della R. Società di Storia Patria, vol. XII 1889 and XIII 1890

Somerset, Anne. *Elizabeth I*. New York: Knopf, 1991.

Spagnesi, G. *La Pianta di Roma al Tempo di Sisto V (1585–1590)*. Rome: Multigrafica Editrice, 1992.

Thurston, Herbert. *The Holy Year of the Jubilee, An Account of the History and Ceremonial of the Roman Jubilee*. Westminster, Maryland: The Newman Press, 1949.

Webster, Daniel, *The White Devil*. Boston: D.C. Heath & Co., 1904.

Welch, Evelyn. *Shopping in the Renaissance*. New Haven: Yale University Press, 2005.

Wiel, Alethea, *The History of Venice: From its Founding to the Unification of Italy*. New York: Barnes & Noble, 1997.

Williams, Neville. *Elizabeth the First, Queen of England*. New York: E.P. Dutton, 1968.

ARCHIVAL DOCUMENTS:

FOLGER SHAKESPEARE LIBRARY, STROZZI COLLECTION, WASHINGTON, D.C.:

Vita del Sommo Pontifice Sisto V ovvero Annali del Suo Pontificato (opera supposta del P. Maffei). W.b. 132, volume 14.

Conclave di Urbano VII. W.b. 132, volume 14.

BIBLIOTECA DEL MUSEO CORRER, CICOGNA COLLECTION, VENICE

Conclave nel quale fu creato papa il Cardinal Montalto li xxiiii di aprile MDLXXXV e chiamato Sisto V. Vol. 2236

Conclave di Sisto V. Vol. 546

Difesa di Francesco Filelfo. Vol. 3053

Lettera di Lodovico Orsino alla moglie. Vol. 2547

Lodovico Orsino. Vol. 2349

Maritaggio e morte di Vittoria Accoramboni, prima maritata con Francesco Peretto, Nipote di Sisto V, e poi con Don Paolo Giordano Duca di Bracciano. Vol. 1293

Morte della Corambona e dell'Orsino. Vol. 782

Strani accidenti occorsi in Padova l'anno 1585 dopo la morte del Sig. Paol Giordano Orsino duca di Bracciano. Vol. 1439

Vita di Sisto V. Vol. 1204